The Group Process and Family Therapy

lupt price £4

The Group Process and Family Therapy

Extensions and Applications of Basic Principles

A complete revision of
The Group Process as a Helping Technique

by

SHEILA   THOMPSON

and

JACK   KAHN

PERGAMON PRESS

OXFORD · NEW YORK · BEIJING · FRANKFURT
SÃO PAULO · SYDNEY · TOKYO · TORONTO

U.K.	Pergamon Press, Headington Hill Hall, Oxford OX3 0BW, England
U.S.A.	Pergamon Press, Maxwell House, Fairview Park, Elmsford, New York 10523, U.S.A.
PEOPLE'S REPUBLIC OF CHINA	Pergamon Press, Room 4037, Qianmen Hotel, Beijing, People's Republic of China
FEDERAL REPUBLIC OF GERMANY	Pergamon Press, Hammerweg 6, D-6242 Kronberg, Federal Republic of Germany
BRAZIL	Pergamon Editora, Rua Eça de Queiros, 346, CEP 04011, Paraiso, São Paulo, Brazil
AUSTRALIA	Pergamon Press Australia, P.O. Box 544, Potts Point, N.S.W. 2011, Australia
JAPAN	Pergamon Press, 8th Floor, Matsuoka Central Building, 1-7-1 Nishishinjuku, Shinjuku-ku, Tokyo 160, Japan
CANADA	Pergamon Press Canada, Suite No. 271, 253 College Street, Toronto, Ontario, Canada M5T 1R5

First edition 1988

Library of Congress Cataloging-in-Publication Data
Thompson, Sheila.
Group process and family therapy.
(Social work series)
Rev. ed. of: The group process as a helping technique, 1970
1. Group psychotherapy.   2. Family therapy.
I. Kahn, Jack H.   II. Thompson, Sheila. Group
process as a helping technique.   III. Title.
IV. Series.
RC488.T46   1987   616.89'15   87–10413

British Library Cataloguing in Publication Data
Thompson, Sheila
Group process and family therapy.
Rev. ed. of: The group process as a helping technique 1970.
1. Family psychotherapy
I. Title   II. Kahn, Jack   III. Thompson, Sheila. Group process as a
helping technique   IV. Series
616.89'156   RC488.5

ISBN 0–08–034787–8 Hardcover
ISBN 0–08–034786–X Flexicover

Printed in Great Britain by Richard Clay Ltd, Bungay, Suffolk

Foreword

Few innovations into the field of psychotherapy have made such a universal impact as that of family therapy. Now, a generation after the pioneering contributions of Ackerman, Bateson, and Bell, the aspirant to knowledge is likely to find a bewildering nomenclature representing a variety of theoretical formulations, each making claims for particular treatment strategies. Sooner or later a book had to appear which addressed itself to those so engaged with an invitation to pause, take stock, regain a sense of perspective and, refreshed by the exercise, set off again with a clearer vision and renewed vigour. This is such a book. The authors, whose experience is long enough and broad enough to have lived and worked before and into the family-assessment and family-therapy era, take the reader through a deceptively simple account of the origins of various forms of group work culminating in the therapy of family groups, illustrating in turn each form of group process with succinct examples from group counselling, social casework, child-guidance, family psychiatry, and mental health consultation. We are led gently, sometimes amusingly, through a scholarly discussion, which assumes some familiarity with basic psycho-analytic concepts, and enlightens the discourse with excerpts from Jane Austen, Conan Doyle, George Eliot and Bertrand Russell as well as from Sigmund Freud, Ezriel, Bion, Foulkes, Caplan, Skynner, Satir, and Melanie Klein. The references, indeed, are notable for their quality and not, as is so often the case, for their modernity. I commend to the reader this original and major contribution to the understanding of the principles of family functioning on which therapeutic endeavours so largely depend. It should prove of particular value to those engaged in teaching and supervision within the whole range of the helping professions. It is a text to ponder and re-read, and therefore to find its place on one's own bookshelf alongside *Unwillingly to School, Human Growth and the Development of Personality*, and *The Cry for Help*.

Emeritus Professor PROFESSOR FRED H. STONE
Department of Child and Family Psychiatry
University of Glasgow

Acknowledgements

We would like to express our gratitude to our teachers; to our colleagues; to the families with whom we have worked; and to the members of the groups with which we have been associated in diverse capacities.

We would also like to acknowledge our debt to the group pyschotherapists who have influenced our thinking, amongst whom special mention must be made of Dr. S. H. Foulkes.

Contents

Part 4   The Family Process

9.   *The Family Group*   137

10.   *The Family in Action*   149

11.   *Splitting and Scapegoating*   163

Part 5   The Family Process in Practice

12.   *The Therapist in the Family Group*   173

Part 6   Wider Applications of the Family Process

Part 7   Epilogue

1

Prologue

1

How Problems are Shaped

The problem is introduced

"It's my leg, doctor", says the man in the general practitioner's surgery.

In this statement we have an example of shaping. With this opening remark, the man is indicating clearly the shape that he has given to his distress, and with this shape is justifying his choice of one particular helping person. Perhaps in this situation this shape is inevitable; the leg may be injured and require the doctor's specific skills. Perhaps the doctor, in his turn, has no option but to accept the problem in this shape and deal with it within a straightforward transaction in which further inquiries do not have to be made.

Today few transactions between members of the helping professionals and their patients or clients are as straightforward as this one (at first glance) may appear to be. Some reshaping of the distress is likely to take place so that the helping person can respond effectively with the resources available: and it could be that the distress will in time come to be shaped and reshaped and shaped again as part of that complex series of transaction between the parties concerned that has become known as the helping process.

This process of shaping and reshaping distress is fundamental to a consideration of work of the caring professionals. It is also fundamental to a consideration of a main theme of this work, that is, to *a consideration of the impact that the advent first of group therapy and then of family therapy has had upon the helping process*. We therefore propose to introduce this theme with a discussion of shaping.

Before any distress can be presented for help, some sort of preliminary shape, however indeterminate, will have had to be found for it by the client or patient, and some helping person or agency selected. The helping professional is brought in after this preliminary shaping has taken place, and very often the first task is to recognize the proffered shape, to search behind it for the original unshaped distress, and then to reshape the distress so that it can fit within the professional framework.

This process of shaping and reshaping distress can be considered through the activity of the distressed person, through the activity of the helping professional, or in relation to what the two of them are doing together. It can

3

also be related to the range of help which is currently available, and to the social and cultural background of the time which may permit some shapes and provide no room for others. Yesterday's permitted shapes may seem as old fashioned today as yesterday's hats.

Shaping by the client

An injury to a leg may leave little choice. But there are other situations where an inevitable shape does not present itself, and where there is no clear pathway from the distress to the shape, and from the shape to a helping person. Sometimes the distress which is presented in one form could have been presented in many others.

An overburdened mother, with many children and few resources either material or psychological, may look for relief in a number of different ways. She may go to the doctor, the health visitor, the headmaster, the housing department, or the priest. She may blame her troubles upon her husband, the hostile neighbours, the unhelpful teachers, her poor housing conditions, her legs, her back, her nerves, her children's health. Somewhere in this confusion, she may find a shape which offers a course of action, a helping person, a possible remedy and a future hope.

So the helping professionals, in office or surgery, are presented with distress which has already received some shaping for their acceptance.

Various factors will have played their part in influencing the shape which the distress has acquired by this stage. For one thing, the range of helpers known to one particular individual may be limited. One particular and well-worn path to a particular agency's door may suggest itself, and may determine whether the distress takes the form of a problem of physical or mental illness, housing, child-rearing or education. Our overburdened mother may have had help in the past from a responsive headmaster, or from a health visitor, or from the chemist on the corner; and so her current difficulties may cast themselves into a pattern that will enable her to go to the same resource again.

The professional worker reshapes

Once the person's distress reaches the office, consulting room, surgery or chambers, another set of factors is brought to bear upon the problem. The task of shaping has only just begun. There are two different parties to the process now, and together they have to work on reshaping the problem so as to find an area relevant to them both on which they can work together. Some agreement or contract has to be made.

The helping person does not stand alone. He, or she, is the representative of a particular profession, and probably also of a particular service or agency which operates within defined terms of reference. It is the helpers' job to bring to bear upon the problem their professional training and any resources which are available, augmented by personal skills, perceptions and inclinations, and augmented, too, by concepts added through additional training or through borrowing from other disciplines. Professional helpers have to pick up the problems that are presented, distinguishing the distress from the subsequent shaping, identifying the people concerned. They have to look for things which can be treated, areas suitable for intervention, and they may have to consider transposing problems into different areas, adding to what is presented or subtracting from it. Some reshaping is, indeed, inherent in all professional functioning.

Alternative shapes: a hypothetical encounter

To illustrate the process of shaping and reshaping that can take place in the transactions between client and helper, we can return to the general practitioner's surgery where the doctor and the man complaining about his leg are working together to define the area of their joint concern.

The patient has begun with the following statement:

1. *"It's my leg, doctor."*

With this statement, the problem is defined by the patient as the problem of part of a person. If he stops at this point, and if the doctor accepts this definition and also stops here, the doctor would presumably limit his area of concern to the leg. He would only ask the patient to take off the one sock. (There must be many doctors who still remember the days when there were patients who would resist any request to take off the second sock because they had prepared for the consultation by only washing the one leg.)

A number of situations occur in which it seems appropriate and sufficient to remain at this level. The dentist pulls out the bad tooth and the medical practitioner excises the wart or straps up the sprained ankle. This is similar to the situation in which one leaves one's watch with the watch repairer or one's pans with the tinker without feeling the need to supply information or submit to questioning about other areas of one's life. In such cases it seems legitimate to treat all other bodily activities and personal relationships as irrelevant to the problem presented. At this level one may go to an expert to obtain some information or some tool, or to have some part of one's personal property repaired, without finding it necessary to present the whole of the problem. The person seeking help is considered to be entitled to retain control of the situation and is left to define the problem and decide which areas to hand over for expert attention.

This level of working is not much favoured among the helping professions, where it is often criticized as being shallow and superficial. Since there is always more to the problem than the fragment that is presented, it can be argued that the additional areas should at least be sought out and examined. This viewpoint is not always shared by the patients or clients.

Conversely, it can also be argued that this level very often is sufficient, and that whenever possible the helping person should remain at this level without seeking any authorization to take the enquiries further. Different levels of work are appropriate in different circumstances: the optimum level should be that which achieves a "good enough" result with the minimum of disturbance.

This level, at which the doctor limits his interest to the leg, is characteristic of the "tinkering trades" described by Irving Goffman.[1] By tinkering trades he means those services in which the server deals with a disordered possession brought by a client, and in which there is an implicit bargain that the server should maintain a disciplined unconcern towards the client's other affairs and even towards the reasons which brought the client to request the service in the first place.

Within the helping professions, work of the tinkering kind requires closed and discernable physical symptoms if it is to be adhered to consistently, something like a disordered leg in fact, or a housing or financial problem which may in some circumstances need action on these criteria alone. This work requires that a distinction be made between the client and the client's malfunctioning object, and that these two entities be kept strictly separate. The problem of the helper is to distinguish these cases from the others where it is proper and necessary to make enquiries that extend beyond the presenting facts.

It is Goffman's contention that the profession of medicine has attempted to pattern itself upon the tinkering model, and that this attempt has been carried to extremes that have resulted in some strange and inappropriate practices. Patients may find themselves being treated as if they were not social persons at all, but possessions that have been handed in for repair. And becoming possessions, they may find that the role of client or customer has been taken away from them and transferred to others. It is not unknown for a relative to be pressed into service as the customer who brings a malfunctioning object for attention, to be given information about the patient, to consult with the experts, and to make decisions about the treatment and the handling of the case.

If our doctor accepts the leg as the object to be tinkered with, it may be because he has an image of himself as an expert repairer of defective objects. Or it may be that he is aware that there are other possibilities, but judges that this level is sufficient in this instance, or else that the other levels are not of medical concern and should be attended to by members of other disciplines.

However, either doctor or patient may be dissatisfied, at their encounter, with intervention at this level alone. It may not be so easy to stop at the knee.

The patient may wish to continue and the doctor may (or may not) permit him to do so. The doctor may wish to explore further, and the patient may (or may not) respond to his continued interest. Should they agree to continue, they could pass on together to position 2.

2. "It's my leg, doctor. *But I don't feel well in myself.*"

Now the leg is no longer a defective object to be tinkered with on its own, but has been related by the patient to the rest of his person. He presents the whole of himself to the doctor as being disordered, and the leg can no longer be understood without this context.

This is the level at which the watch mender might extend his interest beyond the watch to the owner, feeling that the information given by the watch alone is incomplete, and ask "Have you ever dropped it?" And the garage mechanic might turn from the car to the driver and ask "Do you drive with your foot resting on the clutch pedal?" A doctor or a social worker may take the initiative, turning from the symptom or situation presented to ask "How do you feel about it yourself?", ready to put the presenting problem into a wider context and to link it to the additional information which will come. The professional worker is assuming authority to reshape the problem, extend the area and enter into other aspects, reserving the option to direct treatment to something other than the leg.

3. "It's my leg, doctor. But I don't feel well in myself. *My wife isn't being much help to me either.*"

Here we have another major extension. The problem is no longer bounded by the person of one individual, but has been widened to include a relationship with someone else.

There are two main possibilities at this level. The patient has disclosed his wife's involvement in the problem, but he still keeps the problem as his possession; his wife is being no help to *him*. The doctor, while accepting this extension, can still remain focused upon the one patient, accepting the wife as one of the factors in the patient's environment with which he needs help, and which may have to be modified in the patient's interests. To this end, he might advise the patient how to behave towards his wife, or he might seek to talk to the wife in an attempt to explore her attitudes and feelings.

But there is another possibility. The doctor could redefine the boundaries of the problem so that it is no longer confined to one person. The problem could become a joint possession of the husband and wife, and the focus shift to the relationship between them and the way in which each of them affects and is affected by the other. We move from the intrapersonal level of concern with the inner and outer life of a single person to the interpersonal level where it is the interaction between two people which is important. This is a level in which many family doctors are beginning to take an interest, although it may be even more familiar to marital counsellors.

The doctor might say: "Next time you come to see me, would you ask your wife to come along too? I would like to talk to the two of you together about this."

4. "It's my leg, doctor. But I don't feel well in myself. My wife isn't being much help to me either, *but it's not just that. The children seem to have got out of control since I've had this bad leg.*"

This new situation brings a move from an interpersonal to a transpersonal level, from the dyad to the group.

When we are focusing selectively upon the relationship between two people, we are likely to have in mind a closed, two-way interactional system in which an action performed by A has an effect upon B, and B's reaction comes back to have an effect upon A in its turn. But with the introduction of the children we move into a wider arena, and have to have in mind a model of a much more complex pattern of relationships: we are now confronted by the family process itself. A watch mender would be unlikely to try to enter this area, although one might conceive of him asking "Do your children ever play with it?" if he thought that the problem being presented could not be understood without an extension into this area.

At one level, a problem can be considered to belong to a single individual: at another level, the same problem can be considered to belong to the family as a whole. An anecdote can be used to illustrate this.

The patient was a man with bowel symptoms who had had extensive and repeated examinations including X-ray of the bowel and sigmoidoscopy, all negative, and all, it appeared, carried out in the spirit of the tinkering trade. Only after these procedures had failed to help the patient was he sent to a psychiatrist in order that the disorder might be related to the whole person.

After listening to the patient's description of his symptoms and the way in which they troubled him, the psychiatrist put the following question.

"I know that these symptoms are painful, and that you are in constant discomfort. But sometimes symptoms like these do serve a useful purpose in the life of a person all the same. Can you think of any way in which these symptoms have done you any good?"

The answer came back without any hesitation. "No good at all. Quite the contrary. They are only upsetting to my mother, my sister and my wife!"

It needed very little more acquaintance with the family history to realize that the upsetting of his female relatives was a consummation devoutly to be wished.

This patient continued to retain his symptoms.

An awareness of family interaction, and a readiness to enter into this area, can be used in different ways. Some workers might continue to focus upon their primary patient; and yet find it relevant to question what meaning the problem that has been presented might have for other members of the family, and how the patient perceives this.

Other professional helpers, faced with a problem which has become identified as family property, might try to separate out the component parts. This might involve dealing with the different individuals in turn in their special roles as husband, wife, parent, child and sibling, against a background in which all the other relationships have their place. This work often goes by the name of family treatment, since the problem is defined as one of family life, but the work is essentially focused upon the separate individuals.

A third method would be to take the family as a whole and treat it as if it were a single entity.

At this level, a worker who has been trained to work with individuals, and with specific interpersonal relationships between people in particular roles, such as parental and marital relationships, has to add a new dimension to the original training. This dimension involves the ability to look beyond the individuals to the group as a whole; and to look on the group as a single entity subject to its own group processes which include, but transcend, the activities of any individual member. An extension into this dimension has been made possible through the work of group therapists.

But all this is not enough. The family is a very special group which differs in many important respects from the artificial treatment groups from which the concepts of dynamic group psychology have been largely derived. The worker will also need to have access to concepts relating to the family as an entity, and to conceptions of a family life cycle, and of family growth and development, in which different patterns can be recognized.

Our doctor still has a primary patient with a leg condition. His role is not that of a family therapist *per se*. But, nevertheless, he can make his interventions with an awareness of the family dynamics as a whole, and of the part which he himself may be playing within them.

5. "It's my leg, doctor. But I don't feel well in myself. My wife isn't being much help to me either, but it's not just that. The children seem to have got out of control since I've had this bad leg. *A very rough type of person is moving into our street now and it's having a very bad effect on our boys.*"

Now the boundaries of the problem are extended yet again. We pass beyond the family to its social context, and find relevance in the relationships between the family and the society of which it forms a part. In order to understand this relationship, there are certain new questions which need to be discussed. What are the boundaries of the family? How are these boundaries maintained? How does the interaction between the family and the surrounding society take place? How does the family see itself in comparison with other families? What are the crucial differences which help to give this family its sense of identity?

Some workers may wish to study the social context in order to understand the family better. Some workers may attempt to intervene at the interface between the family and the community of street or neighbourhood. Some may even, within the terms of their job descriptions, feel called upon to consider a whole community as their client and help this community to work towards a solution of its problems. Most doctors would not feel that they had the authority to turn neighbouring families into patients (even as parts of a greater whole) but there are group and family psychotherapists and community social workers who have felt able to do this. There have been well-documented cases in which psychotherapists have formed whole neighbourhoods into treatment units, intervening in the first instance in the interests of one disordered family and then locating the pathology in a social network or tribe and bringing upwards of forty persons together in one therapeutic enterprise.[2]

6. "It's my leg, doctor. But I don't feel well in myself. My wife isn't being much help to me either, but it's not just that. The children seem to have got out of control since I've had this bad leg. A very rough type of person is moving into our street now, and it's having a very bad effect on our boys. *I've been up to the Town Hall about it, but they don't seem very interested in our case.*"

This last level is that of the more formal social and political structure in which the family carries on its existence, including the helping agencies and those agencies which the family sees as withholding help.

The staff of these agencies may be treated as colleagues or auxiliary workers, to be approached, co-opted or manipulated in the interest of the patient. They may be seen as an integral part of the problem, to be included in any treatment plan. The boundaries of the problem may need to be redrawn to include housing department officers, if a family has a claim to be rehoused, or if it has difficulty in paying the rent. A school may have to be included in the area of work if the problem involves the failure of a child to learn, his fear of his teacher, or his disruptive behaviour in the classroom. Our doctor might wish to influence what is happening in housing department or school, he might know who to approach at the Town Hall, or he might feel he should help his patient to present his appeal more effectively. Or he might well feel that none of this is of direct medical concern, and put aside this aspect of the patient's problems. Or, yet another possibility, he might be one of those doctors who work as part of a team with social workers and health visitors, and who are thus able to intervene therapeutically within a wider field, and include more dimensions of a problem than would be possible were a single discipline working on its own.

In moving by stages from the part person via the family to society at large, we have been considering the possible boundaries of the identified problem within one dimension. In the interest of a tidy formulation, other aspects have been left out.

One important area that should not be omitted here is that of employment. Suppose that the patient were to say to the doctor:

7. "It's my leg, doctor, *it's not right, and it's making it difficult for me to carry out my job.*"

Here the disorder, located in the leg, is linked to the whole man in the role of worker and breadwinner, and so is linked to the work situation which includes him.

Starting from this point, there are again a number of different ways in which the problem could be approached, and a number of different contexts in which it could be placed. There is the leg; there is the man as worker, with the focus upon his capacity to do his job; there is the work situation which may need to be modified if he is to continue in the same job; and there are the alternative jobs which might be available to him now with his reduced capacity. Then we have the man as provider for his family, and here we are back in our mainstream again, taking into account the family relationships. It might be necessary to explore, for example, his fears that his family will suffer hardship, and his fears that he will lose status in the family or will have to put up with criticism or hostility. There may be an unconscious wish to punish his family, or a conscious feeling of gratification at the prospect of giving up an irksome responsibility and taking up again a more dependent role. We could go on adding to the possibilities, and the range of our perceptions will depend upon the range of the shapes that we are able to carry in our minds. If the doctor has only one shape available, then there is no problem of alternatives.

Inward and outward-looking professions

We have been using an artificial example in which doctor and patient are seen to shape and reshape the problem in a progressive sequence. The patient is given the option of taking part in this process because the doctor is ready to listen and respond, and appears to have extended his original training, taking in concepts from elsewhere and carrying in his mind a range of different models which could be applied to the understanding of the problem.

There are many other helping professions at work today whose job is to respond to distress that will have been given some sort of shape in order to be presented to them. Some professions offer a particular and specific method of treatment, and only take on patients who are suitable for that treatment. There are other professions which take on particular problems or particular client groups and have to find appropriate treatments for them all within their existing repertoire.

Marital therapists, for example, are likely to have a primary commitment both to a particular treatment approach and to a small and selected group of people in distress able and willing to benefit by that method. Their responsibility is limited in range (though not in depth) and does not extend to distress at large.

Generic social workers in area offices have a more general orientation. They may indeed have their specialist and preferred areas and their statutory responsibilities, but their primary commitment is not to one particular method but to a range of problems or forms of distress. They do not so much select clients suitable for treatment by their one method, as try to include among their wider repertoire a treatment plan for each of the clients who come.

We can look on these two groups as the inward-looking and the outward-looking disciplines. The inward lookers, for example the neuro-surgeons or the traditional psychoanalysts, have been accustomed to keeping themselves separate and exclusive, seeking to deepen and refine their skills rather than to extend their range. They maintain their boundaries and mix mainly with their own colleagues, reading the same journals and learning from one another.

The outward lookers, on the other hand, have been concerned to extend the range of their treatment methods, and to provide more choice, more variety and more flexibility, in the skills they have to offer. They are more likely to look beyond their own profession and to learn from others.

Finding a fit and failing to find a fit

Both inward and outward-looking professionals have the task, at the first encounter, of responding to the distress as it has been shaped by the client. They have to hold in mind the different options that come from the patient and those that they themselves can provide, and they have to try to find a fit and make a bargain about the treatment.

In this encounter the inward lookers often offer a clear shape of proven effectiveness in which they have total and justified confidence. In such a case there is no need to look for any further options. Nevertheless it is too much to hope that this one good practice can apply to all cases and all problems. There is always room for the outward-looking professionals who are searching for a new shape that will fit the problem before them.

The more options that the helping professionals have in their repertoire, the more options are likely to be discovered within the contributions of the clients, and the greater will be the flexibility that can be brought to the reshaping process.

Sometimes a bargain cannot be made. Sometimes the person in distress has come to the wrong door, or has brought an inappropriately-shaped problem. Sometimes the gap between the conceptions of the person seeking help and the conceptions of the helper are too great to be bridged. Sometimes the helper tries to reshape the problem in a way which is unacceptable to the other party.

An extreme example can be found in the case of a young man suffering from distress about the size of his nose. He wished to have plastic surgery, and accepted referral to a psychiatrist hoping for the recommendation which would enable him to have the operation performed free of charge under the national health service. The problem had been placed by others, but not by the patient, in a psychiatric framework; though the psychiatric framework, in this case, was intended to be a means to an end.

The psychiatrist did not accept the assignment in these terms. He interpreted the patient's complaint about the shape of his nose as a symptom of a psycho-sexual problem, and made an offer of psychotherapy in lieu of surgery, an offer which was indignantly refused. The interpretation may have been valid, but in the circumstances it did not lead to effective action because the patient and psychiatrist had each started with preconceptions from which neither was prepared to budge. The young man had settled his distress into the shape of his nose, and the psychiatrist was determined, with some theoretical justification, to locate it in another aspect of the personality. There was a rigidity on both sides, and a refusal to reshape together in order to find a meeting ground. Too few alternative shapes were available on either side.

In another case, where psychiatrist and patient have a more viable area of negotiation, they may together be able to shape the miseries into some sort of agreed pattern so that the two of them can work together, perhaps even finding a pattern which can be matched with the descriptions of an illness in psychiatric textbooks. For traditional psychiatric diagnosis can be considered as a process of shaping and selective matching, in which the imperfect approximations of the patients have to be measured against the model or "ideal" illness of the textbook. In the past it has sometimes been a rather one-sided exercise, and there are psychiatrists today who find that the process of shaping and naming is diagnosis enough. An example of this is when the diagnostic term is merely the translation of the symptoms presented into Latin or Greek. A diagnosis of agoraphobia, for example, does not appear to add anything new to the patient's own description of his fear of open spaces.

The professional response

Professional workers respond to the shapes that are brought to them in their different ways. Some may try to narrow the area that is presented, calling their patient or client back to the point, wishing to concentrate more upon one specific area which appears relevant to their own particular framework and to the model that they are carrying in mind. It may be the bad cough, the sexual problem, the child's failure to learn or the need for supplementary benefit. "I tried to tell them all about it," the client may say afterwards, "but they didn't seem to be interested. They only wanted to hear about the cough". These are the cases in which the client, (for example, a regular hospital outpatient) may say, in retrospect, "He asked the same questions every time, so he couldn't have been listening to the answer". The mother of a child about to be taken into care complained, "They only seemed to be interested in the baby". Granted that the baby was indeed the primary concern, she still felt that some thoughts should have been spared for her, as yet unexplored, personal distress.

In some other cases, attempts to widen the area of discussion may be equally unwelcome to the clients. Unsupported mothers, seeing their problems as economic rather than psychological or even social, can be indignant when a social worker enquires into their personal relationships and offers casework help in addition, or even instead of, the practical support which they are seeking. Social workers, no less than psychiatrists, have their framework in which financial difficulties seldom stand alone and are often taken as symptoms of a wider maladjustment which needs exploration, a "cry for help" that the crier does not always wish to acknowledge.

The power of individual professional helpers to reshape distress may be considerable or it may be very limited. Their professional training and their terms of service within the context of their clinic or agency gives them their primary authorization. In some clinics, such as those providing psychoanalytic treatment, the staff have the task of deciding whether a particular person will or will not profit from the treatment they are able to provide, and any redefinition of the distress will be done to include it or exclude it from their terms of reference. Social services, or more eclectic psychiatric services, may have less power to exclude, and be under more pressure to provide some sort of help or treatment. In this case, their reshaping will be linked to the need to make a selection from the different approaches at their disposal rather than a selection from the applicants for treatment of those most likely to respond. The approaches vary from finding suitable cases for treatment to finding suitable treatments for cases.

Apart from the requirements and limitations of their agencies and services, and the frameworks of their specialist trainings, professional workers bring to this task of reshaping their own personal talents and inclinations and the sum of their personal and professional experience. They also bring all the extensions and developments of their original training, and the concepts and models which they have created for themselves within their own professions or have borrowed from other disciplines and made their own. They will have a range of different shapes at their disposal, and an understanding of some of the different shapes which are at the disposal of colleagues in other disciplines. They will have the capacity to collaborate with these colleagues, and this will help them to place the problems in a wider context than that of their own particular specialization.

Professional boundaries

Although at times it seems as if there has been of recent years a great increase in the number of specific helping methods with exclusive adherents, there has also been, in many of the helping professions, a marked breaking away from former stereotyped roles. With this has come a greater readiness to experiment, to cross professional boundaries and to draw upon the experience and knowledge of other disciplines. This means that it has come to seem less and less appropriate to look at problems in limited terms, dealing with them within the boundaries of one profession or specialization, and ignoring or failing to observe other aspects.

Many professional workers have had to become aware of a wider range of possibilities, and become sensitive to a larger number of aspects, as knowledge and techniques originating in other disciplines have become available to them. They do not have to cover all these aspects on their own, and they do not have to leave their own discipline. They can take their own particular tasks and relate them to a wider perspective, refining their own responses and at the same time opening up the possibility of collaborating with a larger number of colleagues of different trainings and different orientations.

Members of a number of different professions who have a knowledge of group and family psychodynamics can now carry a range of models in their minds which enables them to recognize the existence of processes at different levels, and which makes it possible for them to respond to the material presented at these levels, whether their clients come singly, in couples, as families, or in groups.

This does not mean that we only work with groups or family units. It is our experience that, by and large, most clients still come singly, most problems are initially presented for help by individuals, and most distress first comes to notice as individual distress, even though it may well contain a complaint about another family member, and even though the translation of individual problem into family problem may be swiftly made. We still find that our starting point is usually an individual, and the individual has to remain an ever present preoccupation. We find that when we work with families we need the foundation of a knowledge of individual growth and development and of individual psychodynamics (supposing for the moment that there is such a thing as individual psychodynamics). And conversely when we work with individuals we need a knowledge of the dynamics of the groups and families of which individuals form a part.

When these concepts of group and family dynamics first began to be formulated it was as if they had come in response to a need, at a time of dissatisfaction in which new approaches were being sought. Existing concepts and existing treatment methods based upon an individual psychology were then no longer seeming adequate as a response to the problems that clients and patients were bringing. Perhaps there had been a change in the problems themselves, or perhaps there had been a change in the way that they were being presented, or perhaps the change was in the perceptions of the helping professionals.

Wherever the change came from, it brought a search for new concepts, and for new forms of treatment, and for ways in which existing practice could be extended. And as a result of the changes that came, it is now possible for us, along with colleagues from a number of different professions, to work with whole groups and whole families in mind, whether the clients or patients come singly, or in pairs, or in larger aggregates, and whether they themselves present their problems as individual ones or as part of a larger disturbance.

But in no sense have these changes made work with the one individual (or even with the one leg) obsolete.

Notes and references

1. Goffman, E. *Asylums* Doubleday, New York, 1961.
2. Speck, R. V. and Rueveni, U. *Network therapy*, Family Process ed. Ackerman, Basic Books, New York, 1970.
   Schoenfeld, P. *et al. Long term outcome of network therapy* Hospital Community Psychiatry, 37–373–376 April, 1986.

2

The Group Process

2

Crossing the Frontiers of Professional Practice

New concepts

If it is true that a single idea can dominate a generation of professional workers, then the theory and practice of group therapy would have had a claim to this distinction within "the helping professions". At the present time, family therapy is its heir.

During the last few decades, we have seen a number of different schools of group and of family therapy emerge, establishing their own bodies of theory and technique, and training their own specialist practitioners. Many books have been written and a literature has accumulated.

But this is not all. Like individual psychoanalysis in the previous generation, therapy making use of the interaction of a group of people has had an influence that has spread far beyond the consulting rooms and clinics in which the treatment is being carried out.

Excitement and controversy surrounds the actual application of the concepts, and this brings a fresh source of inspiration and encourages a more widespread questioning of accepted theory and practice. Even the creation of a new vocabulary within a new dimension of therapy can be sufficient to have an influence on the work that goes on in allied professions.

With all this, problems have come as well as opportunities.

The transmission of concepts between disciplines is a complex process, and difficulties can arise when insufficient attention is paid to the actual process of transferring material from one discipline to another.

The communication of ideas between professions is an important theme throughout this book, which is itself a product of interdisciplinary communication. One of the authors is a psychiatric social worker, the other a psychiatrist. Neither could have written it alone. The book makes use of concepts basic to both these professions, of concepts from common areas to which they both lay claim, and of concepts which they have borrowed from elsewhere. It also attempts to enter into other fields of work to which these concepts have a practical application, and to make some suggestions about ways in which the concepts might be applied. It is up to the practitioners in these other fields to decide whether they wish to take up the concepts or to leave them alone.

This book is addressed to the members of the authors' professions, but it is also addressed to many others. There is no copyright in ideas. But ideas have to be communicated in order to become available, and there are barriers of various kinds that may have to be crossed. In order to write this book, the authors have had to make themselves aware of the issues which arise when a member of one profession is communicating ideas to a member of another profession.

Professional identities

Before one is able to communicate profitably with a member of another discipline, whether as teacher and student, borrower and lender, team members or co-workers on a shared task, one needs first to be sure of one's own professional identity and traditional boundaries.

Professional identity grows in complex ways. In some respects, professional identity can be compared with that personal identity which comes as the growing child incorporates qualities from others: in the first place the child takes in qualities from the parents or other primary care givers, and later from members of the extended family, from teachers, and from all the others who pass through the child's life. Selection is always taking place, and some of the attributes which others deliberately try to inculcate may not be accepted. A personal choice has to be made and a personal identity established, making use of all the sources that are available, And so it is with the professions.

Professional trainings provide a framework within which a variety of source material is offered; and out of this some minimal requirements are laid down with an expectation that there will be a recognizable end product in the qualified entrant to the profession.

Learning from other professions

Some professional teaching may remain in the hands of members of that profession. But often members of other professions are involved in the teaching process as well. For example, in the various courses for social workers (a profession always prone to look outside its own boundaries and to go in for extensive borrowing from others) there may be lectures from psychologists, psychiatrists, physicians, administrators, sociologists and others who are not themselves practising social workers. Whatever these people are teaching, it cannot be social work; and the role models which they are offering are not those of social workers. What these teachers from other professions can do is to make concepts available for the students to borrow, and to find ideas, and linkages between ideas, in the hope that some of their hearers will derive enough from the experience to construct something new for themselves. It is the task of the student rather than of the teacher to make the final integration of separate systems of thought.

The member of the medical profession most familiar to the public is the general practitioner, but it is only in recent years that the work of the general practitioner has been specifically included in the teaching programmes of the medical schools. Until this happened, the teaching of all doctors was carried out by specialists of distinction who had little or no experience themselves in the work of general practice, and who therefore demonstrated a professional identity different from that of the general practitioner. The general practitioner, nevertheless has always had a recognised professional identity; and the existence of a powerful oral tradition of general practice preceded the acquisition of a systematized theory practice and literature of its own.

A number of general practitioners, meeting once in a discussion group with a psychiatrist, addressed themselves to this problem and they arrived at the conclusion that the medical school teaching that they had themselves received bore no relationship to the actual work that they were doing.

The psychiatrist asked how they thought it came about that the general practitioner had a distinct and recognizable identity, such that patients usually knew what to expect.

One of the general practitioners replied:

"It comes from the memory we have of the way a family doctor treated us when we were children."

If this be true, then this identity is passed on from doctor to doctor without going through the medical schools. But it cannot be altogether true, because the teaching of all the medical specialisms is absorbed into a complex identity incorporating practical and theoretical knowledge from a range of different sources, And, in addition, although the general practitioner works as a general practitioner and not as a sub-specialist, the range of his general practice is extended by his understanding of the various specialisms. Perhaps it is extended even more by his perception and absorption of some of the personal qualities of a selected number of his teachers.

The same process is part of the continuing education of every professional worker in practice, and it is a process which becomes ever more important as the knowledge base expands and as the perception of problems becomes more and more complex. Professional workers are expected to acquire a deepening knowledge of their own profession, and, in addition, a knowledge of the range of work that colleagues are carrying out beyond the range of their own experience. They are likely to have a continuous exposure to teachers and workers in other professions, sometimes because of multidisciplinary work and sometimes because of deliberately arranged training courses bringing different disciplines together to discuss specific themes. Shared areas of theory and practice need to be recognized in addition to the areas where each profession can lay claim to exclusive authority.

The knowledge that is exclusive and the knowledge
that is shared

Some knowledge is specific to a particular profession. But, in addition, each professional worker also draws upon a wide area of knowledge that is shared with others, and it is these overlapping areas that make professional collaboration possible. Without this overlap, members of an interdisciplinary team can only work separately and in parallel, and the co-ordination then has to come from an overlord who gives orders concerning the final objective.

We can look on the knowledge used by any profession as being figuratively, contained within three concentric circles.

First, there is the inner circle containing the knowledge that is exclusive to that profession.

Secondly, there is the middle circle containing knowledge that is shared with other professions.

Thirdly, there is the outer circle containing knowledge that is very relevant to professional practice, but which is outside that profession's specific training and professional experience.

The expansion of knowledge, and developments in areas belonging to other professions, can remove a particular theme or skill from the exclusive possession of one profession and move it outward into the shared area. Alternatively, there can be a movement in an inward direction, as when a change in thinking brings a piece of formerly shared theory within the territory arrogated to one particular profession.

For the purpose of illustration, it is convenient to apply this model to medicine, for here the exclusive area ia more clearly differentiated than in other caring professions. We find within the doctor's inner circle the special medical knowledge and skills, the authorization which the doctor has to deal with acute illness and with questions of life and death, and the responsibility which the doctor has for the conduct of treatment. Here the doctor carries full responsibility, and any work done by any other profession is done "under doctor's orders". It is what the doctor should mean when he speaks of his clinical responsibility.

Within the second circle are the problems of family interaction, many aspects of the development of children, occupational problems and knowledge of social conditions, and all such knowledge which is shared with social workers, psychologists, administrators, educationalists and others. The doctor makes these areas part of his enquiries, but cannot make prescriptions based upon them alone, although they influence his decisions and he has influence in his turn. It is influence, but it is not exclusive professional authority. If he does elect to speak with authority in this area, he cannot speak with finality, for here there are other professions which have a different but at least equally valid voice.

In the outer circle are all the questions of public policy and of everyday living which affect the lives of the doctor's patients, which the doctor has to know about, and should have opinions about, but in relation to which has no more authority to speak than a layman. The doctor can speak with the authority that comes from personal qualities and everyday knowledge, but cannot speak as a doctor.

A distinction has to be continually made between decisions that come from the trained part of the doctor's personality, and which carry medical authority, and those which come from the doctor's general level of worldly experience and personal interest.

"What do you as a doctor think about modern youth?" may be asked. The doctor may have a lot of opinions about modern youth, but they are not strictly medical opinions although they will influence his work. Observations that come from this area may well be valuable and valid, but the doctor should be careful not to invest them with medical authority himself, and should discourage other people from doing so.

Professional boundaries are always shifting

An example of the shifting boundaries of professional areas that comes to mind is the response to the failure of some children to attend school.

This behaviour was first dealt with within the educational system, having at first been considered to be a social and legal matter. At this time, psychiatrists made no studies of it. However, some cases remained intractable with this treatment; and when parents began to consult family doctors, searching for additional explanations of the behaviour, a number of cases found their way to psychiatrists.

The involvement of psychiatrists led to the invention of the term "school phobia", after which it became possible to recognize a syndrome and place it within the province of child psychiatry and child guidance clinics. Criteria where then laid down in order to distinguish "school phobia", which was now recognized as an emotional disorder, from "truancy" which remained a social problem. However, the boundaries were not altogether clear. For some time it remained a matter of dispute between the clinical and educational services as to whether school phobia had any existence or was just a fancy name to excuse particular children from the consequences of their refusal to go to school.

Gradually, the concept of emotional disorder related to school attendance came to achieve general recognition. This was followed by the further recognition that there were social aspects to the school phobic cases, and emotional factors in many of the so-called truancies. The result of this was that the condition was renamed. The term "school refusal" began to be preferred to the term "school phobia" in order to recognize a continuity of problem behaviour (in interpersonal terms) which could include food refusal in infancy and occupational problems in adulthood.

During all this time, these problems were considered to be personal to the child, or appertaining to the area of family relationships; and for the most part the school was disregarded. The school was merely the place where the behaviour came to light.

The next stage came when the workers in the educational field, including the teachers, began to recognise a psycho-social dimension in their work. The practice of advising or counselling began to form part of the general or specialist teacher's activities. This brought back an educational interest in the whole range of the problems of school attendance, and made it possible to think of ideas of prevention and treatment outside the range of the psychiatric services.

Thus there has been a shift back and forth, from education to psychiatry, and then from psychiatry back to education; with the inclusion along the way of psychology, social work and general medicine as the different professions have been drawn together into multidisciplinary teamwork. Wherever such a shift is made, it brings members of different professions together to work alongside one another, at the same time allowing the professions to continue their own independent approach within their own disciplines.

Boundaries are shifting in many other areas. To take another example, as the understanding of dynamic psychology has increased, new treatments have become available within psychiatry for forms of personal distress hitherto not considered treatable. These disorders are then taken into the inner circle of the psychiatrist, until such time as the spread of skills to other professions (who meanwhile have been making independent progress of their own) brings these disorders out once more into the circle where knowledge is professional but shared.

Expectations of teachers and students

Where members of different professions meet in a situation in which one is designated teacher and the other one is designated student, what is the one expecting of the other?

There are various possibilities.

Is the student expected to take within himself the attitudes and ethos of the one who is designated teacher? Is the student expected to become the teacher's disciple, or his subordinate, or his rival? Is he, in some way, expected to become associated with the teacher's profession, even if barred from joining it? These are among the expectations which often appear to be present, implied even if not stated, to the confusion of the students and often of the teachers too.

Alternatively, the purpose of the encounter could be the development of something new that will become the property of the student's profession.

Or, to take the process one stage further, perhaps the student and teacher, both together, could develop something new in a fresh area which they both could share. For, where members of two different professions meet, each could and should have something to learn from the other; and the roles of student and teacher may be shared, and even at times reversed, with benefit to both parties. Teaching is then turned into a creative experience, and both professions grow.

A prime area of growth, into which more and more professions are edging their way, seems to be the psycho-social area.

There are few professions today that do not face demands from their own public for an extension of their work into areas which are concerned with feelings, motivations and relationships. Doctors and nurses, teachers and clergy, are now expected to take part in "counselling", and this means that it is psychiatrists, psychologists and social workers who are the most frequently cast in the role of teachers of other professions. Willingly or unwillingly, many of them accept this role; and they also take part in the teaching of each other.

Psychiatrists, for example, may take part in the teaching of social workers, but they do not teach them to be psychiatrists. Neither do they teach them to be social workers, for that would not be within their competence. In some medical schools, social workers teach undergraduate and postgraduate medical students; and this, in turn, is not intended to teach them how to do social work, nor how to practice medicine. Each teacher presents a method of approach to topics that are of common concern, within the area that they share with their students, and they do this in the belief that there is a point of contact at which something new can be created.

Requisites for teaching members of other professions

The authors believe that there are three requisites that have to be kept in mind by anyone who is teaching members of another profession.

1. Respect for oneself.
2. Respect for the immediate occasion.
3. Respect for the profession of one's students.

The respect for oneself has to include a respect for one's own profession. The psychiatrist who teaches other professions should not denigrate psychiatry, nor the social worker social work. It is their original training as psychiatrist or social worker that gives them the authority to teach others. It is their capacity to see the relevance of this to other fields that justifies an invitation to teach other professions. However, they must not become so infatuated with the new applications, and the interest of working on the outer boundaries, that they cease to acknowledge and value the work that is carried out in the mainstream of their professions.

The respect for the occasion includes punctuality.* It includes an appropriate amount of preparation for each meeting, and the collection of any factual material required about some topic or document. It includes the devotion of attention to the communications from the student members of the class or group. It also requires that the teachers bring with them the totality of their professional experience, and that they do not consider that any lesser order of skill is required here than in their own professional practice.

* This point may seem elementary but experience suggests that it often gets overlooked when time is scarce.

The respect for the other profession must be genuine, and it requires that the teachers should not imply that their students from other disciplines will provide an inferior substitute for what they themselves would do, entering their field in a subordinate position to carry out routine tasks. It can never be satisfactory for members of one profession to be considered to be working as second best on jobs which ought, in an ideal society, to be done by another. The purpose of the teaching should be to provide concepts that can be used to make a job into the *actual property* of the people who are going to undertake it. The concepts then cease to be the property of the teacher, and the teacher has to be ready to acknowledge this.

The same three requisites are obtained when someone from an academic discipline is teaching field workers. Sometimes an academic approach appears to undermine the value of work which has a practical aim. There are those who use the word "scientific" exclusively for the organization of data which can be measured; and who make a distinction between observations which are objective, and therefore absolute, and those which, being subjective, depend upon value systems. This in itself is a value system, in which the student's ultimate profession, if directed to personal social service, is given a lesser valuation than engagement in the making of "scientific surveys".

Example: in-service training group

As a practical example of the problems which arise at the meeting of disciplines, a psychiatrist was given the assignment of conducting a series of discussion groups with medical, nursing and social work colleagues working for the same local authority.

At the first meeting, with a group of assistant medical officers of health, not knowing how to begin, he asked "What do you expect of me?"

Immediately, one of the medical officers replied: "That you should understand our work".

The psychiatrist said: "That's fair enough", and then it occurred to him to add, "But it is more important that I should understand my own".

As the discussion developed, it became apparent that the medical officers were expecting him to claim that he knew more about their work than they did themselves, and they had come prepared to challenge such a claim. They knew that they had problems with their work, and that they wanted help. But they were doubtful whether it was possible to get this help from someone who, whatever his claims, could not have their experience with the problems that they wanted to discuss. What then, they wondered, did he have to offer?

The contribution that came to be offered to them was the psychiatrist's own tentative thoughts about problems that were new to him. It was the fact that the problems were new to him that made it possible for him to respond to this situation. He had his own experiences and the medical officers had theirs, but they were going to deal with topics on which they could share their ignorance. Some of the thoughts that would arise would be new to them all. What the psychiatrist had to offer was not his greater experience of some particular problem: his contribution was his method of approach. He was not expecting the members of the group to exchange their own methods for his: he was expecting them to be prepared to look at their methods in a wider context.

The very nature of the problems which were brought to these meetings made it appropriate for discussion of them to take place in that setting. Many of the problems concerned patients already in contact with various specialist medical services and with different social work departments. The problems were those which straddled the different professions and involved a number of different statutory and voluntary services. Many of the issues referred to cases for which the practical decisions had already been taken at meetings of co-ordinating committees. In this new group, the participants offered different viewpoints on the problems brought for discussion, and were also able to recall similar or comparable problems.

The reformulations that were made were not the exclusive property of the one who suggested them in the discussion nor were they the property of the leader. They belonged to the group as a whole, and to every individual member of it.

Requisites for learning from members of other professions

The relationship of teacher and student is a reciprocal one. The students respond to the attitudes of their teacher, and they too play a part in shaping the situation. The three requisites for teaching in this context have their counterparts for those in the student role.

The three levels of respect can be respecified as follows for the student.

1. Respect for oneself and for one's own professional identity.
2. Respect for the practical procedures that one undertakes.
3. Respect for colleagues in other professions, including those from whom one hopes to learn.

These conditions are all basic to the central theme of this work, viz. the application to the helping process, in all its complexity, of concepts of interpersonal psychology in which the individual is subsumed within the family or group.

Many members of the helping professions who have become interested in the application of these ideas, and who wish to extend their work to include groups and families as a whole, are having to look outside their own profession. They are having to make use of concepts not originally their own, and integrate these concepts with their existing skills. They are having to turn to the formulations of the different schools of dynamic group and family psychotherapy which make it possible to use the group and family situation in a conscious and disciplined way.

These concepts are, however, complex in the extreme; and they cannot be transferred wholesale out of the specific psychotherapeutic settings in which they were first developed. They have to be adapted before they can be assimilated, and first of all they have to be understood. It is up to the borrowers or students to understand the material they are borrowing and the use to which it is to be put, bearing in mind the ultimate aim for which the work is being carried out.

Different professions have different needs. Some professions are adventurous borrowers. They reach boldly outside their own boundaries, and there may even be times when they are uncomfortably flooded by the material which is brought back. Others, in contrast, are reluctant and grudging borrowers, (and these are likely to be reluctant and grudging lenders too). They attach more importance to preserving the purity of their own discipline and to maintaining the integrity of their boundaries against the incursions of others.

The impetus for any extension of existing practice must come from within each separate profession, and arise from the actual needs of that profession as these are seen in its day-to-day practice.

It must be assumed that every potential group (and family group) worker will have an original professional framework in which to incorporate the material taken from elsewhere, and will therefore be capable of a disciplined approach to any group work which is undertaken. The knowledge of group work that is added will bring new experiences, and new forms of co-operation with members of other professions. The student's original profession will be enriched.

A teacher, for example, who receives a group work training, will have added a new dimension to his work with his pupils and their families, and may acquire additional authority to work as a counsellor within the educational setting. He does not have to leave this setting. Similarly, a clergyman might be able to provide himself with an additional framework for some of the pastoral duties which are traditionally his, but he would not have to enter a new profession. It could, indeed, be looked upon as an impoverishment if entering into group work separated the student from his own colleagues.

Group work, as we are envisaging it, cannot exist *in vacuo*. It requires a base and it requires a context.

It is a discipline of its own for its own specialists, within the schools of group (and family) psychotherapy, and there are indeed those in the helping professions who turn to it for a more formal training and a qualification for entry into a new profession. But its applications are wider than this. For many others, as for ourselves, it can be used to provide an extension of existing practice in work with those who come, singly or together, seeking help.

But due regard must first be paid to the foundation upon which the extension of group work is to be built. And, no less important, due regard must be paid to the nature of the teaching process which will make the building of the extension possible.

3

The Formation of a Group

The family is the first group

The ideas of group work and of family work are intertwined. The family is the first group that anyone experiences. The child is born into the family group and grows with it, forming from the moment of birth a part of the family process. Family relationships are unequal, and the child enters at the bottom of the family hierarchy. A little later in the child's life come contacts with people in the outside world, and then the transition to school which has its own rules and its own legends: here the child for the first time has a peer group in addition to people in authority. From then on follows membership of one group after another; and throughout all this, and through all the relationships that individuals make during their life spans, it is possible to find the transferences that link these situations with each other. It is also possible to link all these group situations with the family group of origin, finding this original family situation present as a model in all later group networks.

In individual psychotherapy the notion of transference is used to explain behaviour and also as a therapeutic tool. With the advent of group therapy a new dimension was added, and a new language had to be invented to make it possible to refer to the multiple transferences of a group. All the new developments, however, can be traced back to the familiar primary concepts of the relationship of parents, children and siblings. The family remains a presence within the therapy group.

Today, in family therapy, we have a reservoir of experience of group therapy which can be brought back to the understanding of the processes taking place in families. The ideas of group work and of family work are intertwined and have to be considered together, but they also have to be considered, separately.

Our first task here, then, is to identify the group.

Group defined in Gestalt terms

Proximity is not enough to turn a number of different objects into a group. There are other requirements which have to be fulfilled. If they are to be considered a group, the different objects must contain some property in common, and they must also be related to each other in such a way that it is possible to consider them as a single entity. There must also be an observer, since such forming of objects into a group is a function of their perception. It is the observer who recognizes the common property and who finds the unifying relationship, and who thus confers upon them the status of group.

There are several trees on the skyline, more than a pair, yet not enough for us to describe them as a wood. We recognize that they are all trees, and that they have this property in common with each other and in distinction from the other objects around them. They are so placed in relation to each other that we are able to pick them out from their surroundings and consider them as a whole. Our perception of the trees turns them into a group.

This concept of a group is similar to the concepts used by the Gestalt psychologists who base their ideas of perception upon the capacity which human beings have to organize the elements of perceived objects into a composite whole.

As with trees, so it is with people. A group is bigger than a couple and smaller than a crowd. In our perception of groups of people, we look for a point in common and a relationship that unites the different individuals as parts of a single whole.

What the common point might be, and what type of relationship we would look for, would depend upon our context. A painter, interested in visual properties, may "see men as trees, walking", finding a common element in the shape that each one makes, and a spatial relationship between them that creates a unity. Another context, that of dynamic psychology, has other requirements, and seeks different resemblances and relationships. The common factor may be found in a shared purpose or concern, of which all the individual members are aware; and the relationship, linking all the parts of the group together in a unique way, may be found in the psychological interaction which follows upon the shared purpose. People may be turned into a group through the activity of an external observer, but equally they may become a group through their own recognition of each other.

A number of people sitting in a railway compartment might be considered a group by a painter able to fit them all into one composition. But if each sits reading a newspaper, or sleeping, if little or no communication takes place among them, they cannot be considered to form a group in any psychological sense. Suppose, however, that there is a breakdown, the train is delayed, and their immediate future becomes uncertain. Suppose that under the impact of this external event they exchange and share feelings of indignation, anxiety, and distress, (and despite the discomfort, these feelings may have overtones which are not unpleasant) each communicates something, and each responds to the communications of the others. These communications and responses can be looked upon as a pattern of interaction, relating each part to each other part. This pattern of interaction is the psychological counterpart to the relationship of shapes and colours with which the painter is concerned. For us, it is the existence and recognition of this interaction that turns a collection of people into a group.

We use the Gestalt psychologists' explanation of the way people discover patterns in unrelated objects to illustrate the fact that we need some dynamic systems of psychology to explain the pattern of group behaviour that we perceive when people meet and interact together.

Thus a number of people congregate, sharing some purpose, interest, or concern, and stay together long enough for the development of a network of relationships which includes them all. Recognition of this network brings the concept of a group. Each member of the group, though continuing to behave in habitual and characteristic ways, is influenced by the behaviour of each of the others and also by the prevailing mood or climate which is present in the group at any moment of time. This mood or climate is something to which every single member contributes, but which no single member can control.

Assumptions of group processes

The group may consist of a number of colleagues having a drink together after work, a reunion of old students, a discussion group, a committee meeting, a psychotherapeutic group, or any one of the small face-to-face gatherings in which most of us spend a large part of our working lives. Equally, it could consist of a nuclear family sitting round the dinner table, or an extended family brought together for a special celebration. After such a meeting, one may look back and wonder why one member talked so much and another so little, why one was listened to so eagerly and another relatively ignored. Why was this topic pursued with interest and that topic allowed to drop? Why was so and so never mentioned, and such and such only treated flippantly? Why was everyone so lively at one point, and so much quieter a little later on? What forces, in fact, determine the proceedings of a group, and, supposing there are such forces, how can one begin to study and understand them?

A student of individual psychology might focus upon the behaviour of each individual member in turn, and attempt to give separate explanations for each one in the light of what could be learned or observed. But the student would find this approach insufficient to account for the complete pattern of events, or to answer the questions posed above. It might be compared with an attempt to explain the shifting pattern of a kaleidoscope by taking the tube to pieces and listing the fragments found inside. Something more than this is needed. It becomes apparent that in studying groups we are not dealing with a collection of different pieces of behaviour happening in juxtaposition, but with a complex and dynamic interaction.

In order to try to understand this interaction, it is necessary to take all the individual pieces of behaviour, the contributions of each different group member, and treat them as if they were parts of a meaningful whole. In order to do this, we have to make certain assumptions about the nature of groups. We have to form a concept of the Group (and just this once we spell the word with a capital "G") as a separate entity, to ascribe forces to it, and even to endow it with capacities for decision and action. We have to do this in order to describe and explain certain aspects of human behaviour, and we are entitled to do so as long as we do not forget that the group is an abstraction. Such a concept can be compared to the many other concepts in psychology which do not refer to anything with an actual, concrete existence, but which provide the language which is necessary for the description of psychological phenomena. The superego, for example, is not a material object; it is an abstract concept which embodies inferences from observations of behaviour and perceptions of experience.

If we treat this concept of the group too concretely, we may be led into another error, namely, the naive transfer of properties pertaining to the individual to the group as a whole. Some of the mechanisms familiar in individual psychology may have their counterparts at a group level (and we shall presently be considering ambivalence in this connection), but their presence cannot be assumed and each needs to be discovered afresh.

For our purposes, it is necessary to consider the group as a separate psychological entity; but this necessity does not alter the fact that a group has no existence apart from the activity of its individual members. Any property or activity that we may ascribe to the group arises solely through the normal psychodynamics and the psychopathologies of people meeting together, through the ways in which they interrelate, and through their reactions to the external realities of the situation in which they find themselves. The activity of the whole and the activity of the parts must be recognized and studied.

If we are to assume that some connection exists between all the events taking place in a group, then we must also assume that, at some level, there are forces in existence that exert an influence over every single thing that happens there. To these assumed forces we give the name of group processes. These processes must belong to the group situation; they are created by the group, and they are present inevitably whenever several people meet and form a relationship with each other. So if one is to understand the meaning of the behaviour of any particular person in a group context at a moment in time, an exhaustive knowledge of that person is not enough; one must also look for the processes operating in the group which will have played a part in eliciting that behaviour. These processes are not usually within the conscious awareness of the group members who are participating in them, but they may be more readily apparent to a detached observer.

Hypothetical example

To illustrate this point, let us consider a summary of events at one particular group meeting.

A number of students meet together for a drink on the evening before an important exam. Several of them immediately start to talk about their work in a flippant and frivolous manner. Two of them begin to discuss an academic point, but the discussion soon peters out and they fall silent. A reference to exhaustion due to hours spent in study is ignored. A shipwreck, reported in the day's news, is mentioned, with the fact that some of the ship's crew were drowned because they could not all fit into the lifeboat. An absent student with a reputation for hard work and academic success is mentioned, and criticized as unhelpful and unfriendly. Several students discuss his way of life with pity and with some contempt, deploring its narrowness and lack of social and sexual content. There is an argument about payment for the drinks, a refusal to let any one person undertake this, and finally an agreement that each member should contribute an identical amount. No one seems to want to leave, and they stay together until closing time.

If we look for some underlying process linking together every single separate incident that took place at this meeting, we find an attempt to reconcile two distinct and incompatible sets of feelings. On the one hand, there is the wish that the group should continue to exist and provide the companionship and support of peers: on the other hand, there are competitive and disruptive feelings, the fears of arousing envy and hostility in others by examination successes, or, alternatively, fears of experiencing envy and hostility oneself if the success is lacking. These are the feelings that are activated or emphasized by the actual group situation, and, whatever other needs and preoccupations the individual members may have, they all share these feelings to some extent. Thus we find an area of common ground where the different problems of individuals meet in a group problem. The behaviour of each individual at this particular group meeting can be regarded as part of an overall pattern of behaviour which has as its aim the reconciliation of the two opposing sets of feelings, and which represents the group's struggle to survive under the pressure of disruptive forces.

In the light of our assumptions, the events taking place at the students' meeting can be interpreted in the following way. The group at first decides that exams are not to be taken seriously, and therefore the threat to the group can be treated as if it does not really exist. This solution is not unanimous at first, and some covert pressure has to be exerted to make it so. The students' wish to remain "all in the same boat", and their fears that the group might break up violently, are then expressed symbolically, since the anxieties are too strong to be dealt with effectively by denial and need to be expressed outwardly in some other way. They then find that they can broach their competitive feelings more directly, without endangering the group, by denigrating an absent rival while at the same time maintaining the fiction that none of them is actually seeking academic honours. No one is allowed to take on the superior position of host. At the end of the meeting anxieties and fears are still present, since nothing has happened to relieve them; and a sense that a threat still exists makes it difficult for the group to disband.

This interpretation is based upon assumptions that we need to make in order to examine group behaviour. To sum up, we assume that all the different events taking place in a group, though contributed by different people, can be treated as if they were the product of a single entity. We assume that these events are all connected through the operation of forces that we are calling "group processes", and which are a property of the group as a whole. We assume that, through the operation of group processes, attempts are made to reconcile the opposing tendencies present in every group, which by their opposition arouse anxiety in the group members and even threaten the group's continued existence.

Anyone familiar with the literature on group work will recognize that these assumptions belong to a particular dynamic viewpoint which derives ultimately from psychoanalysis. We will return to these assumptions and to their origins in the chapter on group psychotherapy; for the moment we are simply stating them in order to set the scene for what follows.

Purpose and structure in groups

In our example, the group of students had from the beginning one overriding preoccupation in which all members shared, and it also had very little of the structure that can impose formal patterns and through its formality hinder the spontaneous development and expression of a common group theme. In other, more structured, groups we are likely to find that the group processes appear more complex and devious, and are influenced by a greater number of variables.

In order to consider the processes taking place in any particular group situation, one has to consider first of all the expressed purpose for which the group is meeting. Every gathering that is more than an unrelated collection of individuals will have a purpose, as the purpose of our students was the enjoyment of the companionship of their fellows. This purpose supplies a reason for meeting, establishing a framework and a context, and providing members with roles to play and expectations about the behaviour of other members; it may also impose a considerable degree of control over the proceedings.

A committee, convened to carry out a specific task, will need to have a structure designed to further this task and to exclude irrelevant elements. There will be a leader, or chairperson, an agenda, and rules of procedure. Members will know that a certain type of behaviour is expected of them, and equally they will have expectations about the behaviour of the other members. If one looks at the record of the proceedings of a committee meeting, one would expect, and one might find, a greater coherence in the discussion, and a greater consistency in individual behavior, than is usual in less structured groups. In this situation, as in all group situations, the group processes play their part, but their presence is likely to be more difficult to detect.

A social gathering, on the other hand, will have another framework. There will be no chairperson, although there may be a host. There will be no agenda or rules of procedure, but there will be certain conventions influencing the way in which people behave and their expectations of the behaviour of others. The purpose of the meeting is enjoyable social intercourse, and the members will be expected to behave pleasantly and refrain from introducing any disturbing elements which might interfere with the enjoyment, or disrupt the harmony, of the group.

It seems that it is necessary for our comfort that the groups in which we take part should have a structure, which can impose some control over what may take place, and set some limits to the behaviour of ourselves and of others. It could be frightening to be in a situation where there seems to be no form of control, where we can have no firm expectations about what may happen, or where we do not know how we ourselves are expected to behave. Such fears have been shown to exist in experimental leaderless groups, and in groups that are kept unstructured for a psychotherapeutic purpose. Typically, in the beginning stage of these groups, there is a period in which the members experience considerable anxiety; and they may try to press someone into the role of leader, or attempt to devise some rules of procedure or agreed conventions of behaviour, even where this is quite inappropriate.

Individual contributions within the group as a whole

Within the group structure, which may be firm or weak, explicit or implicit, are the individual members, each with his or her own psychological make-up, own problems and own needs.

Every one of us is driven by certain emotional needs. Though we may not be conscious of the way in which they influence our conduct, we all try to arrange our lives and our relationships with other people so that these needs can be satisfied. We are each of us aware that we feel more at home in certain situations and less at home in others. We like to play certain roles, to make certain types of relationships, and to be treated in certain ways. We are attracted to the company of people who will allow us, or encourage us, to behave in the ways that we wish to behave, and who will give us the responses we seek. Wherever we are, we try to influence or manipulate our associates so as to elicit from them the behaviour that the satisfaction of our needs requires. We try to avoid situations that we find unsatisfactory, or disturbing, or frustrating. If we cannot avoid such situations, we look for some way in which we can change them or lessen their impact. These basic emotional needs, which determine so much of our behaviour, in groups as in other situations, have their origins in our constitutional endowment and in our earliest relationships; and they are shaped and influenced, modified or confirmed, by all our subsequent experiences.

Different needs will be activated by different circumstances. When a person is with a group of other people, the situation in itself, and his feelings about the other people present, will determine which of his habitual needs he will experience and how he will endeavour to satisfy them. His behaviour will also be influenced by his feelings about the group as a whole, and about the relationship prevailing between the group and the outside world.

To take a specific instance: in a group meeting one male member is lively and talkative, responding to every topic and entertaining the gathering with his wit and fund of stories. This could be part of a characteristic pattern of behaviour which he habitually employs in such situations; if an interpretation for it is sought, it might be found in terms of early experiences which have made him equate lack of notice with lack of love and feel frustrated if he is not given attention. Alternatively, this behaviour might be the result of interrelationships in this particular group and be specific to this situation; there may be a woman present whom he particularly wishes to impress, or a man who arouses strong competitive feelings. At another level, it could represent his reaction to a particular topic under discussion; he might want to divert attention from this topic or he might try to ensure that it is only treated flippantly. Finally, his behaviour might be the result of his feelings about the group as a whole; for example, a wish to keep the group in existence because it is serving some need, juxtaposed with a fear that it is going to break up. At social gatherings similar behaviour is sometimes shown by anxious hosts.

How our man actually behaves will depend upon the other people present, each of whom will also be trying to arrange matters so that a predominant need is met. His behaviour will help or hinder the attempts of the others, and so will meet with support or with discouragement in varying degrees. If one considers marriage as a permanent group of two, one can observe unions which appear to bring together pairs of complementary needs: to talk and to be talked to, to dominate and to submit, to protect and to be protected. These marriages may be harmonious, but are hardly likely to encourage personal growth and development since they provide no incentive for change. It does not seem probable that Jack Sprat and his wife ever changed their eating habits.

Such a consistent dovetailing of needs is not to be expected in most group situations. There we are likely to find constant adaptation and change as each member tries to influence the others to behave in a way favourable to his own particular and personal requirements. The more structured the group, and the more stereotyped the roles that the members are expected to play, the less apparent will be the tensions and needs that each individual brings into the group. The needs will be there, and they will exert some influence, but they will be masked by the formal procedure and there will be less opportunity for them to obtrude into personal relationships.

One will not willingly remain for long in a situation in which personal needs are not being met in some way or other. If unable to influence a group to provide some minimal satisfactions, one will seek to leave. The committee member whose needs are only satisfied when in a predominant position will aspire to be elected to the chair. If unsuccessful in this, other means to satisfy this need may be sought. It is possible that hard work might bring a prominent position as an authority on some aspect of the subject at issue, or, alternatively, as leader or spokesperson of a minority group. If unable to obtain any of these satisfactions, the committee member may find fault with the committee's composition, terms of reference, or method of procedure, declaring it unworkable (which by now it very well may have become).

If attendance at a meeting is compulsory, the dissatisfied member may perhaps withdraw into sleep or daydreams, or express dissatisfactions through overt or covert destructive behaviour aimed at damaging or ending the group. Such behaviour would be satisfying the newest and most pressing need, a need that has been activated by the specific conditions and reactions encountered in the group. It is not necessarily a position of comfort that is being sought: there may even be some who find a perverse satisfaction in demonstrating that none can satisfy them.

This example, illustrating the disruptive effect of a single dissatisfied participant, is likely to be familiar to those experienced in committees, and, equally, those experienced in committees will realize that this is only part of the story. It leaves out of account the constructive and cohesive forces within the group forming the committee, expressed in the consensus of opinion and the decisions which lead to action. It is this aspect which gets recorded in the minutes. The destructive forces operating in the group are not likely to be observed as such, and certainly not in the terms that we have used. The individual expression of such forces is more likely to be described, and may even find approval, under such labels as "sticking to one's principles" or "upholding the rights of minorities". A group that accepts such labels is, in fact, offering its destructive forces a legitimate means of expression, and may be able to contain them in this way.

Despite its complex motivations, our behaviour usually remains appropriate to the different situations in which we find ourselves. We observe regulations and conventions, we pay some respect to the personal needs of others, and we still manage to achieve some satisfactions of our own. If a particular need is so compelling that it must be expressed, and if it cannot find expression through approved behaviour, then we have to behave in unapproved ways, and we run the risk of being designated unconventional, unreliable, eccentric, maladjusted, ill, or simply mad or bad. But most people are able to function at more than one level, satisfying at the same time, and through the same actions, their own needs and the expectations both of society in general and of their own immediate company.

If it is to continue in existence, and if it is to retain all its members, a group has to make some provision for the needs of each of the individuals who compose it, conflicting though these needs may be. Therefore the total proceedings of any group meeting can be seen, at one level, as a compromise which contains some part of the personal preoccupations of each member and which goes some way to meet the requirements of each. This is a dynamic position, and we mean by this that the compromise is continually being adjusted as the interaction taking place among the group members stimulates the perception of new needs and offers new solutions.

The success of the member who seeks to dominate a group will depend upon the ways in which the other members react. Such an attempt might be welcomed by some, for complex and personal reasons, and may come to be justified in terms of providing the group with a new direction, giving a firmer lead, introducing new ideas, or changing an existing unsatisfactory position. For converse reasons it could be resisted by others. If there is open competition for leadership, then the group will only survive if it is able to find a way of accommodating these rivalries. Such competition would pose a problem for individual members: it also poses a problem for the group as a whole, and one must look at the total pattern of behaviour in the group to see the way in which this problem is met. One of the possible solutions to this problem would be for all members to take turns. This could be formalized in arrangements for different members to take the chair in rotation; or, informally, it could just happen that each member finds him or herself taking the lead in succession, while the other members acquiesce. Certain provocative topics which stimulate rivalry might be quietly dropped, as if by some silent agreement. Alternatively, some member who is not personally involved in the leadership conflict might take the position of arbiter and referee.

All these different patterns of group behaviour can be explained as alternative possible solutions to a problem belonging to the group as a whole; they can only provide solutions to individual problems at the point where group problems and individual problems meet. They are not necessarily reached through any conscious decision, individual or shared. Rather, they are reached through the operation of the group processes which shape the proceedings of the group into a form which will provide a common ground on which the needs of each can meet and achieve some satisfaction.

Cohesive and disruptive forces

It is this need to reconcile opposing drives, present in every group situation, which, according to our view, brings the group processes into existence. These group processes are complicated in the extreme. No observer can stand so far outside them as to be able to understand them all. If it is necessary to force upon them the simplification of basic laws, then these laws can be found in the assumption we make that there are regularities in the group processes, no matter in what form they show themselves. Such an assumption is made by all writers on group work, and, in fact, there are comparable assumptions which underly every attempt to study the world in which we live. Science is based upon two acts of faith. First, there is the belief that the universe can be understood; and, secondly, there is the belief that the same causes produce the same effects. These beliefs are not subject to proof or disproof. An alternative set of beliefs would be, first, that the universe can never be completely understood, and, secondly, that every event is unique. But in order to study science we have to be content with the assumptions that serve us for the time being and hand over our doubts to the philosophers who open up new dimensions of enquiry.

To return to our particular concern with the limited subject of group processes, we believe that it is possible to provide a working basis for our study by assuming that two fundamental and conflicting drives exist in every group, originating in two fundamental drives present in every individual: on the one hand, there is the wish to be separate, and, on the other hand, there is the wish to be one of a group. Both these components are always present, though not necessarily in equal amounts.

The quality and strength of these drives shown in any individual will owe something to constitutional make-up and to previous history as well as to the nature of the group situation in which the individual is placed.

All of us try to obtain, at one and the same time, the advantages of belonging and of not belonging. We conform to the customs and standards of our immediate social group, but within this conformity we try to establish the fact that we are different. We fear loneliness and isolation in being separate, and we fear loss of personal identity and of freedom in being one of a crowd. Anyone who seeks to be the leader of a group is trying to achieve a position in which he can maintain an extreme degree of separateness while still retaining membership of the group.

The existence of these two opposite drives is shown in the two conflicting attitudes towards groups that one encounters in our culture. On the one hand, one finds the belief that the group is inimical to the individual, and that membership of a group entails a surrender of part of one's personal identity, a suppression of individuality and a loss of uniqueness, which is to be deplored. On the other hand, one finds an advocacy of group membership as containing a cure for all manner of social and psychological ills, from delinquency to widowhood. Clubs and associations proliferate to meet all tastes and needs, and are regarded as being beneficial to individuals and to society as a whole. Both these opposite attitudes contain some truth; put together they reflect a feeling about the powerful and mysterious nature of group forces, and an acknowledgement that groups contain potentialities for both benefit and harm.

The conduct of individuals can be explained in terms of ambivalence, i.e. in terms of opposing and simultaneously operating feelings of love and hate. We find comparable forces operating at a group level, and these forces are represented by the tendencies of the group to continue, i.e. its coherence, and the tendencies of the group to break up, i.e. its disruptiveness. *The simultaneously operating coherence and disruptiveness constitute the ambivalence of the group.* It may be that only one aspect of the "group ambivalence" will find expression at any one moment, but, in order to understand the behaviour of the group, the other component must be assumed to exist in an undisclosed form.

The first problem facing the group is to survive, just as the last problem is to disband. Groups survive when their opposing tendencies can be reconciled. They also survive when they are able to provide sufficient satisfaction for the needs of each of their members so that the wish to belong is strong enough to overcome the wish to be separate.

Thus, when we consider what happened at any particular group meeting, and wonder why events followed the course that they did, we need to take into account the following factors:

1. The overt purpose and structure of the group.
2. The problems and needs that each individual member was bringing into the group and attempting to solve and satisfy through the group.
3. The conflict that each member was experiencing about belonging to the group, as the wish to break away vied with the wish to remain.
4. The totality which adds up to a basic group problem, and which cannot be equated with the problem of any one individual but which belongs in some way to them all. This problem is that of ensuring the group's survival through the promotion of its cohesiveness and the containment of its disruptiveness. It is within this basic problem that the group processes operate.

Example: counselling group

A final illustration can be provided from the record of a group consisting of mothers of young, mentally-handicapped children, who met together every week with a social worker. This is an example of one of the types of group that will be considered in more detail in a later chapter. The aim of the group meetings was to help the mothers in relationship to their children, and the discussion, though focused upon the children, was otherwise free and unstructured.

In the first few meetings, the mothers related anecdotes about the behaviour of their handicapped children, and a marked uniformity in opinions and in attitudes was shown. When one mother described the behaviour of her child at table or at bedtime, one or two of the other mothers would join in eagerly, claiming that their children behaved in exactly the same way. Inconsistencies and contradictions soon became apparent, and it appeared that the mothers were less concerned with giving accurate descriptions of their children's behaviour than with maintaining unanimity at all costs. Only one mother, at the second meeting of the group, described her child as being different, and she received exaggerated sympathy from the others. She did not attend the next meeting, and the group immediately referred to her and discussed her problems at length, dwelling on the abnormality of her child's behaviour, and criticizing the ways in which she handled him.

These were women who found it difficult, because of their children's handicaps, to take part in the usual range of corporate activities available to the mothers of young families, and they all, to some degree, felt painfully different from mothers in general. Their behaviour demonstrated the strength of their wish to be in a group where they could share freely and did not have to feel exceptional. But it also indicated the strength of the disruptive forces threatening the group. Side by side with the wish to belong to the group there were strong competitive and hostile feelings which the group situation tended to intensify. Most of these mothers were prepared to fight to obtain special provision for their children, and were reluctant to have them classified with other "subnormals". Not all the mothers, of course, experienced these negative feelings to an equal extent. But the conflict between disruptive and cohesive forces posed an immediate problem and led to the adoption of a group solution in which most participated actively and a few acquiesced. The one mother who refused to acquiesce left the group.

It was the strength of these two opposing drives, the drive to belong and the drive to be separate, which was responsible for the establishment of this artificial uniformity. This behaviour on the part of the group members ensured that the group (minus the one who left) could continue to exist over the early sessions. It was not until the group was more securely established, and relationships among the mothers, and between the mothers and the social worker, were stronger, that this restricting solution could be gradually abandoned and some tolerant expression of separate feelings could be allowed.

References

1. Koffka, K. *Principles of Gestalt Psychology* Harcourt Brace, New York, 1935.
2. Ezriel, H. *A psychoanalytical approach to group treatment* B.J.M.P. Vol XXIII Parts 1 and 2, 1950.

4

The Group Situation

The quest for change

Imagine a small number of people coming together regularly, perhaps at weekly intervals, and spending about an hour and a half in each other's company. They meet as equals, and they sit in a circle and talk together. There is a leader, with special knowledge and skills, who is there to help them. He (or she) seems to exercise less direct control over the proceedings than one normally expects from a leader, and may even appear to follow rather than lead. It is not a business or committee meeting that has brought these people together, since there is no agenda, no chairperson, no reference to any external task. It is not a social or recreational occasion, since there appears to be a serious purpose. No systematic instruction is given, so the purpose does not seem to be formal education. There is no discernible ambition to bring about changes in the wider community, so it is not a political meeting. There is no reference to supernatural forces, moral code, creed or body of doctrine, so it is not in any sense a religious assembly. The focus is upon what goes on in the group, the dynamic interchanges, the contributions of members and of leader, and on this alone. Whatever it is that the members are seeking, it seems to be contained here.

Such a meeting as this could be taking place in any one of a variety of different settings. It could, for example, be in a private consulting room, hospital, clinic, social work agency, prison, school or university. The members could be patients, clients, inmates of an institution, members of a youth club, or professional students of such disciplines as medicine, psychology, social work, teaching or nursing. The leader could belong to any one of a number of different professions, including those listed above, each with its own techniques and its own distinct body of professional knowledge. Thus the groups may vary considerably in their settings, in their composition, and in the disciplines of their leaders. They may also differ widely in their purposes and in their proceedings, in what the individual members hope to gain, and in what the leader attempts to contribute.

These are the groups that form the subject matter of this section. For the moment we are not dealing specifically with the family group. We are trying first to identify the properties belonging to a group which allow change to take place, and which, when identified, can be purposefully used to that end.

What type of change is being sought in these groups?

Each member of the different groups we are discussing has come because he or she is dissatisfied at some level or in some degree with current circumstances. It may be a dissatisfaction with the whole of present life, or with one small part of it; the dissatisfaction may be severe or slight. What is being sought may be relief from a severe mental disturbance, or help with some family difficulty, or something that will ease the transition from one stage of life to another; or there may be a wish to extend the range of certain professional skills. But whatever the problems and dissatisfactions of individual members, or whatever new satisfactions are being sought, they all have this in common: each of them is concerned with relationships between people. It is in this area that the dissatisfactions are expressed, and it is also in this area that the remedies are being sought.

We know that we cannot carry on life in isolation from our fellows, and that it is on the quality of the relationships that we make with other people that so much of our happiness and success depends. Through these relationships we either meet, or fail to meet, most of our basic needs. These relationships are not only central to our intimate, personal lives: they also affect every activity in which we have contact with other people, at home, at work, and at play; and they play a part in the use of most professional skills.

There are professions in which the contribution made by skill and sensitivity in interpersonal relationships is explicitly recognized. "The doctor-patient relationship" and "the casework relationship" are discussed as professional techniques, and they have their counterparts in other disciplines and other occupations. Every relationship between two people is a two-way process to which both contribute, and any professional practice concerned with living beings in face-to-face situations may require from the worker a deeper understanding of his own behaviour as well as of the behaviour of others. In this way such work differs from work dealing with inanimate objects, which alone can be "objective". Such deeper understanding is not easy to acquire, and it cannot be achieved by an intellectual process alone. It may sometimes be sought (as may the relief of mental illness and the resolution of personal problems) through participation in the activities of a group.

The members of all these groups, with their different motivations and their different degrees of commitment, are seeking to improve the quality of the relationships which they make with other people; to learn to recognize the contribution they themselves make to every personal relationship in which they are involved; and to take responsibility for that contribution. To this end they are prepared, in the groups they have joined, to expose themselves to new situations which contain the possibility of personal change. This brings us to a further point that all our groups have in common; the change that is being sought includes a degree of personal change in each of their individual members. This change is not something that takes place through the influence of any external factor, nor is it change in some determined direction. The members of the group are not converted, nor are they indoctrinated, nor, for this purpose, should they be instructed. The agent of change is participation in the group itself and in its processes, operating under exceptional and disciplined conditions. Though all groups have their dynamics, and there are potentialities for change, growth, and development in every human encounter, we are considering very particular situations in which an attempt is made to be aware of these potentialities and to influence them.

The fear of change

Change in itself may be frightening. It can lead to something not yet experienced and the thought of this may be painful. Change is not necessarily beneficial, and even where it is beneficial it involves the surrender of some present good. We tend to spend much of our energy trying to avoid change, endeavouring to maintain an existing situation because we fear that any alteration might involve loss rather than gain. This perhaps explains the increased vulnerability that comes at transition points in personal and family development, and the way in which people often experience depression at moments of change even when the change is for the better.

In every individual, and in every group of individuals, there are forces that resist change. Singly and together, we have our defences. We possess certain beliefs which we do not wish to have questioned; we have standards that we like to assume are self evident. Even when we are conscious of certain inadequacies and failings in ourselves, we may not be prepared to have them brought to the attention of others. We try to present ourselves to the world in a favourable light, concealing our less acceptable side, pretending that all is well. It is not easy for us to abandon this pretence, and moreover, any attempt to do so is likely to be discouraged by others who will feel it as a threat to their own security. The frankness of one person can be a challenge to the concealments of everyone else; and those who speak plainly of their own shortcomings may, in fact, expose others more than themselves.

For many of us, it is hard openly to acknowledge a need; for we fear that, if the need is known, it may be ignored, and then our burden would be doubled. It is hard to acknowledge ignorance and incompetence, for we fear contempt and loss of esteem. We are afraid that others may take advantage of any weaknesses that we reveal. Thus our insecurity makes us assume positions that are hard to relinquish, and that discourage change. Others of us, on the other hand, may cling to weakness as an entitlement to a special care and consideration that we are reluctant to surrender, fearing any change that might bring greater challenges and greater demands.

At another level altogether, there are aspects of ourselves that we struggle to conceal not only from our associates but even from our own conscious selves. There are illusions and concealments that seem necessary not only to our standing with others but to our very existence. We are afraid that any slackening in our self-control could reveal and release primitive impulses of which we are only dimly aware; and which we fear might overwhelm us even to the point of disintegration and madness.

We have seen that unstructured group situations are felt to be frightening. They contain a danger that too much will be revealed. The less structure there is in a group, the less are we able to hide ourselves in stereotyped roles and the less predictable will be our own behaviour and that of the other group members. The less, too, will be the restrictions on the free play of group forces, which are also feared. But the group situations in which we customarily find ourselves in our day-to-day lives have much of their challenge removed through rules and regulations, social conventions and agreed standards of behaviour. These preserve our accustomed roles, and protect us from unexpected encounters and embarrassing revelations.

The groups that we are considering now differ from these other groups in a fundamental way. If the members are ready to expose themselves to the possibility of change, they must also be ready to abandon some part of their defences, to relinquish some part of their controls, to reveal more of their weaknesses, and to be more honest both with themselves and with others. Some of the conventions of social intercourse, with which they would normally protect themselves must be abandoned. It has to be learned that there is no safety in numbers.

The safety provided by the group leader

Changes may be desired, but they do not come about merely by willing them. The ways in which we habitually react are not entirely within our conscious control. If members of a group are going to be able to behave in a different way, then they must feel that they are in a different situation: if they are to modify the defences they are accustomed to use in order to feel secure, then, initially, alternative sources of security will have to be provided. The margin of safety has to be extended. This will not happen all at once, and the extra security of the group will have to be built up by degrees, as the members are able to test out and thus extend the permitted limits. They will be helped in this by the knowledge that they all have similar or comparable purposes, and by the gradual sharing of confidences and experiences.

But whatever may happen in the group to help or hinder the development of this process, the safety of the group and of individual members is ultimately the responsibility of the group leader. It is part of the group leader's function to ensure that free exchanges can take place without danger, that no one is subjected to more stress than can be tolerated, and that the group does not break up until it has accomplished its purpose. No leader can expect always to be completely successful in this.

It is also the leader's responsibility to see that the aims of the group are preserved. These aims set bounds and limits to the proceedings, and any self-exposure should not overstep the limits set by any group's particular aims. The group members have to relinquish some part of their normal controls, and, in doing so, they vest these controls in the leader. Removing a layer of outer garments, they rely upon the leader to ensure that the room is kept warm enough for their body heat to be maintained. They also rely upon the leader to prevent them from taking off so many clothes that they will either catch cold or be improperly exposed.

In every one of these groups, an implicit bargain is made between each group member and the leader. Within the terms of reference determined by the aims of the group, the leader guarantees that the difficulties can be discussed and feelings can be ventilated in safety. Outside these terms of reference, the leader guarantees that privacy will be respected. In some groups, the terms of reference will be drawn widely, and in some they will be drawn narrowly. In each situation, the group members will only be prepared to expose themselves to the extent that confidence exists in the power of the leader to guarantee safety when conditions in the group itself cannot do so. This confidence may be helped initially by the acknowledged position of the leader, but it depends in the longer run upon the leader's skill in this role.

The leader may not be required to make any direct interventions. Sufficient conditions of safety at each stage may come to be provided by the group itself as it develops and matures. Through the operation of group processes, a broad, tacit consensus of opinion can be expected to develop about the behaviour of individuals in the group, the honouring of confidences, the tolerance of divergencies, and the level of reciprocal disclosures. The leader will not wish to interfere with the free development of such a consensus, which, though constantly shifting, will be far more effective than any imposed ruling would be. However, the leader's presence is necessary as the ultimate guarantor, and will be a personal reassurance when the strength and cohesiveness of the group seem insufficient.

Some members of a group will always be more vulnerable than others, and sensitivity in different situations will vary. Sometimes one member will introduce a topic, make comments, or ask questions, for which others in the group are not ready and which they find too disturbing. For various reasons, and in various ways, individual members may find themselves isolated and criticized. The result of all this may be one or more members who become unable to participate, or who may even leave the group. The disruptive forces in the group, of which all are afraid, will need to find some expression; but if they are expressed too early, before sufficient cohesion has developed to contain them, they may lead to the disintegration of the group. In any of the groups we are considering, the leader may be required to intervene to protect a particular member, or to protect the group as a whole; to increase the safety of one of them or of all of them; and to help the group to develop sufficient strength and cohesiveness for its purpose. The leader may also have to intervene to see that any necessary limits are observed and that the privacy of members outside these limits is respected. In this way is the leader's side of the bargain fulfilled.

The bargain with the leader

The concept of a bargain between group member and group leader, "implicit" because it can seldom be explicitly formulated at the outset, plays an important part in our argument. It is included in the concept of the "mandate" which is given by the party seeking personal help to the party offering it, and which must not be exceeded.

This concept has been questioned.[1] It has been argued, in relation to social work, that the client of the social worker is rarely in any position to appreciate the nature and the limitations of the help being offered, or to forecast what is going to be demanded, and that therefore it is an act of self deception for social workers to speak as if there were a contract freely entered into by both parties. By the same argument, the individuals who join any of the groups that we are considering may well have no clear and accurate idea of what will be involved, but this does not mean that they are agreeing to participate in an unlimited process. One joins a group for some particular purpose, and one expects that the leader will do everything in his power to see that this purpose, and none other, is achieved. In this sense the leader is empowered to act in certain ways: if the individual members do not understand what these ways are, they are able to support the uncertainty because of the belief that the leader understands them.

The fact that group members and group leaders are embarking upon a joint task of uncertain direction and outcome makes it all the more important that its ultimate aims and limits should be understood and respected by the leaders who must take responsibility for them. The consent of the members may often be based initially upon an act of faith, but this consent becomes ratified by their increasing involvement in the groups which they have joined. The leaders are fully committed at the beginning, but the members must extend the area of their commitment gradually. For them, the bargain is not a static one but a living experience which makes possible the organic growth and development of the group as a whole.

Reference

1. Halmos, P. *The Faith of the Counsellors* Constable, 1965.

3

The Group Process in Practice

5

Three Systems of Group Work

Distinguishing three systems

A number of different types of group, differing considerably in their aims and in the methods used to realize these aims, have so far been considered together. We are now going to separate these groups and divide them into three categories which we shall call group psychotherapy, group counselling and group discussion. This use of categories involves introducing into the discussion some rather more concrete formulations than we have been able to use elsewhere in this work, particularly in the latter section when we go on to discuss family group work.

We are attempting to base the distinctions between these three systems of group work upon a consideration of what actually takes place in the groups, and not upon a consideration of the designation of the leader, the status of the members, nor the nature of the setting, nor even upon the avowed purpose of the meeting. These distinctions are made in order to provide a framework which will help to differentiate group psychotherapy (which to many is the prototype of all group work) from other group work methods. In doing this, we are attempting to provide these other methods with a firmer conceptual base, and to facilitate teaching and communication in this area. It is hoped that this will also help to give these other methods a validation and an identity in their own right which is independent of the separate schools of group psychotherapy; and that it will help to free the ideas of dynamic group processes from dependence upon any closed system. In a later section, we hope to be able to do something similar for family group work too. We must emphasize that in doing this the last thing we would wish to do would be to introduce another closed system of our own making.

A clearer understanding about the use of terms in this field is badly needed. Thus in a report of a Home Office Research Unit entitled *A Survey of Group Work in the Probation Service*, the authors deliberately avoided using such precise terms because they considered that "at our present stage in understanding what takes place in these groups there does not appear to be a clear cut distinction between the methods". They added the warning that "attaching a label to a type of treatment can give a misleading impression of a unified body of theory and treatment practice, which may not exist". This warning is still pertinent, and we heed it; and we go on to offer our framework as a contribution to the remedying of this deficiency.

Group discussion, group counselling, and group psychotherapy all share the area in common that was outlined in the last chapter. They all have aims which include the promotion of a degree of personal change in each member; each member is prepared to expose the self to change to a greater extent than would be done in other circumstances; and each member relies on a leader with special skills to be the ultimate guarantor that it is safe to do so. Any change that takes place in individual members comes about solely through participation in the processes taking place within the group itself. The differences between these three group work systems are to be found in the aim of the groups; in the role played by the group leader; and in the psychological level of depth and particularity at which each group operates. The three methods have an additional point in common in the derivation of their theoretical bases from theories of dynamic group psychology, but each also has its own separate roots in a different individual helping process.

Individual psychotherapy and group psychotherapy

Group psychotherapy will be considered first, since it is from here that much of the theory of group behaviour common to all three systems is derived. Group psychotherapy has its counterpart in individual psychotherapy. In the latter, the aim is to bring about a radical and permanent change in the personality of the "patient". The setting is traditionally a medical one; the psychotherapist will either have a medical qualification or be working in conjunction with somebody else who has one. The patient is prepared, at any rate theoretically, to reveal private thoughts and fantasies, however painful this may be, holding nothing back; and relies on the psychotherapist for protection from the feared and real consequences of such a surrender of his defences.

There are a number of different schools of psychotherapy, but, for the most part, use is made of the concept of transference. The psychotherapist will base the work upon the interpretation of transference relationships, going back to the deeply unconscious feelings that the infant had for the original love objects, and which are currently transferred into the therapist-patient relationship. Though the patient may have sought help on account of some particular difficulty, the therapist will focus upon the person, and not upon the problem, while trying to effect a total change. The therapist's concern is with the patient's inner world, and with this alone.

We are considering a notional, and perhaps idealized, model of psychotherapy in order to point out the contrast between the different systems. For our purpose we are confining the term "psychotherapy" to a specific process taking place within a precise framework within which patient and psychotherapist have an implied contract to devote themselves to the purpose of the treatment. The principles of psychoanalytic psychotherapy have penetrated in varying degrees into the general culture and into the practice of social work, education, and other professional frameworks; and in this way psychotherapeutic principles have enlarged the scope and deepened the effect of the practice of the other caring professions. None of these extensions is included in our consideration of psychotherapy here; we are treating it for the moment as a procedure confined to the consulting room.

Much of the above, which is derived from the consideration of *individual* psychotherapy, also applies to *group* psychotherapy. The declared aim of group psychotherapy is to effect a significant change in the personality of each member of the group. As with individual psychotherapy, normal social rules are suspended, and each member of the group is expected to reveal thoughts and feelings with complete freedom, on the understanding that the psychotherapist will be able to maintain the safety of the group and protect each member from any adverse consequences. The transference is now a multidimensional one, and at any one time a wider range of unconscious attitudes are brought into the treatment situation. The role that the group psychotherapist plays will depend upon the theoretical framework that is being used, along with the conception of the nature of the group processes. The therapist may focus upon the behaviour of the individual in the group, or, at the other end of a continuum, may use interventions in such a way as to effect those processes which take place within the group as a whole.

Social casework and group counselling

Compared with group psychotherapy, group counselling has a more definite and directed aim. It is concerned with relieving particular problems and with modifying specific situations. To this end it may be necessary to bring about changes in some attitudes and relationships, but fundamental changes in the structure of personality are not specifically sought. Group counselling may be carried out by members of different disciplines, and is not a technique exclusive to any one profession, but for its individual counterpart one must look to the one-to-one casework relationship which has been developed by social workers.

Social caseworkers are employed within specialist agencies, and have definite terms of reference. A client will be referred to a particular agency because of specific problems which fall within its terms of reference. Although the caseworker will need to make a complete assessment of the total situation in which the client is placed, and may try to bring about a general improvement in the client's circumstances and system of personal relationships, the caseworker does not lose sight of the problem for which help was originally sought. The client is expected to talk frankly about the problem, and expects that it will be safe to do so, but there is no expectation that everything is to be revealed and nothing held back. Should the client choose to enter into other areas, caseworkers need to respond, and must handle the situation within the limits determined by their training and experience, making such use of the client's contribution as they can within the particular framework set by their own agency. Caseworkers need to be aware that there are dangers in extending the treatment process to include a form of psychotherapy which has not been sanctioned, and in which they are not trained.

Caseworkers make use of the relationship which they have established with their clients, and this relationship furnishes the context in which other forms of help may be offered, material as well as psychological. They need to be aware of the transference, but, even though they may recognize it, they do not need to interpret it in the way that a psychotherapist would do. Their training and terms of reference have other aims in areas in which, conversely, psychotherapists would be ill equipped and ill at ease. Caseworkers may need to demonstrate how a client is carrying over attitudes and feelings from the past into the present, but the attitudes and feelings will be conscious or near-conscious ones, and they will be the ones that affect the practical issues in the client's life.

Compared with the psychotherapists, the caseworkers have more freedom to select and set limits to treatment aims and to the themes that are to be discussed. Although they may have to limit their focus to specific problems, they can select from a range of different helping techniques, and they do not have to avoid behaviour that might conceivably interfere with the untrammelled development of the transference relationship.

Group counselling derives from casework, and its counterpart is found in some particular aspects of the casework process with the individual. But it cannot be tailored to meet individual needs in the way that casework can, nor can it include such a wide range of individual helping methods. Members of a counselling group will share some common problem or situation which provides a point on which to focus, and to which everything that takes place in the group needs to be related. It is the task of the group counsellor to maintain this focus and to make the links that establish the relationships. Thus the proceedings of the group and the interactions between all the group members, the contributions and the responses of each individual, are all made to play their part in the problem-solving process. Group counsellors may themselves play an unobtrusive part in the proceedings, keeping their own personality in the background, and in this respect their behaviour may appear to resemble that of group psychotherapists. But they have other options too. There may be occasions when the counselling needs of individual members and of the total group require the leader to play a more active role and make a positive and direct use of the relationship between them. Here too we can find a counterpart in the different uses that caseworkers in an individual setting may make of their relationships with their clients.

Education and group discussion

Group discussion, in its turn, differs from group psychotherapy and from group counselling in having an aim that is primarily educational. The focus of the group work is not upon particular difficulties of personality or of relationships, nor upon specific problems: it is upon topics that are presented for development and elucidation. The processes that take place in the group are used to develop and elucidate the topics, and thus they become an educational tool.

One important application of group discussion is as a means of helping workers in the field of human relations to increase their insights and skills. The application has to counterpart in the individual supervision or consultation process, in which a student (or it could be a qualified worker) will bring problems for discussion with a supervisor or consultant. This is a form of learning which cannot take place through intellectual means alone; the general problems that the students encounter in their work, and their specific difficulties, are likely to be linked to factors in their own personalities, and resolution will largely depend upon the growth of self-awareness. However, the relationship with a supervisor is not a therapeutic or a casework relationship. This means that the supervisor has no sanction to intervene in the student's personal problems and should seek no direct knowledge of them. Both parties should understand this, and both should know that the other understands it. Details of the student's behaviour on the job and the relationships that he makes with others in the course of the work may have to be discussed, but the supervisor will make no direct links between them and any other aspects of the student's life revealed in other contexts. Students capable of personal growth may be able to make use of the opportunity to do this for themselves.

In practice, some information about students' personal histories is likely to be disclosed, and cannot be thrust aside altogether. Supervisors have to make a response to such disclosures, and it may be necessary to distinguish this response from other supervisory activities, and place it outside the narrow professional framework in which they and their students have their disciplined and functional relationships. Even though a supervisor's responses are designed to be helpful, it is important that the occasion should not be converted into a therapeutic encounter. If more than this is needed, the student should be referred elsewhere for casework or therapy on a formal basis, which would include the right to disengage.

Group discussion, like consultation or supervision, can be used for the development of professional skills and understanding, but the method is more indirect, and the focus is more upon the general than upon the particular. The topics that are discussed are concerned with human and interpersonal behaviour, so the behaviour that takes place in the group cannot be ignored but will be used to illustrate and test the validity of some of the concepts put forward. Members of the discussion group will expect the leader to refrain from intruding into their personal lives, and to prevent others from doing so. They expect to be able to expose their work problems without encountering personal criticism or ridicule, and in the knowledge that the other members are prepared to do likewise. In discussion, members will necessarily reveal the nature of their defences and the areas in which they feel less secure, and they will need confidence to reveal these areas. The leader may comment, as in individual supervision, on details of particular cases or individual professional difficulties described by members, or may concentrate comments on matters involving the group as a whole. The leader will need the skill to make use of the contributions of the less confident and to construct a framework in which the contributions of all can be included. He (or she) will need to protect the vulnerable, and is more likely to repair defences than to interpret their nature.

However, the group discussion leader may have more scope than the consultant or supervisor working with an individual to use interpretation of the immediate situation as a professional technique. Attention can be drawn to a group process without any personal intrusion, whereas a supervisor with one student would have to be much more circumspect in commenting upon the current relationship between the two of them.

Sometimes group discussion is used for education about group work itself, in any of its forms. Through participation in such a situation, with the help of the group leader, the members will hope to develop their awareness of the group processes. The topic on which such a group is focused is group behaviour, which must include the behaviour of this particular group. The leader needs to be able to make appropriate use of the example that the behaviour of the group supplies, and to help members to increase their insight and understanding, but at the same time avoid implicit or explicit references to personal behaviour that are not sanctioned.

So far, we have been looking at group discussion as a means of professional education. The method can be used for other purposes and in other settings. There are, for example, the classes in human relationships that are provided in many schools and youth clubs; and there are the marriage preparation courses for engaged couples that are part of the activity of the Marriage Guidance Council. Though these groups may differ markedly in many significant respects, such as their homogeneity, the level of sophistication of the members, and the ability of the members to withstand stress, the same basic principles apply to them all. The focus in all these groups is upon topics. The leader helps the members to respond freely to the topic. The leader constructs a framework by relating together all the individual contributions. The privacy of the individual is respected.

Activity groups

No mention has yet been made of activity groups. These are groups in which the members come together in the first instance to take part in some shared activity such as acting, painting, boat building, or photography; and in which the leader attempts to make use of the occasion provided, and the group situation, to help members in other ways. These groups are found in such settings as mental hospitals, prisons, special schools and probation offices. Much of what has been said applies to these groups also; they too have their dynamics, and a leader able to recognize and work with the group processes may significantly influence the development of the groups and the progress of individual members. Successful participation in any group activity, no matter what that activitity may be, can bring considerable benefits for the individual. It can provide a positive experience in human relationships, helping to promote the growth of capacities which can then be transferred to relationships in other settings, and helping to develop qualities such as generosity, tolerance, and the capacity to share. All groups, not excluding psychotherapeutic ones, derive no small part of the benefit they confer from the opportunity provided for successful participation in a social activity.

Although we wish to recognize the existence and the importance of activity groups, we propose to confine any detailed consideration to groups whose main business is carried on through verbal communications.

Obstacles to clarity

The terms that are used to designate the three group work systems, group psychotherapy, group counselling and group discussion, are all in common usage; but there is little consistency in their use, and they normally convey little clear information about the treatment or educational process actually taking place in the groups they are being used to describe.

The imprecise use of language is one difficulty. Another difficulty comes from the fact that some concepts and techniques are shared by all three of our systems, and this overlap sometimes gives an impression that there is only one basic group process which can be applied at different levels of depth and intensity in different circumstances. Such an impression is based upon a failure to appreciate the importance of the differences in the aims of different groups, and also of the differences in what has been sanctioned. These are decisive factors which require to be clearly formulated at the onset, as they provide the context which determines what techniques are appropriate.

A number of different factors add to the current confusion. The following have all played their part.

Group psychotherapy is the only one of the three group systems we are considering in which considerable progress has been made towards the establishment of a firm conceptual basis, or which can make claim to be regarded as a scientific discipline. It is from group psychotherapy that the knowledge of group dynamics necessary to all group workers is derived. Social workers who wish to work with groups are frequently, and by their own choice, trained and supervised, if not by group psychotherapists, then by social workers who have themselves been trained and supervised by group psychotherapists. It is not surprising that such social workers often appear unable, or unwilling, to consider their work as belonging to a separate system; they often appear to look on it as a diluted and attenuated form of psychotherapy, and see advance in skill in terms of an ever closer approximation to the work described by group psychotherapists. While usually disclaiming use of the actual term group psychotherapy, they do their best to adopt the methods and much of the terminology.

Social workers may disclaim the term, but others do not. The difference between the three systems is further obscured when the term psychotherapy is treated as medical property, and "group psychotherapy" is used to indicate that the leader of the group has a medical qualification, and tells us nothing about the purpose of the group or about what is taking place at the group meetings. Sometimes the qualifying adjective "limited" or "superficial" is added, and this may or may not be a disclaimer indicating that the leader is untrained in both group work and in psychotherapy. It is unfortunate if group leaders who have a medical qualification feel precluded from using a more appropriate terminology to describe what they are actually doing only because they do not feel able to make use of terms which they associate with the work of other disciplines.

Members of many different disciplines are called upon to lead discussion groups. There is not always sufficient recognition of the fact that group discussion is a separate technique, and that competence as a group discussion leader is not automatically conferred by training or experience in group counselling or group psychotherapy. Discussion groups have on occasions been turned into psychotherapeutic groups simply because psychotherapy has been the only technique that the leader has had at his disposal.

A group work project is sometimes undertaken without any prior formulation of aims and terms of reference, or any appreciation that such a formulation is needed. This may be the result of a belief that therapeutic forces reside in the group itself, and that the act of bringing people together is itself therapeutic. This seems to be a half-truth. A group contains both therapeutic and anti-therapeutic potential, and the group forces may help or harm the individual. Group work can always be hazardous, and this is particularly the case when it is unfocused and undirected.

In order to provide both a framework and a basis for future discussion, we have put our emphasis upon the separateness of the three systems, and stressed their differences. We may have implied the existence of a uniformity within these differences and of definite boundaries and distinctions which do not exist in practice. In fact, not only do all the groups we are considering share many concepts and techniques, but there are also areas of overlap, and the boundaries can often appear blurred rather than clear-cut. There are different schools of group psychotherapy, differing in their theoretical bases and in their techniques. The members of some psychotherapeutic groups may be selected on the basis of some problem such as drug addiction, which they all have in common. Group counsellors define different aims in different groups, and vary in the use they make of interpretive techniques and of their own relationship with the group; some may widen their focus to include more aspects of their clients' past and present experience. Group discussion can be used to serve different needs; and it can be adjusted to meet the different needs of groups which may be very varied in terms of age, education and degree of personal commitment. Some discussion groups may focus upon a topic containing personal and intimate preoccupations of its members which cannot remain unexpressed.

The proceedings of each of these groups will be influenced not only by the particular disciplines to which the group leader belongs, but also by the leader's own leadership style, interests and experience, personal make-up, and even psychopathology. This influence cannot be considered an improper one, for group leadership is not a mechanical skill; rather, it is a process in which the spontaneous use of the leader's personality plays an important part. There is much that can be learnt, a disciplined framework and a theoretical base are essential, but within this framework and upon this base each group leader develops a personal style of leadership and gives the group something that no one else could give.

Leadership roles illustrated

The context of the group, its aim, its focus, and its sanctions, must never be forgotten. The way in which the role of the leader in each of the three systems needs to be related to the purpose of the group is illustrated in the following example: it deals with a situation that must be familiar to all group workers.

Let us suppose that a new group assembles and that at the first few meetings a predominant feeling in the group is anxiety at being in a new and uncharted situation. Although they react in different ways, all the members share in this group tension and in the efforts that are made to deal with it. Typically, they turn to the group leader and put pressure on him (or her) to take a more active part and to give more structure to the proceedings.

To group psychotherapists, this tension provides the very material with which they work. They will do nothing to lessen it in order to allow the group members to feel more comfortable. On the contrary, they will allow it to develop until it becomes expressed and resolved, or until it seems appropriate to make an interpretation, or other intervention, not primarily to lower the tension but rather to permit further development. Painful experiences are necessary to psychotherapeutic progress, and members of such a group must be prepared to face some discomfort.

If a similar tension were to develop in a counselling group, it would be dealt with in a different way. Here there is no sanction, in the bargain between leader and members, for the same level of discomfort; and outside a psychotherapeutic framework it would be likely to have a disruptive effect, perhaps even leading to the break-up of the group. In a counselling group, there is not the same need to foster free communication and the unhampered growth of transference relationships, so the leader has a wider choice of approaches and is free to play a more active part.

Group counsellors have to decide what to do in the light of the particular aim that has been defined for their group, and in the light of the needs of its members. It might be appropriate to accede to the wishes of the group for the time being, and to play the more active part that the members are asking for. For example, in a counselling group of ex-mental hospital patients, a common problem for all the members might be difficulty in leaving the ordered regime of a paternalistic institution. Stress in the group will involve stress on individual members; and such members may, temporarily or permanently, have both a limited capacity to tolerate stress and a need to form a dependent relationship with the group leader during the period of transition. The behaviour of the leader would need to be adjusted to meet the needs of such a group. Alternatively, or in addition, to making direct use of the relationship to help the group, the leader might decide to make an interpretation or draw a comparison. This could be done through a comment on what is taking place in the group, linking it to the problem which provides the group's focus, in this instance the problems of adjustment to life outside the hospital. The relationships that are finding expression within the present group could be compared by the leader with the new relationships that individual members have yet to make outside the hospital.

In group discussion the leader would have to handle the tension in relation to some aspect of the group's topic; using it, if possible, to clarify and stimulate, but avoiding such a degree of stress as would expose the inadequacies of the most vulnerable. Such a situation would be very relevant to the particular theme of groups concerned with discussing problems related to dependency; this could be dependency in relationships between parents and children, between marriage partners, or in the relationships between professional workers and their patients or clients. It might, in fact, be an advantage to such groups to be able to experience, and then to discuss, a situation in which dependency is both sought and denied. Although, in group discussion, less stress on individuals is sanctioned, the capacity of the group and of individual members to tolerate new and experimental situations may be greater. The behaviour of the group as a whole may be used by the leader to illustrate the theme, but no attention will be paid to individual personal problems that may be revealed in the course of the exercise.

Responsibility of the group leader

So each of the three leaders in the three different group systems may be confronted with a very similar situation in the group. Each will be required to respond to this situation in some way. In their responses, all the three leaders use an understanding of the dynamic processes which take place in all groups, and all three look beyond the individual members to the group as a whole; but each one handles a comparable situation in a different way because each relates the response to the aims of the group and each gives regard to what has been sanctioned.

Members may join a group with ideas about its purposes and processes that are distorted, inaccurate, and incomplete; the responsibility is not theirs. The responsibility belongs to the leader, and it is his (or her) ideas which must be clear. The leader's perception of the group is all important, and determines much of what will follow. The dangers of a blurring of boundaries and consequent confusion as to what is, or should be, taking place in a group are very real.

In each of the three systems of group work we are describing, the actual proceedings of the group, and the group processes taking place, form a principal vehicle through which the purpose of the group is achieved. In all three, the leader is required to recognize, understand, and in some way influence, these proceedings and processes, without unnecessarily distorting or hindering their natural development. Some of the different ways in which this may be attempted will be discussed in the next chapters. It is, however, impossible to say that anv one technique belongs exclusively to one particular system and has no place in another. We cannot say, for example, that interpretation is a technique of group psychotherapy, and that direct intervention to divert the course of the proceedings of the group from a particular path can only be considered in group discussion. This very lack of explicit technical demarcation highlights once more the importance of a clear conceptual basis in every instance rooted in an understanding of aims and limits.

6

Group Psychotherapy

Different theoretical systems

The practice of bringing small numbers of patients together to share their psychotherapeutic sessions may have been undertaken by a few pioneers even before the First World War, but it is only since 1945 that it has been practised on any large scale. It is now a familiar and accepted part of the psychiatric and social work scene. The development of theory has followed upon practice, in the same way that psychoanalytic theory did not become formulated until Freud had used the psychoanalytic method for the treatment of patients. But there is no single theory of group psychotherapy as such; instead we have a bewildering variety of different theoretical systems, some differing radically from one another, and some separated more by degrees of emphasis. The present position of group psychotherapy could be compared with the early days of psychoanalysis, when Freud's followers were all laying their separate claims to new discoveries and new formulations. Today, there is a similar wealth in the contributions of group psychotherapists, and, as techniques become more refined, and are used more precisely, so the terminology becomes more complicated. The prominent group psychotherapists have their adherents, sharing common assumptions about group dynamics and about processes that are considered to be therapeutic, but it would be premature to speak as if coherent schools of thought existed. It is possible for the group psychotherapist in training to become familiar with, and to make use of, a wide range of different theories.

Classification of theoretical systems

In order to study these different theories, it is important to be able to classify them in some way. One way in which they differ is in the importance that is attached to any single event taking place in the group, and the context or perspective in which that event is placed. Thus, a single event taking place in a group can be seen as the product of one particular group member, as the product of the interaction between two or more group members, or as the product or the sum of all the interactions taking place.

The first viewpoint is represented in theories which treat activity taking place at an intrapersonal level, within the individual, as the most relevant and significant. Here the therapists make use of a model drawn from the two-person situation of individual psychoanalysis. They set out to treat the individual within a group setting and conduct something resembling psychoanalysis in public with a participating audience. Some exponents of this method claim that it is an improvement on individual psychoanalysis because the support that each member derives from being a member of a group increases tolerance of anxiety and enables deeper levels to be reached more quickly. Slavson, Locke, and Schwartz are the best-known group psychotherapists who take this position.[1]

Others have placed their main emphasis upon a conceptualization of events at an interpersonal level, i.e. as transactions taking place between more than one individual, and the products of dynamic interpersonal relationships. An example is the "games" that Berne has uncovered.[2]

A third point of departure is to regard each group event as being determined or influenced by all other happenings in the group, and by the complete network of relationships that includes all members. Thus each event has, in addition to its significance for individuals, a significance at a transpersonal or group level, and the sum of all the intra- and interpersonal transactions has a meaning which can only be understood by considering the group as a whole. The total group situation always has to be taken into account.

This last viewpoint is associated with Bion, Foulkes, Ezriel, and Stock Whitaker and Lieberman. It is also our own viewpoint, which we have already indicated, and which is fundamental to this book.

It is not our aim to attempt a comprehensive description of group psychotherapy, however brief. The purpose of this chapter is more limited. We propose, firstly, to refer briefly to four selected theories of group behaviour: these are theories which, though derived from the practice of group psychotherapy, have an application that extends beyond its boundaries and are very relevant to our formulation. These theories are psychoanalytically orientated and they also focus upon the behaviour of the group as a whole; they differ at many points, however, and at times make use of rather different terminologies. They are concerned with finding answers to the questions that have been considered in the preceding chapters of this book, i.e. "What forces determine a group's behaviour?", and "How does each individual contribute to these group forces?", and "What is the impact of these forces on the individual?" These questions are important, not only to group psychotherapists, but also to others, including those who wish to utilize group methods for counselling and discussion. Anyone embarking on group work of any kind, including therapy, counselling, and discussion, must start from some particular viewpoint and must have hypotheses about group behaviour, a framework, and a vocabulary. Though the data for developing group theories may be available in all groups, it is in psychotherapeutic groups that they are most accessible and have been most intensively studied, and hence it is to group psychotherapists that we owe the dynamic concepts that make the discussion of these questions possible.

Our second aim in this chapter on group psychotherapy is to contribute to the development of a theoretical basis for group counselling and group discussion by indicating where the boundaries of the three systems may be drawn. For this purpose it is necessary to postulate a model "group psychotherapy", belonging to all schools and likely to be recognized by none, and to attribute to it certain features which we believe belong essentially to group psychotherapy and not to group counselling nor to group discussion.

Four psychoanalytically-orientated systems

We shall first consider the four different approaches to group psychotherapy at their point of greatest abstraction, where they deal with group events at a transpersonal level and offer concepts which make it possible to comprehend the interrelatedness of all events taking place in a group, and the existence of a total pattern of behaviour which includes but transcends the individual members.

We do not attempt to do justice to these theories; their importance in this book is apparent. Those with a serious interest in group work as part of a therapeutic system will need to turn to the works of their originators (see Bibliography).

The psychoanalytic approach is characterized by the belief that every piece of human behaviour has meaning at two levels, the manifest and the latent, the conscious and the unconscious; there is the everyday level of conscious response to the perceived realities of the situation in which the individual finds himself, and there is the level at which behaviour can only be comprehended in terms of a response to unconscious drives and basic emotional needs. Although it is a mistake to think that psychoanalytical concepts derived from the study of individuals can be applied directly to groups, the concept of conscious and unconscious levels is fundamental to both fields. The two levels are applied to the behaviour of groups at a transpersonal level by *Bion*.[3] In his theoretical system Bion describes the *Work Group*, which corresponds in many ways to the Freudian Ego and which contains the rational, conscious, orderly aspect of the group's behaviour. This is the level which we all know. At this level members of a group can give some explanation of why they are meeting and what they are doing, and can describe their procedure and purpose. Bion also sees the group as being at the same time in one of three "*basic assumption cultures*" which will be more or less dominant and apparent according to the strength of the work group and the coherence of the group organization. The existence and continuation of the group, according to Bion's formulation, is threatened by a conflict between what he calls the "group mentality", to which all members contribute, and the individual drives of each group member. The function of the basic assumption cultures is to meet this threat and to ensure the group's continuance. The first of these cultures is dominated by the basic assumption *dependency*, in which the group is seeking some leader, external object, idea, or cause which will dominate it and give it protection and greater cohesiveness. The second basic assumption he calls *fight-flight*, and in this culture the group pinpoints a particular threat which must be dealt with by either fighting it or fleeing from it. The last basic assumption is *pairing* when anxiety compels individual members to seek allies, and this may take place actually, vicariously, or symbolically, and can again be seen as an attempt to increase the cohesiveness of the group. Each basic assumption culture requires a leader, to satisfy dependency, to direct the group in the direction of fight or flight, or to permit pairing. The group is always seeking a leader of a type indicated by the particular basic assumption culture in which it finds itself at any one time. The leader of the basic assumption group is unlikely to be identical with the leader of the work group. At any time, in any group, one of the three basic assumption cultures will be operating alongside the work group. When a basic assumption culture ceases to give sufficient protection, there will be a move into one of the other two cultures. Participation in basic assumption activity is "instantaneous, inevitable, and instinctive", and every group contains a spontaneous cohesive factor based upon mutual basic assumption needs. Bion gives the term "valency" to "the individual's readiness to enter into combination with the group in making and acting on the basic assumptions". Every group is engaged in a struggle, which never ends, to make the work group overcome the basic assumption cultures, and "despite the influence of the basic assumptions, it is the work group that triumphs in the long run". This is compatible with Freud's dictum, "Where id was, ego shall be."

We have referred to the use of psychoanalytic concepts. To be more precise, Bion regards the group activity as a regression to the earliest stages of mental life, and therefore finds his explanations in terms used by Melanie Klein.[4] In his work he gives central importance to projective identification and to the interplay between paranoid-schizoid and depressive positions.

Another framework for studying the behaviour of the group as a whole is supplied by the concepts of Group Analytic Psychotherapy formulated by *Foulkes*.[5] Foulkes makes use of the concept of a group matrix, a network comprising all the communications and interactions that have taken place in a group from its inception to the present. The matrix, which is equivalent to the history of the group, is growing and developing all the time and becoming more and more complex. "It is the *common shared ground* which ultimately determines the meaning and significance of all events and upon which all communications, verbal and non-verbal, exist". Specific group events take place against the background of this matrix, and cannot be understood in isolation. It is only when they are "located", that is, related to their context of the group matrix, that their significance and meaning can be comprehended.

It is the concept of the group matrix that makes it possible for the group analyst to regard all spontaneous contributions as equivalent to the free association of psychoanalysis. "Looked at this way it becomes easier to understand our claim that the group associates, responds, and reacts as a whole. The group, as it were, avails itself now of one speaker, now of another, but it is always the transpersonal network which is sensitized and gives utterance, or responds. In this sense we can postulate the existence of a group 'mind' in the same way as we postulate the existence of an individual mind."[4]

The approaches to group work, based on psychoanalytical concepts, assume not only that all the successive events that take place in the group are linked together associatively, but also that these events are related to feelings experienced in the current situation. *Stock Whitaker and Lieberman,*[6] whose focal conflict theory we refer to next, express this with their usual clarity.

"Whatever is said in the group is seen as being elicited not only by the strictly internal concerns of the individual, but by the interpersonal situation in which he finds himself. Of all the personal issues, worries, impulses, and concerns which a patient might express during a group session, what he actually expresses is elicited by the character of the situation. Moreover, a comment is likely to include a number of elements and is responded to selectively by others. An individual may make a comment which includes a half dozen elements. As the others listen to an individual's highly personal contribution, they will respond to certain aspects and ignore others. The aspects which are picked up and built upon are in some way relevant to the other patients and gradually become an emerging shared concern. . . . The group-relevant aspect of an individual's comment is defined by the manner in which the other patients react to it."[6]

This shared aspect of the group, the transpersonal perspective, the behaviour of the group as a whole, is seen by Stock Whitaker and Lieberman in terms of an attempt on the part of the members of the group to establish a generally acceptable solution to a problem, of which they may not be consciously aware, that is affecting them all. This problem is known as the "focal conflict". Such a conflict, representing the covert shared concern of all members, emerges in every group, but the more structured, consistent, and purposeful the group, the harder it will be to detect. It is a conflict between a wish (known in this context as a disturbing motive) and an associated fear (reactive motive), both activated by the current situation in the group. At any time, the behaviour of members of a small group can be seen as determined by the need to find a solution to the current focal conflict. To be successful, the solution must be accepted by them all and must reduce the fears while it permits the maximum possible satisfaction of the wish.

Ezriel[7] has a similar orientation, as is shown in the following:

"The manifest content of discussion in groups may embrace practically any topic. They might talk about astronomy, philosophy, politics, or even psychology; but it is one of the essential assumptions for psychoanalytic work with groups that, whatever the manifest content may be, there always develops rapidly an underlying common group problem, a common group tension of which the group is not aware, but which determines its behaviour."[7]

In Ezriel's formulation, each member brings into the group an individual unconscious tension, the residue of unresolved infantile conflicts, and attempts to relieve this tension by means of the relationships which become established in the group. To this end, each member attempts to manipulate the other members of the group so that they will behave in certain ways which will satisfy unconscious needs "like pawns in a private game of chess". It is by means of the interaction of each member's individual dominant (unconscious) tension that the "common group tension" is created. Like Stock Whitaker and Lieberman, Ezriel describes the group situation in terms of a dynamic triad of forces. The relationship which the group (or it could be an individual) is attempting to establish he calls "the required relationship". It is required not so much for the gratification which it is expected to supply, as for its power to prevent an alternative relationship. This alternative he calls "the avoided relationship", for in unconscious phantasy it must be avoided lest it lead to a third situation, "the calamity". For example, a group may behave in a docile and compliant way towards their leader because in this way they create the relationship that is required in order to avoid another type of relationship in which hostility to the leader might find expression and which might bring about the calamity of his withdrawal or retaliation.

Despite their differences, the writers on group psychotherapy we have considered share some important concepts about the nature of groups that are fundamental to their theories. They all recognize the existence of certain processes which are present in every group and which are the overall determinants of the group's behaviour. In psychotherapeutic groups, the processes have a special significance, since, in the words of Stock Whitaker and Lieberman, they "encompass and intersect the individual's concerns in such a way that the individual's therapeutic experience cannot be understood except as it occurs in and through the group processes".

Model of group psychotherapy

We find ourselves turning from a consideration of the individual to a consideration of the group, and then back again to the individual. This movement between the whole and the parts is important, for both perspectives only have meaning in relation to the other one. The psychological processes that take place within the individual, and within the group of which the individual forms a part, cannot be understood in isolation.

This is the framework within which the experiences of the individual patient must now be considered. Traditionally, group psychotherapy is practised in a medical setting or under medical supervision, and the group member is a "patient", a designation which implies that he is suffering from some condition which requires treatment and which may be cured. There is dissatisfaction with functioning in one or more areas of life, and a belief that one could do better. Difficulties may be canalized into a specific symptom or symptoms, but in joining a psychotherapeutic group a patient is exposing the self to the possibility of a change that will affect not only a specific area of malfunctioning but the whole of personality, and is (theoretically at any rate) committing the whole of the personality to the therapeutic process. It is an axiom of all psychotherapy, individual and group, that problems of personality have their origins in early disturbances of interpersonal relationships, that they manifest themselves currently in disturbed interpersonal relationships, and that it is only in interpersonal situations that they can be treated satisfactorily. Individual psychotherapy is an interpersonal situation involving two persons, whereas group psychotherapy involves more than two. Group psychotherapy, it is claimed, provides each group member with experiences which can bring about comprehensive and beneficial personality changes, curing neurosis, removing difficulties, and enabling one to relinquish habitual maladaptive ways of behaving. The testimony of patients is not enough to substantiate this claim. In addition, the total experience of the individual member in a therapeutic group needs to be examined, and the specific therapeutic components of that experience identified. There seems to be some agreement among writers on group psychotherapy about the presence of these components, but opinions differ as to their relative value and importance.

In our model, the psychotherapeutic group is composed of about eight members and a leader. There will be some selection, although the criteria for selection vary from leader to leader and from group to group. In selecting the group, there is likely to be an attempt to avoid great discrepancies in terms of age, intelligence, educational background and previous experience of therapy. There is also likely to be selection in order to obtain either a one-sex group, or, alternatively, a group in which the sexes are evenly balanced, thus avoiding a situation in which either men or women would constitute a distinct minority. Some forms of illness or personality difficulties may be considered unsuitable for groups altogether, or for one particular group. Stock Whitaker and Lieberman attach importance to selecting a group of patients who are homogeneous in terms of "vulnerability", meaning by vulnerability the extent of the patients' capacity, or lack of capacity, to deal with stressful situations and to tolerate anxiety. There is a danger that if the group is too homogeneous in respect of the habitual methods of dealing with difficulties, the members would then collectively support and reinforce similar habitual maladaptive patterns of behaviour.

Our model group meets at least once a week, and remains together for a fixed period of up to an hour and a half. The members sit in a circle. They are expected to communicate freely whatever is in their minds, including their feelings about the group, about other members, and about the leader. There are no limits to the communications. This form of communication has been described as the group equivalent of the "free association" of individual psychoanalysis, in which the patient is expected to reveal all the ideas and associations which come to mind without regard for their apparent lack of coherence or relevance. Group members cannot communicate in exactly this way, as they each inevitably spend more time in listening than in talking. However, they are encouraged, as far as is possible, to contribute uncensored thoughts and associations, the result being what Foulkes has labelled "free group association". This he treats as the equivalent of the individual's free association although it comes from the group as a whole.

This requires relaxation of the censorship that is normally applied to the expression of thoughts and feelings in social situations. This relaxation is possible only if members of the group come to feel more secure than they would in other settings, and free from the constraints, obligations, and fears that ordinarily prevail. This safety does not mean, of course, that personal criticism or direct verbal attack should be precluded; very much the reverse. It does mean that freedom of expression is seen to belong to them all, that it will be kept by the leader within "safe" bounds, and there will be no repercussions or leaks outside the group.

For this reason, it is important in our model that the members of the group should be strangers to each other, and that any contact between them outside the group meetings be kept to the absolute minimum. Relationships within the group must be kept strictly separated from the personal relationships of domestic and occupational life. These latter are relationships which should not be jeopardized, and the obligations and responsibilities to the continuing life outside the group should not be disregarded.

We must stress that we are describing an idealized model, and for our purposes we are disregarding certain group activities which in other contexts are included within the definition of group psychotherapy by other workers. There are many derivatives of group psychotherapy, for example "therapeutic communities", which have been developed in some hospitals, and in which some of the working activities within the hospital may be intermingled with group meetings. Other types of therapeutic groups include those intended for the treatment of marital disorders, which involve both spouses and family groups to which we shall come later. These need specialized description. For our present purpose we are restricting our descriptions to the type of psychotherapeutic group with the properties outlined above.

This psychotherapeutic group has no other structure. No focus is suggested, nor is any topic for discussion supplied. Any external control, however minimal, would deflect the course of the group's free development and interfere with the expression of fundamental conflicts. Members of the group may be told that they are expected to talk, since ultimately group psychotherapy must rely on verbal communication, but even this requirement involves some interference and some distortion. Talking can itself be a defensive activity, used to prevent the development of revealing silences, and to distract attention from important non-verbal communications.

In this unstructured and protected situation, the newcomers to the group are likely to find themselves attempting to communicate with the other members about their personal difficulties. The other group members may or may not have been selected on the basis of some shared problem, but in any case they will all be people who have acknowledged the existence of difficulties and who are prepared to try to discuss them with others. This in itself provides certain opportunities and experiences. The newcomers will soon realize that they are not the only people with difficulties, and they will find that others too have feelings of fear, shame, resentment or inadequacy, perhaps not very different to their own. This is a simple group phenomenon, which has been labelled "universalization", and which should help to reduce the sense of isolation and shame, and to encourage further communication and even greater frankness.

The responses of others to what is being communicated in the group may help each individual member to see him or herself in a different light. They will all come to have access to information about the effect of their behaviour upon other people, and the different ways in which they are perceived by others, information which may never have been available to them before. This is sometimes known as "the Mirror Reaction", perhaps containing a reference to the distorting mirrors of the fairground. The visitor entering one of these "halls of mirrors" is surrounded by different and often surprising reflections, each of which may contain some truth but none of which gives the "true" picture. This type of "feedback" is something that each gives and each receives, as increasing freedom of expression brings benefits to them all.

"Spectator Theory" is another term which is sometimes used to indicate the benefits the individual may derive from listening to a discussion of some problem resembling one's own, and witnessing attempts to apply different solutions to similar difficulties, even though one may not feel able or willing to contribute to the discussion oneself. Any group will include both talkative and less talkative members. Although the importance of verbal communication is rightly stressed, the silent member will also be participating and communicating, at a non-verbal level, even through silence. Even if one says little, one may be feeling much. None the less, the growth and development of the ability to communicate in words about personal difficulties, to make one's feelings explicit and understood, and to help others to do the same, can indicate the progress of the individual and of the group.

Participation in the group provides the individual members with two different types of information: they hear about the problems of the other members, and they perceive the reactions to their own communications. Each disclosure leads to another, and as some members put more and more of their cards on the table others find it increasingly possible to do likewise. Thus the information available to them becomes more relevant and more important. They may be able to test out the possibility of behaving and responding in new ways, and find that there is no need to be so dominant or so self-effacing, so suspicious or so ingratiating, in their personal relationships. Such disadvantageous behaviour may be part of an individual's habitual pattern because of fears of the consequences of behaving otherwise. In the special conditions of the group one may feel safe enough to relinquish part of this habitual pattern, only to discover that the feared consequences do not follow. This opportunity for reality-testing that the group provides is stressed by some group psychotherapists, who see it as a necessary forerunner to any therapeutic change.

The individual experiences that we have described so far are likely to be familiar to everyone, and are not the monopoly of psychotherapeutic groups. They may be provided fortuitously in any small face-to-face gathering, particularly where one feels accepted and "at home". A person may find that his life has been changed through a conversation in a railway carriage with a perfect stranger, but the method cannot be taught. Psychotherapeutic groups are different from these casual encounters in that conscious attempts are made to foster these experiences, to maximize their impact, and to call attention to, and study scientifically, what is taking place.

Transference

So far we have mentioned the physical setting and the composition of our model group, both designed to promote conditions of greater safety, encourage freer communication, and enable the patient to bring into, or transfer to, the group conflicts and disturbances originally and currently experienced elsewhere.

Though the different theories we have mentioned stress different phenomena and different experiences, all pay some attention to the concept of transference. This concept, central to individual psychoanalytic therapy, needs modification before it can be applied in a group setting. In a two-person setting, the assumption is that the patient transfers to the psychotherapist feelings experienced in earliest relationships that are still inappropriately active in current life. Thus these transferred feelings have two characteristics, their roots in infancy and their current distorting effect on the patient's interpersonal relationships. In most systems of group psychotherapy, it is not considered appropriate to trace transferred emotions back to their historical origins, and emphasis is placed upon their second aspect, the role they play in the "here and now" situation in which all the members of the group are involved.

The transference that takes place in a group differs in several respects from transference in an individual psychotherapeutic setting. Essentially, it has more dimensions. The patient may transfer to the leader, to other members of the group and to the group as a whole. The leader, as a recipient of transference of relationships, aims to remain neutral, and to keep his or her own personality from intruding. This is not true of the other group members, who will react spontaneously and repudiate any transference roles that do not happen to meet their own needs.

The patient may attempt to re-create in the group the original "network" of relationships in which the conflict was first experienced, using different individuals, including the leader, to represent different protagonists. Equally the group itself may come to represent or symbolize something important to the patient. This may be a person, an idea, an object, or a situation. The "matrix" of the group may appropriately stand for the mother. Alternatively, it may represent home, a symbol of security, or an experience like the first day at school.

These are not the only possibilities. Any transference relationship may be shared and divided among different members of the group. In the transference to the leader, which is a feature of all groups, each member may express a different and complementary component. The roles that the members take up in the group may have the same complementarity as the roles assumed within a family, where the good son and the bad son enact their parts in relation to expectations which they share with the parents, and thus the whole network may be transferred into the group with a new dramatis personae.

This is the means by which patients bring into the group the conflicts and difficulties that they are experiencing elsewhere. The language used to describe the effect of these transferred relationships will vary according to whichever theory is being used. They influence the development of one or other of the basic assumptions; they contribute to the formation of the group matrix; or they help to determine what manner of group focal conflict, or common group tension, develops. The pattern of the communications in the group will be influenced in some way by the theoretical position which the group leader holds.

The group culture

Up to this point, no specific mention has been made of the role played by the leader, or group psychotherapist, within the group culture. The task of the leader is to influence the development of the group in such a way that each member is able to derive the maximum therapeutic benefit from attendance at the group sessions. It cannot be taken for granted that group activity (even psychotherapeutic group activity) brings automatic benefit.

Groups contain potentialities for harm as well as for good. Fears and anxieties may be confirmed rather than reduced when they are found to be shared by other people; "feedback" may supply distorted and misleading information; maladaptive patterns of behaviour may come to be shared and receive support instead of being challenged. The group may fail to develop and mature; it may encourage regression to earlier levels of development; it may become dependent on its leader, and seduce the leader into playing a directive role. Individual members may be victimized, isolated, attacked, turned into scapegoats, to a degree which they are unable to tolerate. Finally, the group may break up, leaving behind it a residue of disappointment, failure and mistrust.

In the same way that cohesive and disruptive forces co-exist in every group, so the effect of the group on the individual can be ego-strengthening or ego-weakening, therapeutic or anti-therapeutic. Any group will contain both elements. In a psychotherapeutic group, the very factors that support and sustain the individual member, support and sustain, in order to make tolerable, exposure to increasing stress and pain. As endurance increases, so one can be given more to endure. As the group gets stronger, so destructive aspects can be more clearly and openly expressed, and the group finds itself able to tolerate such expression, and survive increasingly greater stresses. This cannot be achieved easily. But if the individual patient does not encounter difficult, and unpleasant, and frightening, situations during group psychotherapy, he or she will leave the group untouched, the conflicts still intact.

The phenomenon known as "scapegoating", for example, which can occur in all societies and in all groups, can be extremely painful both for the scapegoat and for the other participants. Impulses which a number of members of the group find unacceptable in themselves, and which, if revealed, would cause a breaking-up of the group, may be projected on to one group member. This process allows the remaining members to attack and repudiate such impulses. This way of dealing with what is personally unacceptable may not only secure the continuance of the group, but also it may provide an experience that is necessary for both "scapegoat" and "persecutors", involving and highlighting the basic conflicts of both parties. The two roles are complementary and each contains its own opposite. Group and scapegoat alike find that they can pass through a frightening experience and survive it. On the other hand, either scapegoat or attacker may find the experience intolerable, and may even have to leave the group. Therefore the leader must be able to maintain the delicate balance. One side of the balance is to allow sufficient stressful interaction to represent the inevitable conflictual situations that have to be experienced, and which all recur in everyday life. The other side is to prevent the stress on any individual from extending to a breakdown that would damage victim and victimizers alike.

In an earlier chapter we put forward the concept that group processes are determined by the struggle between cohesive and disruptive elements in the group, and, by the same token, in the individuals composing the group. The existence of the group is constantly threatened by the disruptive forces in the group and in the individual members, and measures have to be taken by the group as a whole to meet this threat and safeguard its continuance. Scapegoating can be one such measure. This concept seems to be present, if not always explicitly stated, in most dynamic group theories.

A close analogy may be drawn between the group and the nation state. The disruptive elements in the state can be dealt with in a variety of ways. A confident state may be able to tolerate rebellious and even subversive activity on the part of minority groups such as students and others, whereas a threatened or divided state is more likely to curtail freedom of speech and assembly, introduce censorship, and attempt to secure conformity to its rulings. In a similar way, some groups may develop a "culture" which discourages non-conformity, puts a virtual taboo on the discussion of certain topics, or makes it only possible to discuss them in certain approved ways. Even the theories believed to be held by the group leader may become an ideology which must not (or must) be challenged.

The term "culture" is used in this way by Stock Whitaker and Lieberman to include "the practices, standards, and mutual understandings which regulate relationships within the group and define the character of the group world". It is the culture which determines what is acceptable and what is not acceptable and where the limits of tolerance and acceptance lie. In their focal conflict theory, Stock Whitaker and Lieberman see the culture as being made up of the sum of all the successful solutions to the focal conflicts that have been preoccupying the group at an unconscious or near-conscious level. These solutions are described as either restrictive or enabling. A restrictive solution to a group focal conflict is like repressive state action, the group as a whole deciding to deal with subversive elements by a restriction of freedom.

The role of the group psychotherapist

The leader is also subject to the influence of the group culture, but must be able to maintain sufficient detachment from it to be aware of what is going on and to be able to intervene to influence it. Group leaders need to be able to recognize the group processes, and the way in which they themselves and all the other group members are contributing to them and being influenced by them. They must be able to forecast how the group as a whole will be influenced by any intervention, or lack of intervention, on their part.

We can distinguish a number of different ways in which group psychotherapists influence their groups. Every intervention that group psychotherapists make, or do not make, will have its significance. First of all, there are the leaders' implicit attitudes. Their behaviour will to some extent serve as a model for the members of their groups. It is through attitudes rather than through anything that is said that a leader can show a group the value of tolerance, and promote a permissive and accepting attitude.

It is through their own ability to tolerate distressing experiences that group psychotherapists can help their groups to tolerate them in their turn. Initially, and in the last resort, the leader has to guarantee the safety of the group, and all group members need to learn that their leader is capable of doing this, and that, whatever they themselves do or say, their leader will not be frightened or angry, wounded or destroyed. Such tranquillity provides some protection against the disruptive forces, the fears and conflicts and antagonisms, which might destroy the group. If the leader can withstand the contents, Pandora may open her box.

Group psychotherapists are used as transference figures by their groups, and have to recognize this and accept it even if they do not deliberately encourage it. They wish to help all the group members to become as fully involved as possible, to relate not only to a leader but also to each other, and to look to each other for reactions to, and comments upon, their communications. Such leaders do not wish to be the main focus in their groups, neither do they wish to "lead" them. It is for this reason that Foulkes did not use the term "leader" but preferred to speak of a group "conductor". In this sense, the leader of a psychotherapeutic group is not a leader, nor a teacher nor yet a counsellor. The group may try to impose such a role, and this attempt must be considered along with all other group happenings, in relation to the state of the group as a whole and the processes operating in it at that time.

For example, a group psychotherapist might consider that such an attempt means that the group as a whole is trying to avoid dealing with some particular problem, is showing a reluctance to take the next step forward, is wishing instead to substitute some magical solution and to return to a state of dependence upon a parental figure. The progress of every psychotherapeutic group is hindered by obstacles. These obstacles are introduced by individual members and accepted by the group as a whole because they afford a temporary solution to, or respite from, a current group problem, or because they prevent change in an unknown and therefore frightening direction.

Everything that a group psychotherapist does, or does not do, in such a situation, will affect the outcome. He, or she, needs to be aware of the group processes, of the ways in which each individual is contributing to the group processes, and of the relevance of the group processes to, and their effect upon, each individual. Through tacit refusal to accept the imposed role, by denying to the group a magical solution or a dependent relationship, the leader may be able to re-confront it with the problem which it is trying to evade. It may be judged necessary to put into words what is going on, and to draw the attention of the group to the meaning of its own behaviour. This brings us to the unique aspect of the psychotherapist's role in the group: the analytic function of "making the unconscious conscious" through interpretations.

The interpretations of the leader in our group therapy model differ from those of the individual psychotherapist in that they are not centred upon individuals and, therefore, they do not attempt to trace the transference relationship back to its historical roots. For the past history of each individual is separate and unique and belongs to that individual alone; it is only in the "here and now" situation in the group that individual concerns meet, and that a focus can be found which belongs to all members conjointly and which conjointly affects them all. Each member is a co-author of the theme. Even if the leader does not presume to believe in something as mystical as a "group unconscious", it is still necessary to respond as if every communication can, in some sense, be taken to come from the group as a whole. This means that the assignment is to find the factor in the communication that has reference to a common preoccupation of the group. References to individuals are not necessarily precluded. The leader may need to make an interpretation about the behaviour of a particular group member, where the interests of the group and of the individual require it, but every such decision will be made with reference to the processes operating in the group at that time. It will also need to be made in the awareness that the singling out of an individual by the leader can be destructive to both individual and group, and is not to be undertaken without good cause.

An interpretation has to be well timed. If given prematurely, it may seem like an attack, increasing the threat to the group and the need for a defensive solution; or it may bring a potentially valuable experience to an untimely end. It could also forestall the finding of the interpretation by the group as a whole, and the group would be so much the poorer. Each member in the group has a role as therapist, as well as patient, and needs to exercise that role. Rather than presenting the group members with interpretations (and thereby emphasizing dependence), the leader may help them to find their own, asking questions rather than suggesting answers. For there is no role, whether that of guarantor of safety, protector of the weak, interpreter, clarifier, or therapist, that group psychotherapists would not rather see exercised by their groups working together than arrogate to themselves.

The advantages that group therapy can bring to the individual are equalled by the potential dangers, which are greater than in either of our other two systems. Analytical therapy demands commitment, a greater commitment than in any other structured encounter. No one ever commits the whole of himself to this process, not even in individual analysis. Yet, in analysis, whether individual or group, it is not possible to anticipate nor to define the areas of confrontation, nor to contract out of any one of them in advance. *It is the potentiality of commitment which is without limits.* This potentiality makes group therapy a more dangerous situation for patient and therapist than exists in group counselling or in group discussion, where group members may legitimately make mental reservations which keep some part of themselves untouched. The danger in group psychotherapy lies in the unwitting exposure of vulnerable parts of the personality, the removal of defences, and the release of forces which could well be destructive in and to the personalities of the participants. These are the forces which are the springs of all creative activity; but the same forces, unharnessed and undirected, are the essence of psychosis and violence.

The development of the group's capacity to deal with its destructive forces must not be weakened or impaired, since in participation in this development we find a large part of the individual's therapeutic experience. However, the expression of destructive forces may at times outstrip the capacity of the group to tolerate them without damage, and the vulnerability of different group members will vary. In the language of psychiatric practice we are accustomed to use the phrase "acting out" to describe behaviour which is undesirable or even disastrous, whereas a description of phantasies of the same behaviour would be welcomed as a revelation of unconscious processes. Some of the activities and exchanges within the process of group psychotherapy might well be called "acting out". For example, members of the group may make sexual challenges to each other. These might well represent the recognition of sexual feelings in their manifold form. There is a legitimate place for the expression of these feelings, which exist in human encounters in a variety of forms and which ordinarily must remain unrecognized and unexpressed. However, in group psychotherapy, someone must take the responsibility for preventing these expressions from becoming dangerous seductions or attacks. The absence of limits for discussion is not the absence of limits for action.

The leader has a duty which is similar to that of the individual psychotherapist. Necessary as it is for the deepest unconscious material to be revealed, the psychotherapist must at some point relate it back to conscious material. Insight is not the equivalent of the revelation of unconscious material alone; it is the perception of both conscious and unconscious meanings at the same time. Similarly, in group psychotherapy, the group psychotherapist may have to remind the participants of the existence of the outside world.

We have referred to the skills which the psychotherapist needs to have. These skills include the ability to reintroduce limits in a situation where the limits have been removed. This is not merely the ability to restrict something which one fears or does not understand. One has to be able to perceive the trends and to be able to carry oneself along into the same depths as the participants. One has to have the ability and the experience to keep part of oneself as an observer of the conscious as well as the unconscious meanings, and to predict the way in which the discussion will affect the feelings and behaviour of all the group members. One has to be able to intervene and, equally important, one has to be able to remain silent.

Finally, we can only agree with Foulkes that the responsibility is great and that "no one should embark on this who has not the measure and control of his power firmly in his blood and system, lest he will suffer the fate of the sorcerer's apprentice".

It was intended to be part of our purpose to describe group psychotherapy as a separate process, in terms that would distinguish it clearly and unambiguously from group counselling and group discussion. We believe that we have been able to draw some valid distinctions. We have, however, to admit that in a very real sense group psychotherapy can only be identified as those procedures that are carried out by individuals with the following qualifications: they are psychoanalysts or psychotherapists who have had a training in group methods, who therefore have authorization to treat patients by this means. We acknowledge that this definition is comparable to the definition of psychiatric illness as that illness which is treated by a psychiatrist. Group psychotherapy is that which is practised by group psychotherapists.

Notes and references

1. Slavson, S. R. *Analytic Group Psychotherapy with Children, Adolescents and Adults.* Columbia University Press, New York, 1950.
2. Berne, E. *Games People Play,* Grove Press Inc., New York, 1967.
3. Bion, W. R. Group dynamics: a re-view *International Journal of Psychoanalysis* Vol. 33, 1952. *Experiences in Groups.* Tavistock Publications, 1961.
4. An explanation of the terms used by Melanie Klein may be found in *The Adult World and Other Essays,* Melanie Klein, Heinemann 1963, and *Introduction to the Theories of Melanie Klein* by Hannah Segal, Hogarth Press, 1973.
5. Foulkes, S. H. *Therapeutic Group Analysis,* Geo. Allen and Unwin Ltd., 1964.
   Foulkes, S. H. *Group-Analytic Psychotherapy,* Gordon and Breach, London, 1975.
6. Stock Whitaker D. and Lieberman M. A. *Psychotherapy through the Group Process,* Tavistock Publications, 1965.
7. Ezriel, H. *A psychoanalytic approach to group treatment.* B.J.M.P. Vol. XXIII Parts 1 and 2, 1950.

7

Group Counselling

Relationship to social work and to psychotherapy

In discussing group work so far, enough has been said to make it clear that we are not using the term group counselling to describe a form of group psychotherapy that has been diluted in order to allow it to be carried out by less-skilled practitioners. It is used, rather, to denote a distinct process in which a different form of help is offered, with aims, criteria, techniques, and skills of its own. It draws upon dynamic theories of group behaviour derived from group psychotherapy, but it makes use of them to serve its own different purpose. It also draws upon theories of social casework, but this does not make it a technique to be used exclusively by social workers. It is not confined within the boundaries of any one profession. However, social workers are likely to remain its principal and most steadfast practitioners; it is in social work settings that its concepts can be most clearly demonstrated. It is, therefore, in relation to social work that we shall mainly be considering it.

In contrasting group counselling and group psychotherapy, one essential distinction has already been made. In group counselling, as in casework, a particular aim is detected and defined at the outset, providing a focus and setting the limits within which the proceedings of the group take place. Group psychotherapy is not so bound. We stress this distinction because, in our opinion, group work that is not defined and limited requires the sanctions of psychotherapy, and only someone possessing the skills of a group psychotherapist is authorized to practice it. Outside this discipline, unstructured and unfocused work is hazardous for both leader and members of the group.

Thus so far, in attempting to establish a second group system, the emphasis has been placed upon the more restricted purpose of group counselling, the lack of sanction for the type of free disclosure required by psychotherapy, and the less complete commitment of the participants.

The limitation in aims means that group counselling is less intensive and less comprehensive, but, by the same token, it is more flexible and has a wider application, extending to situations where the rigorous demands of group psychotherapy would not be met. Members of a counselling group come for a limited purpose; they are not required to be patients, accepting a status that has implications of weakness and dependency, and neither do they need to be strangers to each other nor to restrict their contacts outside the group meetings. Group counselling need not be confined to the consulting room but can be practised in a variety of different settings, and it can be used to deal with groups that are already in existence as well as the artificial groups created specifically for a treatment purpose, though here care may have to be taken to find an appropriate point of focus. Group counsellors may belong to a number of different disciplines: given a professional competence in one particular area, such as medicine, nursing, psychology, or teaching, individual helping methods can be augmented and extended by the acquisition of group counselling techniques.

To say that group counselling does not deal with the deeper levels of personality is not to say that it is less valuable. It is necessary to emphasize this point because the great influence and prestige of analytic practice has sometimes suggested that any other method is second best. There have been times in the past when social workers themselves have helped to establish this hierarchy of esteem by valuing more highly those forms of casework that make most use of interpretation and the development of insight. Attempts have since now been made to reverse this trend. Treatment in "depth" no longer seems to be the preferred technique in all circumstances. It is now increasingly recognized that different levels of work are appropriate in different circumstances, and the optimum level may be that which achieves sufficient result with the minimum of disturbance. By analogy, you do not need deep mining to obtain open-cast coal, and, for that matter, in some countries diamonds can be picked up on the surface. The only justification for going "deep"[1] is that in some situations it is necessary to do so.

Depth is one dimension. It is not the only one. We need to look at this dimension along with others, and so we need to consider a number of different approaches, involving a number of different professions, to the assessment and treatment of personal problems. This requires a concept of a total treatment process as a context in which different dimensions, levels, or areas of work, can be related as alternatives or complements to each other. This context must be able to include different forms of analytic and psychological treatment, social work, group counselling, and group psychotherapy.

Before adding our own formulation to the many that have gone before, a word or two of qualification is needed. No formulation such as that of a total treatment process can ever be definitive or complete. More than that, it can lead to self-deception, obscuring rather than clarifying the processes that are actually taking place. In describing what we are doing we risk becoming the dupes of our own propaganda and our own legends, and it is often the incomplete formulations of the past that have provided our current myths by which we are bemused. The myth that is currently fashionable, for example, is that we deal with the total person in his total environment. This is indeed the general aim. The aim is unattainable, though there may be increased satisfaction, and an improvement in methods, every time that the area which is dealt with is enlarged. The concept of the total person in his total environment is an abstraction; its purpose is to remind us of the unattainable aim, and to indicate such extensions in understanding as have been achieved.

When we attempt to study the total patient, or client, all that we are able to comprehend and describe are a few fragments of an unknown whole. When the patient or client tells us of his problem, he is offering us one fragment. We may respond to that fragment, or we may add to it other fragments which we have comprehended through our own observations or from other sources. The field to which these fragments belong is complex and unbounded; in order to do our work we have to simplify it and to put in some boundaries, and our concepts and formulations are our attempts to do this.

Three areas of treatment

In our formulation of the total treatment process, we suggest that the fragments which are obtained can be classified under three main headings, representing three areas of the patient's total functioning. Any single process that is undertaken in the way of treatment must be directed to one of these three areas. They are as follows:

1. *The patient's circumstances*, including his material environment, his education or work, and his financial and housing situation.
2. *The patient's personality*, including his state of physical and mental health, his defects and disorders, his capacities and potentialities.
3. *The network of interpersonal relationships* of which the patient forms a part, including his family of origin and his current parental, marital, and social relationships.

Any problem may be presented by the patient or by others as a malfunctioning in any one, or more than one, of these three areas. The area chosen will often determine which of the caring professions is given authority to intervene. A professional helper, though not ignoring the expressed area, may consider another one to be equally, or more, significant. These areas are not alternatives: they exist simultaneously and they are interconnected. If intervention takes place in one area, the others will not remain unaffected. In our view, no one area can be satisfactorily treated in isolation. Neither is any one discipline professionally equipped on its own to intervene directly in all three. Where social workers attempt to deal with two areas simultaneously, they are likely to look on one area as the primary one, and the attribution of primary and secondary importance to one or another factor may depend upon the credo of the worker. There are, indeed, professional people who, as an ideological principle, restrict all their efforts to one of these areas and question the relevance of any of the others. Some psychiatrists, for example, will hold that all that is necessary is to deal with a disorder within the individual personality; they treat the disease, restore the patient to previous good health, and the patient then deals with the external circumstances and finds that personal and family relationships have improved! Others may concentrate on social and family relationships, often finding the pathology there, if not the cure. Other workers again have economic and political explanations for all disorder and consequently find it intractable until such time as these external conditions receive their rightful attention in the society in which we live. Alternatively, there are others who take a more global approach, and feel competent to deal with all three areas, by themselves and at the same time. This at least avoids that fragmentation of problems which is now generally deplored, but those who work in this way need to recognize that in much of what they are doing they are making use of their own personal resources and their experience of life rather than their professional training. A general practitioner, for example, who tries to deal with the problem as a whole may find that he or she is having to be an untrained psychotherapist and untrained social worker as well as a trained family doctor.

This formulation of the treatment process can be illustrated in a simple example. A young man has difficulty in finding and keeping a job. The work that he is equipped to do is in short supply in his neighborhood. He has specific neurotic difficulties which affect his application to his work. These difficulties are fostered by his dependent relationship with the mother with whom he lives. In this example, the problem could be located in any or all of the three areas, and the initial intervention might be directed at any one of them or at more than one. But intervention in each area involves a distinct and different process. Treatment directed at his circumstances, such as the finding of jobs for him, retraining him for a different job, or intervening with his employers, is a process which has no direct group counterpart, and so, although important, it does not directly concern us here. Treatment directed at the area of his personality may be offered on an individual basis or as a group process; as a group process it has been considered in the previous chapter on group psychotherapy. We are left with the third area, and, correspondingly, with a third treatment process. In this, the focus is not upon the intrapersonal conflicts of the patient but upon his interpersonal relationships, and therefore it takes in not only the patient but also the whole network of relationships of which he forms a part. Treatment will consist of intervention at any point in his network; it may involve work directly with the referred patient, or it may involve work with some other key person such as parent, spouse, or with two or more members of the family seen conjointly. We have mentioned a hypothetical case above in which a young man's difficulties were intensified by his relationship with his mother, and therefore, in this instance, the relationship between mother and son might be selected as the focus of a treatment process. Treatment focused upon this relationship might involve work directly with the young man himself: such work would have a limited aim and would fall within the framework which belongs to casework rather than to psychotherapy. On the other hand, treatment might take the form of interviews with the mother in the interests of her son. This would involve working with someone who does not see herself in the role of a patient, and within a different set of sanctions. She may, however, have access to sufficient anxiety about her role as a mother to allow her to question it, and to accept the status of client, in her own right, in relation to a case-worker.

Emphasis on the interpersonal relationships

This area of work is of interest and concern to different disciplines. Many psychotherapists seek to include it within their own field. However, where treatment is based upon team work with a high degree of professional differ-entiation, it is usually seen as a specialist province of the social worker. Thus we have another dimension added to our conception of social casework; it is within the area of interpersonal relationships that it finds a major focus and a primary technique. Other techniques and other forms of help—material, educational, or psychological—are not excluded, but such help can only be considered as casework when it is offered within the context of a personal relationship of a particular kind, and when it is offered in such a way that it contributes to the development of that relationship.

What special techniques, then, differentiate work in this area? We have already considered some of the assumptions that are made about the nature of interpersonal relationships. Each one of us lives within a network of inter-connected relationships, and through them we seek to satisfy our basic emotional needs. It is the whole that gives the parts a special significance, and it is only in the context of the whole that specific events can be under-stood. A new and happier situation at work may help a man to make a more positive contribution in his family circle. Conversely, a frustrated wife is more likely to be a possessive mother and an exacting friend. Our relation-ships with other people are not only interconnected horizontally in the pres-ent: they are also connected longitudinally throughout our life history. The interaction that took place between ourselves and others in the past, particu-larly in our earliest, most formative, years, influences our present needs, and our demands and expectations of others. The extent of the influence varies, as some people are able to achieve a greater freedom from past conflicts than others can, but some influence always remains.

In his or her professional role, the social worker enters the network of sig-nificant relationships surrounding the client and becomes part of it. The rela-tionship that is established becomes part of the client's experience and contributes to the whole, affecting not only the client but also all members of the client's immediate circle, and others with whom the social worker comes in contact. It is in the use of this relationship that a large part of the social worker's own particular and distinctive professional skill is shown.

Lessons from child guidance work

As an illustration of both social work and group counselling, we propose to consider work with mothers in a child guidance clinic. Though such a setting cannot be regarded as typical, it is one with which both the authors are familiar, and in which group work belonging to all three of our systems may take place. Here the different areas of work, and the roles of different professions, can be clearly seen. When a child requires treatment, his place in the network of family and school has to be considered. For this reason child guidance has always attempted to deal simultaneously with several dimensions and has had a multidisciplinary approach.

The social worker in a child guidance clinic is traditionally expected to contribute to the treatment of the child through the family interaction. Let us suppose that this is done by means of a series of interviews with the child's mother.[2] It is likely that the following points will be kept in mind. The client is a woman who is meeting difficulties in her role as a mother, and who has enough awareness of these difficulties to accept treatment for herself, albeit on behalf of her child. The social worker is a helping and caring person, in a position of authority. The mother-child relationship is therefore to some extent mirrored in the relationship with the client. Attitudes that have been carried over from the client's earliest relationship with her own mother are likely to be brought into this relationship. These attitudes are likely to be relevant to the problems on which treatment is focused, since it was from this relationship that the client derived her own primary experience of mothering.

In addition, every theme of family life has its resonance in the mother's conception of herself as a mother. Her past recollection of being mothered by her parents, aunts, uncles, and older siblings are accompanied by present feelings about her role as supplementary mother to other members of her extended family; and there is also the counterpart of this in her continuing need to be mothered herself by these relatives and even by the children. All this is ever present in the mother's relationship with the child who is the referred patient, and also in the mother's relationship with the social worker. The social worker needs to be aware of the range and extent of all these feelings and the part that they play in these two significant sets of relationships: the relationship between mother and child on which the work is focused, and the relationship with the client which is the principal therapeutic tool.

In this professional relationship between social worker and client, social workers will seek to create a situation of safety in which the client will feel free to discuss difficulties, and the feelings about difficulties, without fear of being criticized or misunderstood. The social workers will try to use this relationship sensitively and flexibly to meet what they conceive to be the needs of the client as a person and as a mother. They may use the relationship to augment the client's experience, perhaps to make good some deficiency in the past or present that is adversely affecting her maternal role. The professional relationship of worker and client may be used, for example, to provide a counterbalance to recollections of faulty experiences in the past which the present situation has re-activated. Whatever the social worker may do exists as a model with which the client may identify, providing a pattern of behaviour which can be incorporated and applied in other contexts. Within the particular focus of child guidance, the way in which the social worker behaves towards the client may be taken to exemplify "good" parental behaviour. Ferrard and Hunnybun, in *The Caseworker's Use of Relationships*, discuss the help that can be given to immature people "by slowly building up a relationship with them that offers warmth and understanding, thus enabling them gradually to take over from the worker, as they might from a wise and kindly parent, ideas and ways of behaviour never learnt in childhood."

Within this relationship, the social worker may employ other techniques. One may seek to promote the development of insight and understanding about the problem at a more conscious level. One may use some interpretations. One may encourage the ventilation of hostile feelings, which, once safely expressed and accepted in a casework situation, could lose some of their hurt so that they no longer need to be directed inappropriately elsewhere. One may also try to educate the client about the norms of child development and about different ways in which difficulties with children could be handled. In all this, the skilled use of the worker-client relationship remains an essential prerequisite and is the context within which all other techniques operate. It is only when these other techniques are employed in this context that they become part of casework rather than of some other process, such as education or psychotherapy.

Although present behaviour is affected by all that has happened in the past, the effect is not static or inevitable. Any fresh experience in the present can give a new significance to past events and modify their current influence. Thus help can be provided by means of such experiences, without the need to work at "deeper" levels and to uncover the events and emotions of the past.

Mothers' groups in child guidance settings

Mothers attending a child guidance clinic may have individual interviews with a social worker, or they may join with other mothers and a social worker in a group. In either case the purpose is the same. The focus is still upon the mother-child relationship and the aim is still a development of this relationship in the interests of the referred child. But the instrument to bring this about is no longer an individual relationship and an individual casework process. It has become a group relationship and a group process, making use of free discussion with others in a like situation and the interaction that takes place among the members and the group counsellor.

Attempts may be made to justify such group work as a time-saver, in that one worker sees a number of mothers at one interview. The process may or may not save time, but some groups may well go more quickly and more intensively into the important areas of discussion simply because the situation itself provides a living experience of some of the issues which in individual casework can only be indirectly described. In the group, the mother finds herself in a situation that is more complex and more diffuse than individual casework. Instead of a two-person relationship designed solely to help her, which can be tailored to meet her own particular requirements, she is placed in a group of her peers and is exposed to the demands of competing needs. It is a situation which is closer to real life, to which current problems and preoccupations may be quickly transferred, and in which feelings are more immediately aroused. The relationship with the group leader is a more diluted one, and some of its aspects are spread out over the other members, but its totality is not necessarily less intense.

We emphasize the difference between group counselling and group psychotherapy, but it will be seen that group counselling offers many of the same advantages and opportunities that have already been discussed in relation to group psychotherapy. These advantages and opportunities are no less relevant because the group is bounded by a problem that is known to be shared by all the participants. The group counsellor may work within different terms of reference and different sanctions from a group psychotherapist, and the techniques and skills that are employed may differ in many respects, but both make use of forces that are found in all groups. Whether the group work is limited and problem focused, or whether it is intensive and analytic, engaging the total personalities of the participants, the positive therapeutic factors that exist in the group situation will need to be utilized. Likewise these factors will have their negative, anti-therapeutic counterparts, and these cannot be ignored.

The mother taking part in a counselling group is not the sole recipient: a position sustaining and gratifying to some, humiliating and threatening to others. In the group she is a giver as well as a receiver; she contributes to its success and to its failure, and to the help that the others receive. She listens and reacts to the problems of others, and her own difficulties are not divulged to one helper under conditions of strict confidentiality, but are exposed to the reactions and comments of a wider circle. If, in an individual interview, she were to disclose emotionally charged information about herself, the response would be carefully handled by the audience of one. In a group, her contribution will be received by the other members, and responded to in the light of their different emotional involvements. Any response made by the group counsellor will have to be geared to the needs of the group as a whole, and not solely to the needs of one particular member.

Every contribution adds something to the group and may be of help to others. Each mother brings to the discussion her own experiences as a mother in relation to her children, and these experiences, in which she may feel she has failed, are used to enrich the proceedings of the group and may be treated as a valuable contribution. Thus through her very failure she is given an opportunity to experience the satisfaction and reassurance of being able to help others. This is an example of the support which a group can supply to its members, which extends beyond anything which could be provided in an individual casework situation. Each mother does not depend upon the individual reassurance provided by a social worker, which, if given, would be likely to increase dependency and allay anxieties in an unproductive way. Instead, she creates her own reassurance from her growing ability to contribute to the group, from the use that is made of her contributions, and from the further contributions of others.

The members of such a group come not as patients but as mothers, and the staff of a child guidance clinic emphasize this by using the term "mothers' group". While discussing the difficulties of this role that they share, there are opportunities to build up confidence in the person behind the role. It may even be possible, in this context, to attack the activities within the role without damaging the person responsible for the activities.

In one group of mothers, one member referred to the fact that her own elderly mother of eighty was ill. She described her anxieties about losing her mother, but accompanied the description with a brilliant smile which seemed intended to reassure herself and to tell the other members that all her feelings were within her control. Another member questioned her as to whether she would feel relieved of the burden when her mother died, and gradually in response to further questioning she was induced to admit some of her long-standing hostile feelings about her mother. At this point the group counsellor (in this instance a man and a psychiatrist) was about to draw the session to a close when another member said, "Are we going to allow Mrs. X to go away thinking that she is bad? Oughtn't we to recognize the fact that at the same time she is genuinely concerned about her mother?"

If this point had been brought in too early, or if it had been introduced by the person who had made the attack, it would have been no more than the reassuring smile which the mother had used herself. It derived its value from all that had gone before. This reparative part of the work might well have been carried out by the leader, if he had thought of it, but it was far better coming from a member of the group. Indeed, if it had occurred to the leader to make such a contribution, he might on second thoughts have decided to withhold it. Opportunities need to be given to all members of the group to exercise the functions that would, in a one-to-one interview, belong to the professional worker: functions such as acceptance, tolerance, support, and acknowledgement of both aspects of ambivalence. Thus Phillida Parsloe, in "Some thoughts on social group work",[3] writes that the social group worker "has to find ways of working which allow full scope for the members' ability to help each other. This can be difficult for caseworkers, for we have been used in the one-to-one interview to having all to ourselves the powerful and satisfying position of accepting, enabling, and helping. . . . In a group one hopes such support will come from a member, and this may mean the leader has to control not only words but smiles, nods, and hand movements as well, and thus allow space for members to move in to show their acceptance."

The loss of uniqueness, the knowledge of shared difficulties, should do something to reduce the feelings of isolation and shame which cultural attitudes in our society help to induce, and by which problems are often exacerbated. We have already discussed how one confidence often leads to another, and how we find ourselves becoming franker about our own problems in response to a friend's disclosures. After this, problems often appear less intractable and solutions more attainable. In a social setting, the sequel to frank disclosures may be embarrassment and withdrawal at the next encounter. This may also happen in a counselling group. The group counsellor will have to anticipate this possibility, and perhaps even discourage premature exchange of confidences in the beginning stages of a group. A group psychotherapist, on the other hand, is able to permit greater tensions to develop from the very beginning, and the group then has more time to develop its own means for dealing with such problems.

Each member will not only talk about her own difficulties, but will also listen to the difficulties of others, and their descriptions of attempts to cope with problems like and unlike her own. She may become interested in a problem raised by another member and take part in discussing it, without revealing, perhaps without acknowledging even to herself, that it is in fact a resemblance to some part of her own situation that has aroused her interest. Thus she is working indirectly and vicariously on her own difficulties.

Each member in the mothers' group hears of a wider range of attitudes and reactions to common difficulties in family relationships than her own experience could provide. She learns that there are many different ways in which children can be handled. Through identification, she is able to experiment in phantasy, to try on and adopt, or sometimes reject, different modes of behaviour. She thereby is able to extend the range of her own possible responses and repertoires.

Participation in the group may help some mothers to relinquish defences which are preventing them from dealing realistically with their situation. For example, a mother may be unable to give her handicapped child the help he needs because she is preoccupied with attributing blame to medical or educational authorities. It might take a social worker, who is offering individual interviews, a long time to work through this, as any direct approach to this issue would be seen as one authority defending another, and would be likely to reinforce the mother's attitude. Comments from other parents with similar problems would be very differently received. From an early age, we tend to be more easily influenced, favourably or unfavourably, by the opinion of our peer group than by any other.

The comments of other members in this example are less likely to be helpful if some of them have a like attitude towards people in authority. A group composed of people who all make use of similar habitual ways of dealing with their problems may supply support and confirmation for maladaptive patterns of behaviour in which they all have a share. Though this can happen in all our three systems, it is more likely to happen in groups which are focused upon a common problem. (The record of a counselling group given below provides an illustration.) The danger lies in such behaviour becoming entrenched as part of the group "culture", as may happen when the behaviour offers a solution not only to individual problems but also to the threat of disruptive forces in the group. If the members can unite in attributing blame elsewhere, they are reducing their own feelings of guilt, finding an outlet for action even if it is of a negative kind, and binding the group together against a common "enemy". This possibility should be borne in mind whenever it is possible to exercise some selection procedure for counselling groups. Such groups are likely to make more rapid progress if there is some diversity in the solutions that members habitually employ to meet their common problems.

The capacity of the members of the group to identify with one another, to discover the common aspects in each individual problem, and to give as well as to receive help, forms an important part of the group counselling process in child guidance as in other settings. It is something that the group counsellor may need to promote, intervening more directly to this end than a group psychotherapist would be likely to do. It is therefore important that the group counsellors should be able to identify correctly the cohesive factors that are present in the group, the areas which can be shared, and the conditions under which sharing is possible: otherwise they may find themselves encouraging a spurious uniformity and delaying the discussion of real and importance differences. They must also recognize and not be dismayed by the disruptive forces in the group, and these may have to be dealt with if they are relevant to the problem on which the group is focused, or if they are seriously hampering the group's progress. However, they will not seek to bring these negative forces to the fore in the way that might be appropriate in some stages of group psychotherapy.

This skill, the capacity to recognize, and make use of, such therapeutic forces as are immediately available, can be studied and acquired; it can also sometimes be recognized in an unlearned, intuitive response. A few years ago there was a meeting of parents and staff at a junior training centre which one of us attended. It was a big meeting with about a hundred parents present, and after the speeches the centre head, who was in the chair, invited questions from the floor.

"Please, Miss," came from the back of the hall, "when will my Jenny be able to walk?"

The centre head appealed to the audience, "Some of you know a lot about this. Come along, you other parents with Down's Syndrome children, tell us when your children started to walk."

The meeting at once became lively, with a number of parents eagerly recounting their experiences and an audience listening intently. A large unwieldy meeting had become for the moment an effective group. What the head had done was to make a relationship between the experiences of one member and the experiences of others: a relationship which could then grow and develop.

The context in which group counselling processes take place, and the counterpart of the two-person relationship between client and caseworker, is the relationship between the client and the group as a whole, including the group leader. Just as some mothers benefit from an individual relationship with a caseworker of a kind they have never experienced before, so those who receive group counselling may benefit from a new experience in a relationship with a group. In the group situation different needs will be activated, and a different, perhaps wider, range of feelings will be experienced. Individual casework would be more likely to reveal and deal with particular personal relationships, starting with those with the parents, whereas the relationships transferred to a counselling group will include those with siblings, classmates, and colleagues. Thus the first difficulties to become apparent may be those concerned with rivalry, competing and sharing, rather than with dependency. The mother who, as a child at school, had to demand attention from the teacher which she did not always receive, and had difficulties in making friends with her fellow pupils, may start with similar problems as a member of a group of mothers. The very act of joining the group has some factors reminiscent of entry into school during infancy, when the child has to abandon her position of exclusive relationship to her own mother and begin one that is shared with other pupils. This new relationship depends for its character on expectations regarding the teacher as well as on the realities of her character and behaviour. These difficulties may form one aspect of the mother's nuclear problem, but they are not the aspect that she would bring first into the individual relationship with a caseworker. The group counsellor needs to be aware of each mother's nuclear problem in all these aspects, and also of the ways in which the aspects are inter-related. In this particular instance, the group counsellor's responsibility to the mother is to try to ensure that what the mother experiences is not merely another sterile repetition of the past relationship as pupil to teacher or amongst peers.

We have emphasized the specific foci of counselling groups, and the maintenance of the specific focus in each group is another responsibility of the group counsellor. In the mothers' group, the group counsellor must keep the mothers' problems with their children constantly in mind, and must also maintain a connection between these problems and all the activities at different levels that are taking place in the group. This should not mean an unnecessary curtailment of freedom of expression, nor should it mean the introduction of artificial, or unhelpful, or untimely, comparisons. The discussion will inevitably range over other topics. For example, the mothers may turn from discussing their children to discussing their husbands, and confidences about their marital situations may be exchanged. The group leader will have to respond to this apparent change of theme. There is a danger that the group may lose contact with its original purpose, becoming an unfocused group or, conversely, slipping into a form of group psychotherapy which has not been sanctioned. There is the further danger of entering into the enjoyment of the "pastime", which Berne in his book *Games People Play*[4] described as "Lady talk" with such topics as "Delinquent husbands". This topic can be developed further into one entitled "Aren't husbands awful?", or even "Aren't all men just children?" The group counsellor would not deal with these themes in terms of the individual personality of a particular woman and her absent husband, as in individual psychotherapy; neither would they be interpreted as an illustration of the narrator's unconscious or undisclosed feelings in relation to other members of the group or to the group as a whole, as might happen in group psychotherapy. Rather would they be dealt with as exemplifying the complex interaction between people. They would be placed in a context which includes relationships between parents and parents, parents and children, children and children, either separately or together. The leader is again making links between one relationship and another, and sees them both as part of an interconnected network.

As well as the behaviour of individuals in the group, the group counsellor must be aware of what is taking place at a group level, and will look on the choice of this particular theme as the result of a group process which transcends but includes the activity of each individual member. Discussion of this topic must be meeting some need in each individual member: it is also meeting a need belonging to the group as a whole, and helping to resolve some group tension. The temporary solution that it is providing may be a restrictive one, hampering the further progress of the group. Thus it may be reducing tension by diverting attention from some more sensitive area, enabling members to conceal differences that might become apparent were another topic to be discussed. Another diversion is the direction of criticism to persons not present in the group. The temptation to play some of the games described by Berne does not apply only to the mothers. These lay participants of the group can easily learn a few of the rules and some of the tricks in the game of psychiatry and then they have the power to drag the leader of the group into the by-play at their level. The following passages quoted from Berne will provide an illustration.

E: "I think it's some unconscious oral frustration that makes him act that way."
F: "You seem to have your aggressions so well sublimated."
G: "That painting symbolises smearing to me."
H: "In my case, painting is trying to please my father."

A further example gives an illustration of what happens in some therapy groups where, whatever occurs, the same interpretation can be made to serve.

Black: "Well, anyway, when we're silent nobody is playing games."
White: "Silence itself may be a game."
Red: "Nobody was playing games today."
White: "But not playing games may itself be a game."

These games or pastimes might well be called "diversions" (with a double meaning of the word) and they allow the members of the group and the leader to evade an examination of the nature of their own involvement.

The group counsellor must be aware of these processes, but, in this setting, they do not have the same significance in themselves that they would have for a group psychotherapist. The group counsellor is concerned with what goes on in the group in so far as it relates to the group's terms of reference, and, in our particular example, would look for its significance in terms of the mothers' interaction with their children. One may wonder whether the mothers who discuss their marital situations in such a group are feeling that they have been unjustly singled out to bear the burden of their respective family's difficulties.

One group counsellor has described such a situation in which she made the comment "Perhaps we are feeling that the fathers ought to be here too". She did not say, "Perhaps Mrs. A is feeling . . .", singling out one more vocal member, but rather made a point of attributing the feelings being expressed to the group as a whole. By using the plural pronoun "we" she indicated that she associated herself with the mothers, and that she was not attributing more responsibility to them than to their absent husbands. By using the word "father" rather than "husband" she underlined the fact that it was their relationships with their children that was at issue, and so she helped to relate the discussion to the specific focus of the group.

This group counsellor was aware of the individual relationship that she had with every member of the group, and she was also aware of the relationship which she had with the group as a whole. Her relationship with each member at an individual level could not be ignored; she had to recognize it, and at times she had to direct her intervention to one particular person in the group. For example, when one mother remained silent, and appeared to be feeling isolated from the others, the group counsellor would look for some particular way of responding to her silent presence. The group counsellor might also think it sometimes appropriate to give some personal attention to an over-talkative "monopolist" who was holding up the progress of the group. The behaviour of both these individual members, however, always had to be placed within the context of the total group process in which all were involved; and the group counsellor sought wherever possible to help the individuals through intervention at a group level, aware of the risk that her interventions might be weakening the group and hindering the development of its own capacity to solve its own problems. In the same way that the social worker, in an individual interview, identifies the needs of the client and responds to them, so the group counsellor needs to identify and respond to the needs of the group as a whole.

Suppose that in our group of mothers, one mother were to complain forcefully that the treatment is a waste of time and that the group counsellor is not giving her any help. Suppose that the other mothers allow her to speak but remain silent themselves. In any treatment situation, the expression of existing negative feelings can have value. Many patients or clients, however, while experiencing feelings of hostility, may fear to show them, and others may have to pretend, even to themselves, that these feelings do not exist. The angry mother in the group is verbalizing feelings that all to some extent share, but only she is able to acknowledge and, furthermore, express. She is acting as spokesperson for the group. The group counsellor can respond directly to this mother, accepting her hostility, and demonstrating that angry feelings are present in every relationship and that their presence can be acknowledged without harm. This would be appropriate in an individual situation, but to do this in a group would isolate the angry mother from the rest of the group and leave the unexpressed hostility unrecognized, perhaps by implication making it into something even more dangerous. What is needed from the group counsellor is a group response, an acceptance of the hostility as something offered by the whole group, and an underlining of the point that the professional relationship, which can absorb the anger without being damaged, is with the whole group. It is in this way that the group counsellor is able to make contact with a wider range of feelings in the clients than would be possible in individual work, since feelings which would not be expressed in an individual interview can achieve indirect and vicarious expression through the activities of a group.

Some of the group counsellor's interventions will include interpretations stimulated by particular events in the group but related to types of behaviour in general. The group counsellor coming fresh to the group process need not feel that her interpretations should match those of her mentors, tutors, or supervisors, or, for that matter, the authors of this book. Every interpretation is part of the interaction between her and the group members, her own experience and her own personality are part of that interaction, and the interpretation is her own personal and professional response to the immediate situation. The question is not whether an interpretation is right or wrong, but whether it is appropriate, taking all these factors into account. In all groups some interpretations are noted by the leader but stored away in his mind and not used at the time. Some interpretations will not occur to the leader until long afterwards, and then they will form part of his own personal and professional development, if not of the group's. In this sense one need never regret the afterthought "Why didn't I say that . . .?", because the particular thought will become embodied in what the leader has to offer to subsequent groups.

Example: a counselling group

Let us now look at an extract from an actual record of a counselling group. This group, which was led by a psychiatric social worker, met in the psychiatric department of a children's hospital. It was composed of mothers whose children had been referred because of asthma, and the children were receiving treatment from a child psychiatrist in a parallel group. The two groups were seen as complementary to each other. In this counselling group, a common concern of the mothers was with their children's group treatment; and the focus of the group was upon the mothers' relationships with their children, in the special circumstances caused by the children's illness, and in the current treatment situation. The aim of the group counsellor had two aspects. In general, she set out to augment the help given to the children by affecting the relationship between them and their mothers; more specifically, she wished to help the mothers to express more easily their reactions to the difficulties and frustrations of their situation, and their mixed feelings at being in a position in which they had to accept help from others.

This was the third meeting of the group, and five mothers were present.

Mrs. C started talking as soon as everyone had sat down. She described how she had taken her son to the local authority child welfare clinic to be immunized against polio, and a woman medical officer had refused to immunize him because he was wheezing slightly. The doctor's manner was felt by Mrs. C to be critical and unsympathetic, and, furthermore, the doctor had discussed asthma in the child's presence, something which Mrs. C had always tried to avoid herself. Mrs. C was agitated while recounting this, she flushed and stammered, and her eyes filled with tears. The other members of the group all sympathized warmly with her, and spoke very critically about the behaviour of the woman doctor. Mrs. H and Mrs. Y said that they would not allow such a woman to see their children again if they were Mrs. C, and that they would have told her exactly how they felt. Mrs. C said that she had felt very angry, and would have liked to express this, but "I never can, I always have an inhibition about it". She wished she could express her feelings more easily, in the way that other people seemed able to do. The discussion remained lively and heated, as the mothers talked of the difficulty of knowing what they should do in situations where medical opinion is not unanimous; for example, some doctors advocate immunization against polio for asthmatic children, and some doctors advise against it.

Mrs. Y then asked the group counsellor for direct advice about her boy's nail-biting. The books on psychology that she had consulted told her to ignore it, and she had tried to do this but had no success; her boy was now biting his nails more than ever.

The group counsellor said that there seemed to be a feeling that it was no good looking for help from experts as they did not even agree among themselves, and that psychology was not much help either. Perhaps they were wondering about her, and whether she would be able to give them any help. This was greeted with a short silence, and then Mrs. Y denied that she had meant to be critical of psychology, citing at length the number of books on psychology that she had read. She went on to criticize the staff at her son's school for their handling of him. They made little attempt to understand his problems. She found it impossible to tell his teacher how she felt. The other mothers all agreed that they could not talk to their children's teachers either; and they went on to speak of women teachers as dangerous and powerful figures who needed to be placated, and who might make trouble for people they did not like. The mothers were all in agreement that it was important to appear pleasant and grateful in front of the teachers, and to hide any angry feelings they might have. Mrs. B, whose child attended a special, open-air school, made an exception for one teacher there; this teacher was a married woman, herself the mother of an asthmatic child, and she therefore understood about the difficulties. The other mothers said they wished their children could have such a teacher. The group counsellor said that it was understandable that they could feel that another woman with a child with asthma was, in a sense, in the same group that they were in. She went on to say that they seemed to feel that teachers, and the staff of clinics and hospitals, who had not got the same direct experience of their difficulties, would be likely to blame and criticize them.

Mrs. Y said that the doctors at the hospital, "and I don't mean you", did not seem to understand how much the mothers wanted to be told about their children's illnesses, and to receive direct advice. Several of the others agreed. Mrs. H then said to the group counsellor that she wished that "someone like you" would go to her son's school and explain about his illness and the difficulties that it caused. Mrs. C described her son's demanding behaviour, how he insisted upon having his own way, and how he always seemed to have an attack of asthma if she did not give in to him. Mrs. H and Mrs. C described similar episodes involving their children, and said the children's inability to tolerate any frustration meant that they had no friends, as other children did not want to play with them. Only Mrs. B, who had hardly spoken hitherto, and who was the only mother in the group whose child was a girl, said complacently that she did not have this problem with Jacqueline. The other four mothers then vied with each other in giving examples of the ways in which their boys tried to dominate them, and get their own way in every situation. The mothers spoke of this behaviour as something abnormal, and they strongly approved a firm attitude on the part of parents and of school teachers. Mrs. Y said she had been very relieved when Dr. S (the child psychiatrist) had told her that it was all right to smack Richard. Before leaving, the mothers asked in some detail about the arrangements for the next session.

The group counsellor indicated that she would be looking forward to seeing them all again next week.

Reading through this record, one finds a single major theme predominating. Throughout the session, the mothers seemed to be preoccupied with their feelings towards those people who were professionally concerned with the health, welfare, or education of themselves or of their children. In the immediate situation, these people were assumed by the group counsellor to be representative of herself.

This theme needs to be studied at two levels. First of all, at the individual level, there is the meaning that this theme has to each of the mothers in terms of her own personal needs and her current life. Secondly, at the group level, there is the importance of the theme as an expression of the current situation in the group, and the contribution it makes to the solution of the problems posed by the juxtaposition of cohesive and disruptive forces.

It appears that the mothers anticipated that "the experts" would criticize and blame them. It could be assumed that this anticipation was connected with the feelings which they had about their children's illnesses, and the degree to which they felt responsible for them. It could also be connected with the anger and resentment which they felt at the burdens which they had to carry, these feelings co-existing with their love and concern for their children. Not only did they appear to anticipate a punitive reaction, but their behaviour seemed actually designed to provoke this as if it were what they sought. If the group counsellor were to react in a way that could be interpreted as unsympathetic or repressive, their already-existing feelings of hostility would be legitimized, and a scapegoat found to take the blame for continuing difficulties.

The behaviour of the mothers in the group also needs to be considered as a product of their experience of the parent-child relationship, containing something from their experiences as children in relation to their own parents, and also something of their self-image of themselves as parents in relation to their own children. The group counsellor made no reference to this, although it might well have been a theme of individual casework.

At the level of group interaction, the record shows an attempt to form an in-group consisting inclusively and exclusively of mothers with asthmatic children. Everyone not in this in-group was seen as unsympathetic. This served to ensure sufficient cohesiveness for the time being, and it also helped to contain the urge to compete for the individual attention of the group counsellor, which might have disrupted the group. It also diverted attention from individual problems and allowed responsibility to be attributed elsewhere. But, at the same time, the presence of the group counsellor aroused considerable anxiety, and her relative passivity provoked fears of retaliation and wishes for firmer control.

The first recorded contribution of the group counsellor was a comment on the mothers' criticism of the behaviour of the woman medical officer, an interpretation at a conscious or near-conscious level that attempted to link the description of an outside event, and their reactions to it, with their relationship to her in the group. The purpose of this comment was to help the mothers to express their feelings more openly, to encourage a more direct consideration of significant relationships, and to help the group to find a less restricting solution to its current problem. This intervention on the part of the group counsellor seems to have been premature; at this stage it was too direct and too personal, focusing upon an area which they were not yet ready to consider. The covert attacks on her continued and became more specific, this time displaced on to the teachers, and fears of retaliation were indicated. The next comment made by the group counsellor was more cautious, and was designed to show that she was aware of the hostile feelings without being afraid of them, and without losing sight of the difficulties which had brought the mothers together, and which were real. After this the criticism shifted from the teachers to hospital personnel, and an inclination to test out the group counsellor's sincerity and capacity to help was shown. There was an apparent change of topic when they started to talk about their children's behaviour, but it seemed as if they were also talking about their own behaviour. While they discussed their children they were, at the same time, revealing their own fears of having overstepped the limit, their anxieties at the permissive behaviour of the group counsellor, and their fears that she might retaliate. Before they left they needed to be reassured that they would be welcome at the following session.

Two further points need to be mentioned. This record illustrates the way in which all the different personal relationships that an individual makes can be considered as related to each other, so that each forms part of an interlocking system or network. This system is in a perpetual state of adjustment and change, as an alteration in one relationship will have an effect upon all the others. Thus the mothers in the group could move from discussing their reactions to the doctor in the child welfare clinic, to the teachers, to the hospital doctors, illustrating throughout this their reactions to the group counsellor. They could describe their feelings about their children's behaviour in such a way, and in such a context, that it could be treated as illustrating their view of the group counsellor's relationship with themselves. Thus no single relationship which might be demonstrated in the mothers' behaviour or described in their verbal interchanges could be evaluated or understood in isolation; each had to be considered as a fragment of an interrelated whole, and intervention at any one point could be used to influence the whole field.

The second point concerns the treatment of the material provided in this session as if it were the production of a single entity. It is important to emphasize again that attitudes and feelings attributed to the group as such are not identical with the attitudes and feelings of each individual member. The hostility shown towards the group counsellor has been considered as an attribute of the group as a whole, contributing to the temporary solution of a problem also belonging to the whole group. To the establishment of this group solution each of the individual members made some contribution. At an individual level, this pattern of behaviour in the group must have had some particular meaning for each of the mothers present: for Mrs. C, whose frustration at being unable to express her angry feelings about people in authority began the session; for Mrs. Y, who vigorously developed this theme; for Mrs. B, who indicated through her complacency the satisfaction which she derived as a spectator rather than as an active participant. Though each member would have a different individual attitude from that of the group counsellor, the hostility could be treated as a common denominator. It had a meaning for each one within this particular context, and, therefore, a point was provided at which an intervention affecting the total group process could be made.

Up to now, we have been discussing group counselling mainly in relation to social work, and have taken our examples from groups of mothers conducted by psychiatric social workers in child guidance and child psychiatric clinics; we have also included an example from a similar group led by a psychiatrist. It is in such groups that the essential characteristics of group counselling can be most clearly seen. Here it can be demonstrated that the members of the group are not psychotherapy patients but have a different commitment and different expectations; that their personal problems are only relevant at the point where they impinge on the problems on which the group is focused; that intervention takes place in the area of interpersonal relationships; and that the skilled use of relationships is a primary part of the group counselling process.

Examples from other contexts must also be considered. The contexts are important. Group counselling is more diverse and is influenced to a greater extent by its setting than is group psychotherapy. To some extent it is the setting that determines the aims and supplies the focus of the counselling group.

Group counselling in probation departments

A different example of an agency in which group work may take place is found in a probation department. In this setting, probation officers sometimes conduct groups with young people who are referred to them by the Courts. Such young people come from different backgrounds and have different motivations; they have in common the fact that they have broken some law and that this has led to the making of a probation order. Probation officers will have to elaborate this common factor, or establish some additional and more specific basis for selection if they are to find the focus that is necessary for group counselling and avoid the hazards of unstructured group work in the no-man's land that is neither counselling nor psychotherapy. Attempts are sometimes made to offer a partial explanation for delinquent behaviour in terms of a failure to identify with an authority figure and therefore a concomitant failure to incorporate acceptable standards and modes of behaviour. In this sense, delinquency is not something that has gone wrong, but is a deficiency in the provisions that are necessary for development to proceed normally. It is what had not gone right. Such an assumption is one of many that could be used to provide a starting point and a focus for a counselling group: it enables us to discuss the role of group leader by means of a string of further assumptions. The authors are not probation officers, and these are our phantasies for what they are worth. Probation officers would have the right to disclaim the validity of what follows.

We imagine these group leaders accepting the focus that we have suggested for them, and selecting the members of their groups carefully on this basis. They will have to consider the relationship between themselves and their groups in the light of the deficiency in normal provision that has been assumed, and which it is hoped to remedy. Whatever other feelings may be transferred to the leaders of these groups, the leaders will also inevitably represent that authority, parental, educational, or magisterial, with which the probationers have had their difficulties in the past. The probationers now have an opportunity to enter into a fresh relationship with an authority figure in the context of a peer group.

In this situation, a leader will perhaps hope that through the use of group, rather than individual, methods one can facilitate and expedite the open expression of feelings and attitudes, and enable the group members to test out the limits of the relationship that is being offered. Phantasies will then be more quickly revealed for what they are, and strong feelings will become less frightening when known to be shared. The leader will be likely to take active steps to relate positively to the group, demonstrating tolerance and concern, and a capacity to remain undamaged by overt and covert hostility.

Within this framework, one will need to keep anxiety within the limits of the group's capacity to tolerate it at any moment of time. One will expect to see an increase in this capacity and hope that the group will develop sufficient strength and cohesion to take over some of this responsibility for itself. It may seem appropriate to introduce certain experiences into the group sessions in order to augment their impact and to increase the focus upon the areas considered to be most relevant. One such experience might be an exposure to the demands of authority. In this way the probationers would be given an opportunity to develop new ways of dealing with the challenges they have been unable to deal with successfully in real-life situations.

Group counselling with ex-psychiatric hospital patients

Elsewhere, mention has been made of a counselling group composed of patients discharged to the community after long periods in a mental hospital, suggesting such a group as a means by which the support derived from living in a protective environment might be extended into the community. This provides us with an example of a counselling group in a different setting, and focused upon different aims. If we look for a relationship, significant to all its members, on which this group could focus, we do not find it in that between parent and child, nor between youth and authority. We postulate two sets of relevant relationships: there is the relationship that exists between each patient and the mental hospital on the one hand, and that between the patient and the outside community on the other hand. The group counsellor may be identified with either hospital or community—indeed, one of these organizations may be the employing authority—but in the group the counsellor needs to represent both, and to make a link between the two.

The leaders have to limit the amount of stress within the group, and keep it within the tolerance of individual members who may be exceptionally vulnerable. They may have to play an active role to meet individual and group needs, which could include a need to experience continued dependence and protection. Indeed, it may take time for such a cluster to develop into a counselling group. Given sufficient time, participation in this group may be expected to provide some sense of comfort and security, to reduce the feelings of alienation and stigma, and to provide experience in relating to other people within a safe environment; it may go on to extend the range of responses that are available to the members for meeting challenging situations.

We have envisaged these last two groups as being led by social workers, who may have had some specific training in group work, or who may be transferring concepts derived from work with individuals to a group setting. Group counsellors are not drawn only from social workers. Groups of comparable composition to those conducted by probation officers, and designed to serve similar ends, may be found in approved schools; here they may be conducted by psychologist, teacher, or doctor. Groups of mental hospital patients are sometimes led by a nurse, a hospital chaplain, a doctor, or a social worker, singly or in any combination. Thus in these and other institutions, staff who have no relevant group work training within their own professional framework are expected to take part in group work, or they may choose to do so.

Many other examples may be found. There are special schools where teaching the children can merge into counselling, and where more formal counselling may be necessary for groups of children or of parents. Prisons have their need for group counselling at different levels, and here the leaders of groups might be prison staff, staff specially appointed for the purpose, visiting specialists coming in from outside, or any combination of the three. The use of visiting specialists has its justification, but care needs to be taken to avoid fragmentation of the activities for which the different categories of staff have to take responsibility. The staff of an institution cannot expect to hand over to outsiders the responsibility for dealing with the emotional problems that life in the institution engenders. It could be argued that in each special situation the initiator and leader of the group activity should come from the profession which is primarily concerned with the setting in which the group work takes place.

Other applications

There are many other examples where fields of work, which properly belong to an established profession, bring emotional problems to light, and these have to be faced and cannot be denied or warded off. This is particularly true for those professions whose consumers experience anxiety about the nature of the service which they are receiving, and about its consequences. Here again, it is not possible or desirable always to call in an outside expert to deal with the emotional difficulties which are revealed, and which present problems, in other people's jobs. Many professional workers will rather see this as part of their own responsibility, and will elect to deal with it themselves. These workers need to have an opportunity to extend and enrich their techniques with some of the concepts we have been describing as part of group counselling. Just as social work has borrowed concepts from psychotherapy, and group counselling from group psychotherapy, so other disciplines can borrow from group counselling.

There are many situations outside structured group work where doctors, nurses, psychologists, health visitors or teachers, meet groups of people in connection with some aspect of their own work and have to interpret[4] to them their expectations of one another and the possible outcomes of their techniques. They can enrich these discussions with a knowledge of their own involvement in the group processes. They have to have some idea of the hidden questions behind the questions which they are being asked, and of the alternative meanings of the answers which they are giving. They need to be able to draw comparisons, to detect common themes, and to recognize and deal with some of the anxieties that will be only marginally expressed. They need to be able to answer question with question, so as to extend rather than contract the area of discussion. All this involves the application of techniques which have been developed in group counselling and in casework. This does not make these other workers into caseworkers, and casework is not the object of the exercise. If they can benefit from learning something about group counselling methods, it is not in order to obtain an additional profession but to become more competent in dealing with some of the issues in their existing one. Any skill that they acquire must become built into their individual personal style, and incorporated into the practice of their own professions.

Notes and references

1. We have used the word "deep", in good company, in a rather vague way. "Deep" can mean going a long way back into personal history, and behind the memories that are first paraded. Alternatively, it can mean an exploration of aspects of mental functioning that are normally

hidden by dynamic repressive forces. The word "deep" is used metaphorically, and there are fallacies in any such concept. For example, the content of this "deep" level has features in common with psychotic thinking, and similar material may in fact be that which is first offered by psychotic patients.

2. We wish to point out that this choice is one of several that could have been made. The social worker might have seen both parents, separately or together, or might have joined with other colleagues in family interviews.

3. Parsloe, P. Some thoughts on social group work *British Journal of Psychiatric Social Work* Vol. x, No.1, 1969.

4. Berne, Eric. *Games People Play*, Grove Press Inc., 1967.

5. It will have been observed that we have used the word "interpret" in the above passage. We have done this deliberately. We do not consider that the process of interpretation should be considered the prerogative of the psychotherapist and the social worker, even though these two professions use interpretation in a special and disciplined way.

8

Group Discussion

Group discussion model

In turning to group discussion, we turn away from the field of psychotherapy and counselling, from concern with personal problems and with family difficulties, to the field of education and to concern with problems of teaching and of learning. It would be misleading if we were to think of group discussion as a half-way house, placed somewhere between psychotherapy and education. The purpose of group discussion is always related to education, and, in distinction to the other two group systems, it must always remain within the limits appropriate to a method of education. It is, however, a very special method, a method which makes use of concepts of dynamic group behaviour and insights derived from group psychotherapy and group counselling, and which shares some part of their aims and methods. At one and the same time, it seeks to promote intellectual and emotional growth.

Brief reference has already been made to group discussion in order to account for its inclusion in this study, and in order to outline the features which we consider the three systems to have in common. In group discussion, we should expect once again to find a model containing the physical characteristics of the basic group situation such as we have described: a number of people sitting together in a circle, with a leader, and engaging in "free" discussion. In practice, we find that this model can be considerably modified, and it has been found possible for the principles of group discussion to be applied to larger groups meeting for a common learning purpose in class or conference, even when these physical characteristics are absent.

So far in all our discussions of group work, we have had in mind a small group model, and most of the source material of group work in general has been taken from experiences with small groups in which the size of the network involved recalls the family. In turning to group discussion we now have to include larger groups, since leaders of discussion groups have generally in the past felt free to work with larger collections of people than have leaders of counselling or therapy groups. It is recognized that group discussion can be conducted in a classroom setting for thirty, fifty or an even larger membership. However the large group situation may be seen as an obstacle and a source of discomfort, and so it has often been thought preferable to divide large conferences into a number of sub-groups for discussion, in order to retain something of the intimate pattern of the original model.

Of recent years there has been an increased interest in the dynamics of the Large Group,[1] and a recognition that this situation has, in fact, special features and advantages of its own which can be utilized in a structured way. The concepts and methods developed by Foulkes, and now being applied to large groups by De Maré, have proved particularly relevant in this context. This development has opened up the possibility of conducting therapy and counselling as well as discussion in units of twenty and upwards. There are now therapists and counsellors who feel able to apply their group work skills to larger gatherings, and who are trying to address problems at the level where individual processes interact with large group processes, and individual problems with cultural issues, in the context of a large group or community rather than that of a small group or family.

Before this recent interest in structured large groups, it used to be generally accepted that the process of group discussion could simultaneously engage a larger number of people than could either group psychotherapy or group counselling. It is therefore in discussion that much of the established experience with large groups is to be found. In this sense, therapy and counselling may be said to be following where discussion first led the way.

In group discussion, as in the other two systems, we should also expect to find attempts to promote that positive group development, that active involvement on the part of individual members, which can bring with it the possibility of personal growth and change. The freedom of discussion, again, is made possible through the existence of a definite but implicit bargain between members and leader. But since the purpose of the group is not psychotherapy, or counselling, but education, the members of the group are not patients or clients, but students. They have not come for help with difficulties of personality or of relationships; they have come to learn. The participants may be students for the limited period of a one-day conference or they may be enrolled on a prolonged professional training course. Difficulties can occur with mature students with some previous experience of the subject which is being discussed. They may have engaged in the role of student, but they may have come with the clear intention of teaching. Whether the intentions are fully acknowledged or not, those who come to teach and those who come to learn may frequently find themselves reversing their roles.

Members of a discussion group are not prepared, nor are they expected, to expose either their total personalities or an area of specific personal difficulty in the group. The bargain between members and leader must therefore include an understanding on the part of the leader not to treat them as patients or clients; that when aspects of individual psychopathologies are inevitably revealed in the group, no open attention will be paid to them; and that, when problems are exposed, neither personal comment nor even a change in the procedure will follow. Should it become clear that any member of the group is seeking personal help, the leader would not attempt to use the group as a therapeutic agent. However the leader might, if approached, offer such a member an individual interview in order to discuss the possibility of referral for help elsewhere. Group discussion may also be a group system which aims to promote change in individual members, but such change does not occur as the result of any therapeutic endeavour; rather, it is the result of the members' exposure to a learning process of a very particular kind.

We have repeatedly stressed the difference in method and aim between group therapy, group counselling and group discussion, and yet all these processes are utilized by people seeking help of some kind. The word *help* like the word *change* contains the blessing of vagueness which does not always call for a definition. Yet an attempt at some precision has to be made. We have tried to be most precise when dealing with therapy because here the words imply a specific engagement with a person chosen for a particular range of skill and experience. But in all situations the words *change* and *help* have therapeutic overtones. If a group member's well-being increases while taking part in a group not designated as a therapy group, so much the better for the group process.

Earlier in this book, mention has been made of the individual supervision process as studied and described by caseworkers in particular. While this provides some pointers for the student of group discussion, its application is so much narrower and more specific that it cannot in any way furnish an exact parallel. The use of group discussion methods now extends beyond the field of professional education and disciplined learning. Nevertheless, some lessons can be drawn from the ways in which supervisors may help students to understand, and modify, the part they themselves play in a two-way relationship; while, at the same time, the supervisors refrain from intruding into the students' personal lives.

Learning to use the self in the helping professions

The participants in a discussion group have come to learn, and they have come to learn something which cannot be fully provided by academic methods of teaching or through participation at an intellectual level alone. It could be said that one of the principal things that they have come to learn is to understand and express the feelings which they experience in any task in which the techniques involve the use of their own personalities. This task may be a specific one. Where group discussion takes place in a professional setting, the task will be concerned with the provision of an individual service or material to patients, clients, or customers, or it will involve working as a member of a team in a work situation. All these activities involve the use of personal relationships. In other situations the task may be a more personal developmental one, though still contained within an educational framework; it may be concerned with the entry into adult life, with the assumption of new responsibilities, or with the preparation for some particular period of stress.

In any of these examples, the aim of group discussion will be to widen the capacity of each individual member to use one's own personality in each various enterprise or living activity.

There are some learning situations, some professional trainings, and some tasks and enterprises, where the relevance of an individual's capacity to make appropriate and effective use of one's own personality is clearly seen.

Thus, at a conference of marriage guidance counsellors, the question was asked, "What does a psychiatrist do?" The questioner added, "I know that a surgeon uses the knife, a physician uses drugs, but what does a psychiatrist use?"

The answer, which had to be built up gradually, ran like this. "The surgeon uses his knife, but he also uses his personality. He uses his knife scientifically, but he uses his self unscientifically even if he uses it effectively. The physician uses his drugs scientifically, but he uses his self unscientifically. The psychiatrist (thought not the psychiatrist of every school) has nothing to use but his own self, but there is this difference; he uses his own self scientifically."

The social worker shares with the psychiatrist in the use of concepts which have been developed in order to use the self as a professional tool. In these two professions it has long been taken for granted that the relationship between the professional worker and the patient or client is a major factor in the helping process and that it is necessary to make it a subject for study from both ends. Any social worker, for example, even when dealing with some concrete practical difficulty and using well-recognized techniques, has to be aware not only of the client's complex emotional responses but also of the worker's own. Where there is a selection procedure for membership of branches of these two professions, flexibility and a capacity for personal growth and development are stressed as desirable qualities. During training, the student is encouraged to develop self-awareness and sensitivity. It is recognized that this is a part of the professional training that cannot be provided through academic lectures or the reading of textbooks alone. Well-established teaching methods that attempt to provide it include group discussion as well as individual supervision focused upon on-going professional work or on more general problems. In addition, for some fields of work a training analysis is advocated, but the consideration of this falls outside the scope of this book.

In the training of those who wish to become leaders of groups themselves, group discussion must play an essential part. It alone provides an experience which can help them to understand their own feelings and reactions in a group, as well as to identify group processes, and it can give a living example of the way in which a leader may make use of these processes to further the particular aims of the group.

But an interest in the professional relationship and an appreciation of its importance is not, as we have seen, now confined to psychiatry and social work. The same component, involving the use of the self, is present, though often less well recognized, in many other activities. It is acknowledged in the rules and customs, sometimes unwritten and even unspoken, which exist in many professions and occupations to govern relationships between those providing and those receiving a service; between doctor and patient, solicitor and client, sales representative and customer. Even where it is not considered a specific part of the professional process, there is an ever-increasing realization that the interpersonal relationship through which the professional help is given occupies a central position and can help or hinder the worker's use of occupational skills and the client's readiness to profit by them. This applies particularly to all transactions where help is offered through a face-to-face meeting, and concerns such professions as medicine, nursing, teaching, the law, and the Church, among others. In these professions there is an active demand for an extension of training to include an understanding of human relationships over and above anything which can be derived from academic lectures in psychology. It may be that the skills that are being sought are those of a caseworker or a group counsellor, but the methods by which these skills are imparted are the methods of group discussion. Information provided through lectures can be absorbed at an intellectual level without being converted into increased insight into the behaviour of oneself and others, and may even defeat its own purpose, becoming encapsulated and divorced from everyday experience. Students need to participate actively in this learning process and relate it directly to their own experience if it is not to become a barrier rather than a stepping-stone to further progress.

In industry

Another field in which group methods are sometimes used is found in the in-service training programmes in industry. Here there is not the same focus upon the use of a particular professional relationship, but rather a recognition of the importance of an individual's behaviour as a member of a team and as colleague, supervisor, manager, and subordinate. There is also concern with the capacity of individuals to absorb change, in a field where organizational and technological developments often take place rapidly. The readiness and competence of individuals to alter habitual ways of behaviour, and to accept changes in the organizations around them, depends upon much more than an intellectual comprehension of the situation; it can involve such additional factors as sense of security, ability to trust others, and the nature and depth of the satisfactions derived from their work. Here intellectual methods of training and retraining, such as the didactic lecture, have proved inadequate; indeed, they may have hazards as well as limitations. For example, a lecture describing and advocating new methods of working may be seen as a concealed attack on existing methods and on their operators, who will thus be stimulated to resist the proposed changes. Alternatively, it may serve to change the workers' image of themselves and of the work they are doing, providing an illusion that something is different, without producing any actual, appreciable change in the methods of operation. The illusion satisfies their ambitions and so makes further effort unnecessary.

In this dilemma, industry has turned to dynamic group psychology, and has adopted group methods, known in this context as "T-groups". By this means the advocates of group methods hope that more fundamental changes in attitudes and behaviour patterns can be produced. It is anticipated that an increase in sensitivity and self-awareness resulting from an exposure to group interaction will reduce dependence upon stereotyped, habitual modes of behaviour, and that there will be an increase in flexibility and in readiness to experiment as a result. A T-group may be composed of a number of people unknown to each other and drawn from different industrial settings. Alternatively, firms may set up their own T-groups as part of an internal in-service training programme, despite the complications that could be caused by the prior acquaintanceship and the hierarchial relationships of the people concerned. In each T-group there will be one, or perhaps two, group leaders who are known as "trainers". The trainer encourages the group to focus upon its own behaviour in a deliberately unstructured and leaderless situation, in which the old landmarks and familiar roles that the members habitually make use of are missing or are no longer effective.

It has been suggested by one writer[2] that the difference between a T-group and a psychotherapeutic group is to be found partly in the different composition, T-group members having more adequate defences than patients in a psychotherapeutic group, and partly in the different sets of expectations brought to these groups by their members. These distinctions may be valid. However, it may be thought that these circumstances are not enough in themselves to account for all the differences, nor can they be relied upon to provide sufficient safeguards. The inadequacy of certain defences may be discovered too late, and expectations may not be fulfilled unless they are shared and respected.

The authors have no personal experience of these groups, but it would appear to them that the T-group is designed primarily to be of benefit to the organization that sponsors it, and only indirectly for the benefit of the group itself and its individual members. Traditionally, it has not been thought necessary to give consideration to those who have to leave a post in industry because of inadequacy revealed through the stresses of new demands and the strains of interacting personalities. The use of group methods, in which such stresses and strains may be deliberately introduced, creates new hazards. This gives added emphasis to the importance that we attach to seeing that the aims and limitations of a T-group, and the sanction that is given to the leader by the group, should be formulated and understood as clearly as possible. It should remain the responsibility of the leader of the T-group, as of all discussion groups, to see that the defences of individual members are in fact

adequate (this cannot be safely assumed), and that the stress that is inevitable in such a situation is kept within the tolerance of the most vulnerable
member. Responsibility should also be taken for any casualties of the group.

This is a consideration that does not apply to industry alone. By the same
token, educational establishments have some responsibility for the students
whom they select or accept for a training course in which group methods are
used in such a way that the vulnerable parts of the personality may become
revealed. If, as a result, any of these students have to withdraw from the
course, responsibility remains with the educational establishment, and
attempts should be made to secure appropriate help for them.

Other applications

Professional and occupational training of one sort or another is not the
only field in which group discussion methods may be used; they are equally
applicable wherever an understanding of human behaviour is involved in the
subject at issue. Group discussion, for example, may be offered to young
people in school or youth club as part of a programme of preparation for
adult life and as a way of giving help with the difficulties of this particular
transitional stage. Adaptation to the challenges and opportunities of each
successive stage in life, whether of leaving school, of marriage, childbirth and
the parental problems of child rearing, of divorce, retirement and old age,
can also be looked upon as a task for which preparation is possible, and in
which different areas and levels of the personality are involved. These problems are general rather than specific, anticipated rather than actual. Were
they specific and actual, the group discussants might come instead as clients
to counsellors, selecting a particular agency, accepting a different status, and
anticipating a different process.

In schools and youth clubs, the adoption of group discussion methods has
come with the realization that instruction in the physical facts of sexual
behaviour, coupled perhaps with moral precepts, is not an adequate way of
meeting young people's needs. Sexual behaviour, it is now realized, needs to
be included within the broad context of human relationships, and is by no
means the only preoccupation in this area; other relationships, such as those
with parents, siblings, peer group, and people in authority, also need to be
included. Any such attempt at education in human relationships, if it is not
to be sterile, must be linked with the actual experiences that the young
people have and the situations that most closely concern them, and must
involve them as active participants in the process.

Focus upon topics

We have considered some different learning situations to which the
methods of group discussion can be applied. We now need to make a more

detailed examination of these methods, and of the underlying process that all discussion groups have in common. Whereas group psychotherapy has no directed focus and group counselling is focused upon a particular problem or a particular difficulty in relationships, group discussion is focused at any one time upon a theme or topic. These themes or topics will be of particular interest to all the members of the group and form the basis which they have in common. This is, of course, also true of groups which meet to discuss such topics as the origins of the solar system or the behaviour of the common earthworm. But these are topics which can be treated as external to the discussants.[3]

The topics of group discussion, in our meaning of the term, cannot remain external to the discussants. They may be dependent upon factual information, but they are also concerned with personal relationships. Therefore relationships in the group itself, and the behaviour of individual members, will exemplify what is being discussed. The members of the group are observers, but they also form part of the field that is being observed. It is in this respect that an essential difference between group discussion and other forms of education lies. It is because of this that the experience cannot be one that is exclusively intellectual. No member can escape involvement in the group as well as in the topic.

The leaders then have a delicate task, and a task that differs in some important respects from that of a group psychotherapist or a group counsellor: they must try to maximize the effectiveness of the group as a means of teaching members about human behaviour. They must enable all members to participate in the group, to contribute from their own experience, and to see the relevance of the topic to their own situation. They must help them to study their own attitudes and behaviour and those of others, to question them and to seek to understand them. They must at the same time contain the experience within an educational framework, and within the limits of what has been sanctioned.

The group, as we have seen, will be focused upon a particular theme. The same theme may continue throughout a series of meetings, or the members may choose a different theme for each meeting, or a number of themes may have to be dealt with to meet the requirements of a particular syllabus. This theme will be concerned with some aspect of human relationships. In a group composed of caseworkers, for example, different situations containing casework problems of particular interest or difficulty may be illustrated and discussed. In a group of general practitioners, the relationship between doctor and patient may be considered. A group of school leavers may choose, as their theme, relationships between young people and their elders, or may be concerned with such particular problems as drug addiction or delinquency. These are all themes which have many different aspects and which can be approached in different ways and considered at different levels. They can be related on one level to different systems of thought. To the individual student, a particular theme will have both its academic and its practical aspect. The student will bring to it theoretical and conventional viewpoints and, at another level, attitudes based upon personal prejudgments. All these different aspects can provide material for discussion and it is the leader's job to draw out this material and to make it available to the group. The leader must see that the theme is discussed as widely and on as many levels as possible.

This particular skill of a group discussion leader can be briefly described as that of making appropriate links and pointing out relevant connections and resemblances. In bringing together all these contributions, individual and corporate, verbal and non-verbal, and in showing the relevance that each one has to the topic, the leader has to construct a framework. This framework is the leader's personal contribution. Value is given to each contribution that comes from a member of the group, as the leader takes it, accepts it, adds to it or adjusts it, and places it within the framework.

The different aspects of the theme that could relate to each other will depend upon the richness and variety of the material that the members of the group, including the leader, are able to provide, individually and corporately. The leader's task is to point out to the group such connections as can be discerned between the topics under discussion, the contributions of each individual member, and the behaviour of the group as a whole. It is also to relate attitudes expressed directly or indirectly in the group, and attitudes attributed to others outside the group; to make links between theoretical knowledge and personal experience; and to use behaviour that takes place inside the group to throw light on the behaviour under discussion outside the group. The leader may personally introduce fresh concepts, perhaps linking present experiences with different scientific systems, such as anthropology, sociology, or psychoanalysis, in order to stimulate alternative ways of thinking and to elicit new material. This may also increase the capacity of members to see the same problem at a number of different levels at the same moment.

Many of the topics that are dealt with in group discussion depend upon factual information, but they are all also related to basic personal attitudes. These two aspects are complementary to each other and of equal importance; both need to be brought out. Unless relevant personal attitudes can be discussed with some openness, the proceedings of the group are likely to remain sterile and unproductive, and allow little room for development and change to take place at any level. There are various impediments to such free discussion which may be present; some of them, common to the three group systems, have already been mentioned. There is the widespread tendency towards concealment in which most of us share, a reluctance to expose our true feelings to others for fear of what might be revealed. There is an unwillingness to question standards and beliefs which have proved of value in the past, and in which much may have been invested. Furthermore, many discussion groups are held under the auspices of organizations which embody some authoritarian function, or are known or believed to endorse some particular line—such organizations as university, training body, school, or church, for example. Members of the group may feel it is expedient to adhere to what they imagine to be the "party line", perhaps suggested to them by the nature of the training that is being offered or by the particular sponsorship of the sessions. Their educational experiences in the past may have led them to believe that this is the way to be considered a "good" student and win the approval of their teachers. For converse reasons, others may feel it incumbent upon them to oppose the "party line". But whether it is accepted or rejected, its real or imagined existence provides individual members with roles to play and so protects them from involvement at a more personal level, and from the possibility of personal change.

The leader, at the beginning of the course or at any subsequent stage, may have to take an active part to liberate the discussion from the repetition of textbook knowledge or other conventional opinions, or from an embargo on any exposure of personal feelings. This may be necessary in order to establish certain basic conditions without which group discussion cannot take place at all. Since this is a group situation, an understanding of the learning problems of each individual is not enough; the leader must also be able to relate them to the context of the group as a whole. In order to play the part effectively, appropriately, and economically, the leader must be able to discern the behaviour of the group and relate it to the total situation. The leader must try to identify the factors that are contributing to the development of cohesive and disruptive forces; see what is threatening the group and the individual members, and how both are reacting to the threat; and detect the way in which group processes are operating and the particular problems which they are trying to solve. Some areas which may be particularly relevant to an understanding of the behaviour of a discussion group are illustrated and discussed below. These include the influence on behaviour of the overall task which faces the group, the impact of the specific theme on which the session is focused, and the relationship between the leader and the rest of the group.

Example: in-service training group

These aspects of group discussion are among the points that are illustrated in the following "approximate" verbatim record of one particular group. The record is approximate in that it was not recorded on tape but was taken down in shorthand by a secretary. The group was part of a course of in-service training undertaken by a number of authorized mental welfare officers of considerable experience but without any previous formal training. They numbered about thirty and included both sexes, although men predominated. The course had a syllabus which dealt with human growth and development. At each meeting there was a lecture related to one part of this syllabus, and this was followed by a free discussion. On this particular occasion the formal topic was "Parental Rejection of the Infant", and the psychiatrist who delivered the lecture also conducted the group.

In previous courses, discussions of this topic had tended to concentrate on criticism or support of the scientific basis of Bowlby's formulation regarding the effect of an infant's separation from its mother.[5] Members of the group would argue whether these concepts were "scientific" or not, and the discussion often remained at an abstract level. On this occasion, in the hope that it would stimulate a more spontaneous reaction to such an emotionally loaded topic, the group discussion leader prefaced his lecture by the reading of two news items from the popular press. One item had appeared that very morning, and had been seen by most members of the group in their respective papers. The other article, which had appeared a year earlier, was in the leader's collection of newspaper cuttings, and was fortunately to hand.

First Article

The 25-year-old mother of three children, Mrs. Y, wants to find a home for a fourth baby she is expecting in July.

She would not part with her seven-year-old son . . . or her three-year-old daughter . . . but she said last night: "I don't like babies. I think they are terrible things. They all scream their heads off."

Mrs. Y and her husband insist they could not afford another child. Their third child, a 21-month-old girl, is in the care of the . . . Council.

Mrs. Y said she had asked the social worker at . . . Hospital if she could have the baby adopted. The social worker replied that she was shocked but she would see what she could do.

"Later the hospital said they were not prepared to help me. We wrote to an evening paper to see if we could get help through its columns. We would like the child to go to a good home where there are no other children—to someone who deserves a child."

As Mrs. Y spoke, her two children remained in the room watching television. Amid all the questions and answers, they kept their eyes on the television set. But they know about the child to be born and have been told that it will have to be "given away" or they will not be able to have a holiday this year.

"Babies are a full-time job. Two are quite enough, and this house is not made for a big family. Big families cause squabbling, and the father goes off for a drink to get some peace", said Mrs. Y. "We are a very happy family and I do not want to have anything to spoil it."

Second Article

MRS. Y WANTS HER BABY BACK.
Decision to give child away regretted.

Mrs. Y, aged 26, the housewife who with her husband decided to give away their baby before the child was born, has refused to sign the adoption papers for the baby girl who is now with her prospective foster parents.

Mrs. Y said yesterday, "I never thought it would happen to me. But I keep on thinking about the baby and wishing I hadn't given it away. I can't sleep at night and I lie awake worrying whether she is all right. I suppose it is the mother instinct. After all, she is my own flesh and blood."

Discussion

Student A: Do you think that there is anything important or any problem in a child's phantasy and rejection of its parents? It is so common for children to believe in fairies and to weave tales about this.

Leader: It is not a problem. In fact it is almost inevitable. There is a stage in the phantasy life of the child which includes finding someone to idealize. I did not have time to mention some of the more pathological processes which take place. When a child over-idealizes its real parents it may in fact be a bad thing. Some children so much want the idea that their parents are good parents that they have to find excuses for them if anything is wrong with them. You come across adult people who are full of self-recrimination. It is as if they are saying "I must be bad" in order that their parents could remain good.

Student B: Would you care to comment on the case of Mrs. Y as being relevant to this lecture?

Leader: I wonder if you would like to say what your feelings are.

Student B: I think she is a horror and she does not deserve that child.

Student C: I think her true feelings are those of rejection, but now she has seen what effect this has on people. She is trying to make some measure of atonement.

Student D: I think it was a natural rejection of the child, but now she has been separated from it she wants it back. Separation makes the heart grow fonder.

Student E: With the father just going into gaol and now she wants this child back, could this be a sign that the father was rejecting it?

Student F: I wonder if there was a rejected child in her family?

Student B: She would get quite a considerable amount of money from the press for her story.

Leader: I don't think the press pay for this sort of thing.

Student B: She wrote an article for a Sunday newspaper, "Why I want to give my baby away". She would have got about £500 for that.

Leader: I could be wrong about payment. But let us look at the levels at which it has been discussed. We have had questions of the mother's feelings, internal guilt, external pressure. I think we have to think of it from all these points of view. But there are people who have to make practical decisions. There was perhaps a mental health worker involved here. Would he ask about the consequences to the mother or to the child? And now there is the question of the press and of payment. Do you think this publicity was to the best advantage? Why was there a market for it?

Student G: Well, it's a unique case.

Student E: Mr. Y was said to be earning £15 a week.

Student H: I wonder where he comes into it?

Student F: In the first place he gave his consent quite willingly.

Student H: He left the decision to her.

Student L: She may be the dominating factor.

Student C: There are people who like to have all this publicity made about them. Exhibitionists.

Leader: Yes, the publicity may have done her good in satisfying some of her wishes. Let us leave her for a moment and ask in general why are such things given so much publicity.

Student F: Panders to the taste of the masses.

Leader: Then why have the masses got that particular taste to pander to?

Student H: There is a part of Mrs. Y in all of us.

Leader: Is it then because we ourselves have had at times the same feelings which she has dared to express?

Student B: Oh no, I don't think so.

Student D: Perhaps yes.

Student J: I think we are all angry about things which we might possibly have done ourselves.

Leader: I think we are angry about things which we wouldn't do because we have had the task of learning not to do them. We have learnt some self-control and expect ourselves to have moral and ethical standards. We all have to overcome strong feelings of anger and rivalry and learn to become decent citizens, and if we see some other person who has not learned to control these emotions we feel angry with them.

Student A: I sometimes wonder if these problems occurred a thousand years ago. In the old days there was no press.

Leader: In biblical days, Samuel was given as a baby to the priesthood, and Moses had to be separated from his mother, although in that case the mother managed to get back into the nursing situation.

Student F: I can remember a case just over four years ago where a mother had given her child to a film star and then, five or six years later, wanted her back. There was a lot of publicity about it, but everyone seemed to be on the mother's side.

Student C: I think this Y case has just been a racket. The woman, I will not call her lady, just went into it for financial gain.

Student D: I don't think so.

Student B: But she did write that story for the papers.

Student D: I do not see how she could plan such an eventuality while she was pregnant.

Leader: How would anybody know that this article would sell, and, if so, why?

Student C: Because it is sensational, it is news.

Leader: What makes it news?

Student K: Because people have a lot of feeling for the unborn child.

Student L: It appeals to the masses because at some stage we all have these feelings of rejection for children.

Student B: I cannot understand how a child could be unwanted. If so, what is human right, and why is there such a thing as a human right?

Leader: We are coming to the stage where it is possible to have a married life without children. Why do people nevertheless want children?

Student F: Natural instinct.

Student H: Projection of the parent's personality.

Student A: I wonder if there are more broken marriages without children than with?

Leader: We could check on that. Figures will be available. It might be very interesting to do so.

Student B: In the Y case, I still think she did it for financial gain.

Leader: Do you think people are angry with her because she made money in that way?

Student B: Yes.

Leader: Are we? Are we angry with her because of that?

Student C: No. Not angry, disgusted.

Leader: Why?

Student F: Because it cuts across our moral code.

Student H: Anyone could have to make the same decision.

Student A: Many people have given their children away.

Student H: Sometimes they are given away to Auntie.

Leader: And, in those circumstances, does it upset us?

Student G: No.

Student C: Well, it upsets me.

Leader: Supposing Mrs. Y had not existed and this person and situation had been drawn out of the mind of a dramatist, and we had gone to see the play. We might say that this was true to life or that it was not true to life. Would we be angry with the character and with the playwright?

(*A medley of different comments, some impossible to hear.*)

Student —: I cannot understand why she became pregnant.

Student —: Accidental.

Leader: There is a story about a man whose wife had had a number of children, and on the birth of the eleventh child he announced to his friends that he and his wife were not going to have any more. "But why not?" they asked him. "Well," said the man, "at last I've found out what has been causing it all."

(*Loud laughter*)

Student E (*to secretary*): Have you got that down?

Student A: Surely in these days of family planning she could have been educated enough to avoid having any more children if she did not want them?

Student H: Did she reject it or did the father?

Leader: I think it is clear that the mother needs understanding in her own right. As a person living as part of a community, we each have a right to have the standards of the community and we have just been voicing these standards now. If we are angry with her, we are angry as members of the community. But we are also mental health workers and so we have to consider Mrs. Y as a person with a need. How did she get into that state of mind? It may be that she has abnormal needs for the publicity involved in the situation. There are some people who are the epitome of some fundamental emotion or of some problem. She is expressing herself in this way, and in an exaggerated way she represents something in a large number of ordinary people. We may not be able to do anything for her but we still have the responsibility of asking why this happened to her. Up to now we have been ordinary people and we have been expressing ourselves as ordinary people. But we have to give our opinion as mental health workers.

Student F: Well, my first reaction was that she was a mentally ill woman.

Leader: We have to recognize that a person may be mentally ill in some senses and be beyond the reach of treatment because the person concerned does not look on it as illness and does not seek help.

Student H: We do not know for certain that it is her husband's child.

Student D: I cannot see why we should see her as a mentally ill person merely because she is rejecting her child. This is universal.

Leader: We spoke of the standards which we acquire. We have not yet discussed what the standards are and how they are acquired. It is necessary if you live in a community to have rules. We all of us have the capacity to take advantage of each other. The law alone isn't enough protection. There are many things which are not illegal which we just don't do to each other. For example, as children we don't split on each other and so on into adult life. Somehow or other, this woman has broken the rules. Is this an illness? There were times when only physical illness was regarded as sickness. Then mental symptoms became accepted as a medical responsibility. Only recently have we begun to adopt the concept of social illness in an individual who has not developed the ordinary social standards.

Student A: Mrs. Y has now changed her mind about her baby.

Leader: This may be just as pathological as her initial refusal to bring it up herself.

Student J: I wonder if she would have done this if she had been a Roman Catholic?

Student G: Could we assume that if she were a Roman Catholic and she had done this she would have been mentally ill?

Student B: I cannot see that that is anything to do with it.

Student J: Suppose that the mother had been a Catholic and the child had been given to a convent; what would have happened then?

Leader: I think that brings up another point. There are cultures that are characterized by certain attitudes to child rearing. We have a certain idea in mind as to what the English attitude to bringing up children is. There are some more uniform cultures which have been studied by anthropologists in some areas of New Guinea. Different tribes live quite near to each other with absolutely different ideas on child rearing. In one culture, the children are treated gently and are well and carefully looked after. They grow up into peace-loving adults. In another tribe, however, the children are treated aggressively. They are fed and then bustled away, the parents never spend a lot of time with them and they are treated abruptly. In both tribes, however, there are deviants. It has been said that if the aggressive person was moved out of the gentle tribe into the more aggressive one, he would be happier there. But I do not think so. I think the whole essence of the behaviour is in the fact that it is deviant.

The Chinese and the Japanese are a similar kind of example. In China, children were brought up with a good deal of tolerance and showed no anxiety such as we know in the Western world. As adults, they were serene, peace-loving people. In Japan, the children were brought up aggressively, almost cruelly, and they became a war-like nation. So what is normal depends upon the culture.

Student A: Is it not true that the Japanese introduced some heroic deeds deliberately into their myths and legends to make the children more aggressive?

Leader: Yes. That is directed aggression.

Student L: I wonder whether in the case of the baby farms which Hitler introduced into his régime the girls were right or the dictator?

Leader: I think that there are occasions when we must ask ourselves whether the deviant is "normal" or the people who fit in with the culture. There are people who differed from the social culture of their day who have been the forerunners of a new social system.

Student J: It is said that mentally ill people sometimes see things more clearly.

Student E: There is a story told about the psychiatrist who examined his patient, and at the end of the interview the patient said, "Well, I have listened to you and you have listened to me, and my conclusion is that it is you who is mad!"

Student A: There is another article in the press this morning about a difficulty between teachers: where some teachers are saying that men teachers only should teach in boys' schools and women teachers in girls' schools. Would you like to comment on this?

Leader: I think we will let that come up when we are dealing with the child of school age. We must stop at this point.

Involvement at professional and personal levels

This record of one session of a particular discussion group shows, firstly, the members of the group reacting spontaneously, even forcefully, towards a case that did not come from the professional area of their lives but from the private and personal area, i.e. from their daily newspaper reading. Members of a group, even a group of professional people, and not always excepting the leader, are likely to respond to such a stimulus as members of the newspaper-reading public, escaping from the protection or restraint that they derive from their professional framework.

We have already mentioned one important aspect of a group discussion leader's function as being the making of links and the pointing out of particular connections. To do this, he must select what seems to be most relevant to the group at the time from a complex and varied field. In the particular instance we are considering, the links that he made are those between the professional and the personal areas of social workers' experience. Here the leader had first of all to make it possible for the members of the group to reveal their own personal attitudes to the topic under discussion; when they had done this he was able to relate these attitudes to the professionalized and theoretical formulations, and to attempt to bring them all into the same framework. The technique he adopted in order to confront them with the same phenomenon in a personal as well as in a professional context was almost too successful, and there was subsequent difficulty in trying to return to the use of professional concepts. Individual personal bias was shown so freely, and the divergence of views at one point became so great, that it needed a joke, producing laughter in which all could share, to restore a measure of group cohesion. In the course of the heated discussion, a good deal of hostility was expressed, much of it directed openly or covertly at the leader. Some of this was resolved within the natural action of the group, and some of it was diverted by the introduction of some intellectual themes that were relevant to the topic. At the end of the session one member maintained his independence of the psychiatric challenge to previous attitudes by telling a story at the expense of the group leader. He was allowed to have what was effectively the last word.

The dichotomy between professional and personal attitudes may be more than usually clear-cut in our example, in which the behaviour that is being considered falls outside the range considered as normal. The professional worker in the mental health field is asked to explain such behaviour in terms which help one to deal with it, but one has been accustomed to observing the same behaviour as an ordinary member of the public, making judgements upon it and dealing with it in traditional ways. One may come to substitute a professional language for stereotyped popular explanations, and then proceed to use the professional language in exactly the same way, i.e. to supply a label which serves instead of an attempt to understand the behaviour at a deeper level. The *professional* labels, such as "frustration", "anxiety", "conflict", "oedipal conflict", and the rest, may be no more explanatory than the *popular* labels such as "incompetence", "laziness", and "wickedness".

The use of stereotyped labels of one sort or another has a purpose. If it does not provide an explanation, it may relieve one of the burden of finding an explanation. In a group, it is also likely to be part of an attempt to solve a particular problem or to meet a particular need at an individual and at a group level. It may help to provide a period of apparent cohesiveness, a safe channel for the expression of a feeling, in a group that is not yet ready for deeper exploration or exposure. It may represent an attempt to toe an imaginary "party line", to demonstrate an acceptance of a particular school of thought.

If such labels continue to be used, and no other member of the group is able to challenge or repudiate them, it will become the task of the leader to do so. The leader will have to look for the reason behind the continuing use of these labels, and relate it to the total position in the group, to the way in which the group processes are operating, and to the attitudes, open and covert, towards himself as leader. The leader may, as we have illustrated, respond to the situation by introducing new material which cannot be treated in quite the same way or may make a more direct approach, pointing to the relationship, or lack of relationship, that has been shown between the use of stereotyped labels on the one hand, and the private attitudes to professional tasks on the other. There are certain questions that might be asked. These include "What additional information does the use of this term give us?", "What further information do we need, and for what purpose?", and "Can we put this into other words?"

It is likely that the leader of a discussion group will be working within a narrow time schedule, taking part in a course of fixed and limited duration; having to bear the requirements of a particular syllabus in mind, and to remember the precedent set by the degree of progress a previous group achieved. The leader will wish to promote the development of the group as quickly as possible. And, although required to intervene more frequently and more directly than either a group psychotherapist or a group counsellor would be likely to do, is also bound by many of the same considerations. All group work requires that the major element through which psychotherapy, counselling, or teaching is provided should be the action of the group itself. In every case, the group must be given opportunities to solve its own problems, and establish its own methods of working. The group discussion leader who exerts too great an influence over the group defeats the group's own purpose, and unwittingly replaces group discussion with a form of that very didactic teaching that it is designed to avoid.

The particular problems which all groups, and particularly such relatively unstructured ones, will have to solve are likely to be influenced, and even intensified in the case of group discussion, by the nature of the task before the group and the type of theme or topic on which each session is focused. Both these factors may increase the stress which is experienced by the individual members, and this increase is likely to be reflected in a strengthening of disruptive, as opposed to cohesive, forces in the group as a whole.

The task before a discussion group, within our use of the term, is to learn about some aspect of human behaviour in general in which the behaviour of each individual member in particular is inevitably included. Such learning requires involvement of emotional as well as at intellectual levels. The success of the learning process can best be evaluated by the nature and extent of the modification that takes place in each member's subsequent behaviour.

How far this expectation can be made explicit at the beginning will depend upon the nature, purpose, composition, and level of sophistication, of each particular discussion group. It cannot be determined by intellectual level alone, although some professional groups, whose members have had previous training in this field, could be expected to be more at ease with the concepts involved than others would be. The idea that the provision of opportunities for personal change is an aim of group discussion is an idea that could be misinterpreted at different levels and in different ways. There is a danger that it may be taken to mean change in some pre-determined direction imposed by the leader, and even the leaders of discussion groups have sometimes appeared to see their role in this light. There may be, as has already been stated, some members of a group who have come to teach what they know already rather than to learn, or who are primarily concerned with the defence of existing standards which give them worth in their own or in other people's eyes. The leader of a discussion group may have little or no opportunity to influence the selection of members, either in terms of personal suitability, or in order to try to secure a homogeneous group, a diverse group, or a group selected according to any other particular principle. To a greater extent than the group psychotherapist or the group counsellor, the discussion group leader may have to accept all comers, and to find some way of accommodating them within the group. Therefore in group discussion, the leader may encounter difficulties in making the purposes and process explicit, at least in the initial stages, and these may have to be discovered by degrees. The other two systems are less likely to be hampered in this way.

Four successive stages

Whatever the way in which the idea of change is formulated and understood, the members of discussion groups are likely to feel themselves faced with a new and challenging situation. The stress entailed in such discussions is particularly evident in such courses as the one for mental welfare officers already described. These experienced workers had already established their own methods of work, from which they were able to get some satisfaction, without the benefit of formal training; they were now exposed to a situation in which these methods were being questioned. The problems that this created for them, and the attempts to find solutions for these problems, contributed to the establishment of a characteristic pattern of behaviour throughout each course which became very apparent after experience of a number of such courses in successive years.

Each course, apparently irrespective of whether its length was one day or several days, weeks, or even months, seemed to be marked by four successive stages. In the first stage, an apparently united and enthusiastic group showed its readiness to accept new knowledge in the hope and expectation that this would change the whole pattern of previous work and answer all the problems hitherto found insoluble. The second stage was marked by growing disappointment with what was being provided, and the development of a critical attitude to the ideas that were being communicated. In the third stage open hostility was shown to the leaders, tutors, and lecturers, coupled with an apparent belief that a "party line" was being put forward and that opposition to it would be interpreted unfavourably; sometimes there were two factions, the second opposing the first and expressing enthusiastic loyalty to the "party line". In the fourth stage there was a shift to a position in which much of the initial ambitions and expectations was relinquished, in which small changes of viewpoint could be accepted, and a few new ideas incorporated into a framework which also included previous personal and professional experience.

There were differences in the extent to which each individual student managed to work through the difficulties of each of these four stages, and to make a final adjustment. There were some who remained at any one of the previous three stages, who left the course still waiting to receive "the message", or who were under the impression that they had found it, or who were still vigorously opposed to new explanations which they could not reconcile with those they had accepted in the past. There were some, again, who mastered the jargon and remained satisfied with this, using it more enthusiastically than their teachers ever did. All these students would return to their jobs with a fresh entitlement to success, and a need to find fresh explanations for their failures.

In spite of the importance of the position, and the significance of the contributions of the group leader, the problems that the group has to tackle cannot be solved by the leader alone. Like every other living organs, a group cannot by-pass necessary stages of development. Neither can the *pace* at which a group as a whole progresses be able to take sufficient account of the particular needs of each individual member. The leader may suggest solutions, but cannot impose them. Whatever each group's particular aim may be, some will be less successful in achieving it than others, and even successful groups will contain individual failures. Failures may have to be tolerated by a group discussion leader, just as the psychotherapist has to tolerate clinical failures.

The relationship with the leader

In group discussion each session is likely to be focused upon a particular topic, chosen perhaps by the leader, perhaps by the members, or determined by the demands of a particular syllabus. This topic will have its impact upon the behaviour of the group.

"Parental Rejection of the Infant" is a theme likely to arouse strong feelings and painful associations even among experienced workers. The experience of rejection is universal. All have some share in the condition both of the rejected child and of the rejecting parent or substitute parent figure. The mental welfare officers, temporarily *in statu pupillari*, were at that time playing the role of children *vis-à-vis* their lecturers and tutors, and were sensitive to rejection from this quarter. They were engaged in considering themselves as social workers, members of a caring profession with clients who would sometimes experience them as rejecting. From both these points of view it was clearly a disturbing theme, and this is reflected in the behaviour of the group and in the relationship between the group members and the group leader. Both of these would have been different in response to a different topic.

Reading the record, one sees that some members of the group found it necessary to repudiate the behaviour of Mrs. Y in the strongest terms. Because of this, they were unable to consider her as a potential client, or to look for alternative explanations of her behaviour and of their reactions to it, and the attempts of the group leader to return the discussion to a professional framework were resisted.

Another feature which needs to be considered in this context is the hostility that this particular group expressed towards their leader. Though this behaviour has several aspects, as has already been indicated, it also needs to be related to the particular group theme. The final repudiation of the leader in his profession of psychiatrist, though voiced by one one member, was contradicted by none, and it seems legitimate, therefore, to regard it as an expression of some more general group feeling. It was only paralleled by the equal repudiation of Mrs. Y as a person who deserved consideration and understanding. The leader had presented them with a disturbing experience, and they behaved to him in the same way that they were behaving towards the rejecting parent. In response to the theme "Parental Rejection of the Infant", they behaved as if they themselves felt like unwanted children.

Although the particular discussion we are quoting took place some years ago, the theme has been given greater cogency in the almost impossible position in which social workers are now being placed through having to satisfy public concern about abused children while at the same time attempting to preserve the continuity of families.

In the relationship between the group leader and the members of a discussion group there are present many of the same elements as in the relationship between parent and child or therapist and patient. The leader must be cautious of using this fact in interpretation. In many situations the students would resent comparison with either patients or children—it is quite bad enough to be students! Furthermore, such interpretations might bring specific relationships within the group into the area of discussion, focusing upon feelings towards the leader with a particularity likely to be inappropriate in this context.

Whatever the leader's task in the group, it must be performed with an understanding that the disruptive and cohesive forces existing in the group are likely to be exhibited through opposition and alliance to the leader. The opposition and alliance may be shown towards the leader's person, towards the leader's topic, and towards the leader's profession where it differs from that of the other members. It may be necessary to recognize within responses of leader and of members the repetition of conflicts already experienced with parents, children, tutors and therapists elsewhere.

This is a situation which is shared to some extent with group psychotherapists and group counsellors: the difference lies in the use that is made of it. The leader is aware that the students are responding to the particular topic at issue within a particular context, and that a major part of that context consists of their current relationship, in phantasy and in reality. But since this is group discussion, the aim is not concerned with specific personal problems and relationships. The aim is to enable the discussion to proceed in such a way that it will provide a positive and relevant learning opportunity for the members of the group, within the limits of what has been sanctioned. For this reason, and for this purpose, interpretations, if they are made, are not interpretations at an individual level and nor are they necessarily interpretations of relationships in the group as a whole. Rather, they are directed to the topic that is being discussed and to its implications for them all.

Whatever use the group leader decides to make of the relationship with the members of the group, and this will depend upon its direct relevance to the group's topic, the maturity and strengths of the group, and its readiness to look at its own behaviour, another function with which the leader is invested must be borne in mind. The leader is expected to provide a model with which members of the group may identify. Since group discussion is concerned with some aspect of human behaviour, including interpersonal relationships, the group leader will be looked upon as embodying and exemplifying that aspect of human relationships which is contained within the group theme. This is an aspect of the group leader's role which can provide an effective teaching tool. This is expressed by Balint in his account of groups designed to help general practitioners to become more sensitive to their patients' problems. He writes thus of the role of the leader in these groups. "By allowing everybody to be themselves, to have their say in their own way and in their own time, by watching for proper cues—that is speaking only when something is *really* expected from him and making his point in a form which, instead of prescribing *the* right way, opens up possibilities for the doctors to discover by themselves *some* right way of dealing with the patient's problems—the leader can demonstrate in the 'here and now' situation what he wants to teach."[4]

The model that the leader wishes to supply may differ from that which the group assumes he is supplying. Either model may be tested for flaws. A group of young people may attempt to shock or disconcert a group leader, or inquire into his private life, in order to test his sincerity. The leader of a group of social workers may feel expected to demonstrate an invariably accepting and non-judgmental attitude, and may be presented with case histories of great length and complexity to test a capacity to listen with unwearied patience and attention. There are circumstances in which it is neither necessary nor desirable that the group's expectations should be met.

The particular topic that is under discussion at any moment in time will supply another reference for the model that the leader is expected or assumed to be supplying. With this aspect of the leader's role in mind, we can suggest another explanation for the hostility that the mental welfare officers showed in our example to their leader. Their behaviour may be considered as representing a challenge to the personal position the leader had taken up towards the group topic. The members of the group are disturbed by the discussion of parental rejection, in the particular way in which it has been presented to them by the leader, and in the particular circumstances of this group. The anxiety that is aroused is painful, and they look for a way to relieve it. The way they find is to treat the rejecting person as someone who is beyond the pale, but this is a solution to their problem that the leader tries to deny them.

In effect, a dialogue takes place between the group members and the group leader which could be summarized as something like this:

Group members: The situation you have presented to us is too disturbing. We do not wish to consider it as a part of human experience. We wish to be able to treat the rejecting parent as an outcast and have nothing to do with her.

Leader: The behaviour that has been described is part of human experience and is part of your professional concern. It cannot be separated out and disregarded. Nor need it be. There are other ways in which we can handle it.

Group members: Then you must show us these other ways and make good your claim. We will reject you, and thus give you an opportunity to show us how rejection can be handled.

Several different explanations have now been suggested for the hostility shown to the leader in this group. These explanations are not alternatives, and no one explanation is likely to be sufficient. Any behaviour that actually takes place in a group is an end result of a combination of many different factors. This combination of factors is very complex. Yet, in looking for the cause of any single event, it is important that the leader should not overlook the more open and immediate ones. In our example, it may be thought that the story attacking the group leader as a psychiatrist was a not inappropriate response to his gratuitous introduction of some lengthy and perhaps boring anthropological explanations.

The assimilation of new ideas and the reorientation of attitudes is a process that cannot be imposed or hurried. Within the group discussion context, the members need to have opportunities to explore and experiment freely, to discuss and try out new concepts. Interventions from the group leader may serve to distort rather than foster the natural development of the group. Nevertheless, the purpose is education, and experiences in the group are of value to the extent that they can be used as part of an educational process. The leader is always there as a teacher and has to see that learning can take place in the group. For this purpose the leader is likely to intervene more frequently and more directively than a group psychotherapist or group counsellor would be likely to do. "Reliance on the untrammelled operation of group forces" and "confidence in the group's capacity to solve its own problems" could be explanations offered by inexperienced leaders to account for inadequate leadership. Group discussion may, in fact, never become established in those groups where the leader elects to play a very passive role, perhaps modelled on that of certain group psychotherapists but transferred to a situation where conditions for the practice of group psychotherapy are absent.

The leader's interventions preserve the group

In all the groups we are considering, one can envisage situations in which the groups may attempt to solve an immediate problem by adopting or permitting methods of behaviour inimicable to the very purpose of the group. The solution may be a temporary one, which will be abandoned spontaneously with the next step in the group's development. It may, in contrast, be prolonged to the point where the leader finds it necessary to intervene. In group discussion, the intervention of the leader is likely to occur at an earlier stage than in the other two systems. The danger the leader has to see and forestall is in the establishment of a permanent "culture" or habitual mode of behaviour, which will prevent the group from carrying out its particular function. This may happen if freedom of discussion becomes seriously limited, if certain conventions of speech and behaviour come to be imposed, and if certain topics, or the contributions of certain members, are not allowed. It may happen when a single member, or a sub-group, comes to dominate the proceedings, and other members permit this or find that they cannot deal with it.

The techniques that a group leader might use in these situations can be discussed most readily in connection with group discussion. Indeed, we could not presume to be so specific about the role of the leader in either of the two systems. But the leader of a discussion group has an obligation to teach, and to create and maintain a learning situation, and may be having to operate within a tight time schedule. In addition, the relationships within the group are nearer to the realities of everyday life, and so permit more direct intervention. Group counsellors and group psychotherapists should be able to learn something from considering the methods of group discussion, but their own techniques have to be selected according to other criteria and to serve other purposes.

There is, for example, the situation in which the group allows itself to be dominated by a monopolist. The monopolist, and there may be more than one if this is not a contradiction in terms, may introduce a theme himself, or may use one supplied by someone else, as a vehicle for the transmission of his views. He may attempt to keep the whole of the discussion period focused upon the theme he has introduced or selected, and effectively impede the introduction of other themes and other aspects. He may direct his remarks to another member or to the leader, and use the response he receives, whatever it may be, for a reaffirmation of his viewpoint in a slightly different form, or as an opening which permits him to produce new examples. The topic he selects may be an interesting and important one, and the leader may feel tempted to deal with it if it seems relevant to the group and provides an opportunity for debate. Other members may tolerate or even enjoy this for a time, but eventually they will feel that they are being by-passed and excluded from the discussion. This behaviour on the part of different individuals and of the group as a whole will have its explanations, and the leader needs to try and find these; and may need to have to hand a practical technique for dealing with it. This could be simply to allow such a member to have a second question or interjection as a supplementary to the original one, and then, at his third contribution, to say, "Let us leave this for the time being, we will return to it" (and this promise must be kept), and then, "Can we have another example?", addressing the members of the group comprehensively. If this is done, it becomes the duty of the group leader at some stage to find some connecting links between the subsequent discussion and the first contribution.

Another situation that poses its own problems is the presence of a "paranoid" member within the group, and indeed nearly every discussion group contrives to include in its midst someone who demonstrates these personal attitudes, although the term "paranoid" is not intended in any clinical sense. Such a person is likely to find fault with every formulation, looking for alternative explanations, in one way or another, in the damaging effect of external forces upon individual behaviour. The difficulties under discussion may be attributed to society, to class influences, to economic conditions, or, in a more general way, to established authority. These views may lead to divisions in the group, drawing hostility from some members and support from others. This "paranoid" member may even succeed in eliciting from the group as a whole compassionate attempts to make up for the deprivation so obviously suffered, and from the leader an attempt to provide a "cure". Alternatively, the leader may become involved in a battle, and in an attempt to exclude or secure the withdrawal of the troublemaker, with supporters and opponents among the other members. We can hazard a guess, however, that if this member were to withdraw because of action taken by the leader alone, another would be likely to succeed to the same place. Such behaviour must have meaning for the other members who permit it, and who oppose it, and may represent some aspect of their situation that they wish to have expressed.

Apart from expressing this general aspect, such a member should be looked upon as valuable to the proceedings. The value lies in this member's ability to penetrate the falsity of many established views which might otherwise be accepted uncritically by other members and even by the leader; to challenge the leader's statements; and to prevent an easy and shallow acceptance of points which the leader puts forward. Such a person must therefore be listened to; and, as leader, one must be prepared to be surprised at the validity of some of this member's contributions, and at the comparative inappropriateness of some of one's own.

If, as may happen, some of this "paranoid" member's contributions seem a little odd, it can be a task of the leader to add something to them and give them a structure that will fit into the general theme. Some of these contributions may be disturbing, and the leader will have to repair the situation by remarks which also add something to it. Essentially, these remarks begin with the word "Yes", and not with "Yes, but . . . " but with "Yes, and. . . .". Thus they are used to demonstrate the possibility of a response to the unanticipated, and a readiness to find creativity in something presented in an unfamiliar way.

This procedure somewhat resembles Donald Winnicott's[6] use of the "squiggle" as a device for communication between two people. In this device, each person takes a piece of paper and produces a scribble (squiggle is a more expressive term), and then the papers are exchanged. It is up to the recipient of each paper to make something fresh out of the original drawing handed to him, and it appears to be a point of honour to give shape and meaning with the minimum addition. There is more than communication in this; it is the accepting of something which is apparently chaotic, and, in accepting it, the turning of it into a structure which has value as well as meaning.

This is what a parent does when turning the child's first babbling sounds into words and the child's first tentative movements into purposive activity. It is also one of the functions of the teacher which goes beyond imparting given knowledge. In an incidental way it may be "therapeutic", but it is still related to education more than to any other primary process. The message to be learned is the acceptance the first product as the basis for the final construction.

There is still the problem of the other members' position in this situation. They may openly express frustration, but it is likely that there will be some recognition of the fact that this awkward and argumentative member also speaks for them. The leader's tolerance (which need not be unbounded) is in the long run reassuring to the other members of the group. And perhaps they are glad that one member is prepared to stick his neck out and be the one to risk having his head cut off.

The leader in all three systems

A group leader, in every kind of group, has responsibility for seeing that the group exists as a group and not as a mere conglomeration of separate individuals or a collection of sub-groups. The foremost duty is to help the group to function. Every leader has to lead, and, even in a psychotherapeutic group with unrestricted verbal interchanges, still has to impose some limitations upon what takes place. The leader always occupies a very particular and important role. Even though members and leader are arranged in a circle, the point on the circumference where the leader sits becomes a special position.

Remembering this special role, there are certain types of behaviour that every group leader needs to avoid so that the spontaneous development of the group is not distorted. The leader must make communications to the group in such a way that these communications are not addressed with any particularity; rather, they are thrown into the middle of the group so that any member may be allowed to pick them up. When questioned the leader must answer, but should answer *incompletely* in order to leave room for further comments on the same topic. A complete answer from the leader silences the group.

In all the groups we are discussing, periods of silence are likely to occur. They should be permitted but not insisted on. The leader will not be in a hurry to break a silence, nor permit it to continue so long that it arouses an anxiety that is inappropriate to the circumstances of that particular group.

The leader will need to try to understand the meaning of silence. There are hostile silences, thoughtful silences, and those silences which are a consummation. A hostile silence may need an interpretation to permit the group to proceed. A thoughtful one may need an interruption, since the members may feel, as the length of the silence increases, that the value of the next contribution must attain an increasingly high level. The silence which is a consummation may need to continue until the group feels itself ready for a fresh experience.

Communications from the group leader are likely to take the form of questions rather than statements. Questions open doors in situations where statements would only close them. Questions will be used to point out certain links and make certain connections. This has already been discussed in relation to group discussion, but it applies equally to all the three systems, although the links and connections will be different ones.

The group discussion leader will ask "*What else?*" Focusing upon the group topic, his questions will be "In what other context . . . related to what other themes . . . for what other purposes?" The group counsellor will ask "*How else?*" or "*Who else?*". "How else do you think such a situation may be handled, and with what result . . . how might this seem to other people?" The question "Who else . . . ?" can be used to bring other participants into the discussion and to illustrate the universality of a problem. The question "When else?" can be used to elicit the connections of any event with similar examples in the history of individual members. The characteristic question of the group psychotherapist, with the least direct focus but the greatest particularity, is "*How come?*". This question leads directly to the unconscious processes.

The questions are likely to be phrased in such a way that any personal attribution is minimized. For example, the question is not "How do *you* feel?", but "How does this sort of thing affect *people*?"; it is not "How did you deal with it?", but "How have different people dealt with it?", "Does it make sense to do this or to do that?", "Is there another problem that is similar?", "Is there a different problem?". These may be the questions that would be most frequently asked by a group counsellor, but they illustrate the generality that belongs to all groups.

And if you, as the reader, disagree, as well you may, we would ask "How would you interpret these questions?" and "What questions would you ask *instead* of them? Or in addition?". In fact, more simply, "*What else?*".

Notes and references

1. Kreeger, L. ed. *The Large Group* Constable, 1975.
   De Maré, P. *Large group perspectives*, Group Analysis, Vol. XVIII, No.2, 1985.
2. Johns, T. T-Group traumas. *Journal of Personnel Management*, Vol. 1, No. 7, 1968.
3. These two subjects were the first that came to mind when we were looking for examples of topics that would not involve personal emotion. Subsequently it occurred to us that Galileo had to face the inquisition for challenging established ideas about the solar system; and that the topic of the earthworm received intensive study from that most controversial of scientists, Darwin.
4. Balint, M. *The Doctor, the Patient, and his Illness.* Pitman, 1957.
5. Bowlby, J. *Child Care and the Growth of Love*, Penguin Books, 1965.
6. Winnicott, D. *Therapeutic Consultation in Child Psychiatry*, Hogarth Press & Institute of Psychoanalysis, 1971.

4

The Family Process

9

The Family Group

The beginnings of family therapy

The family, too, is a group, and can now be brought within the same framework as the other groups we have been discussing. For, in considering the processes which operate in all small groups, shaping their proceedings and holding them together, we have also been considering the processes which operate in families.

The realization of this fact came when the pioneer family therapists started to bring parents and children together in one room for treatment. In doing this, they were putting boundaries of time and place around the diffuse and multifaceted family network and so turning it into a face to face group. It was not until this had been done that it became possible to transfer to families the concepts of group dynamics that were then being developed within those other treatment groups composed of strangers, and to demonstrate the existence and nature of family processes comparable to the group processes that have already been described.

This was a very important stage, even a turning point, in the history of the psychodynamic treatment of disorders.

"It is," wrote Skynner, "as if we have suddenly discovered how to apply a lever to the point of balance of a great boulder, previously moved only with difficulty and against enormous forces that repeatedly undid our efforts and restored the previous equilibrium . . ."[1]

And yet work with families was nothing new.

Family therapy, as it now came to be defined, was an altogether new mode of treatment, but treatment centred upon families had been with us for a long time. For some decades before this, case workers had been describing the family as their unit of concern, and their work largely in terms of the maintenance and restoration of family functioning. The voluntary organizations which state their aims in their titles, the family welfare associations and the family service units, have been around for most of this century. So have child guidance clinics.

In all these fields of work, however, despite the recognition given by helping professionals from all disciplines to the key importance of family relationships, the focus had to remain for a long time upon the individual client or patient, or upon separate individuals in conjunction. Interviews with other family members were undertaken mainly as a diagnostic aid, or in support of the individual treatment that was being given to the primary patient. Family casework likewise was broken down into casework with key family members, who were probably seen separately. It was not until the advent of family therapy as a new specialism that concepts and techniques became available for the treatment of the family unit seen as a whole. The target of treatment then shifted from the relationships of family members to the total interaction within the family.

But, before this happened, the ground was being prepared by a growing dissatisfaction with existing concepts and methods, and a growing awareness of the limitations of individual treatment, which reached as far as mainstream psychiatry itself. The helping professionals were beginning to take note of the way in which treatment was often hampered or interrupted by interventions on the part of other family members who often had not appeared to be directly involved. It was observed that there were times when improvement on the part of the patient would be followed by the breakdown or illness of some other member of the family circle. There were other times when a recovery in hospital would be followed by a relapse as soon as the patient returned home. It seemed as if the boundaries of the problem could no longer be equated with the personal boundaries of the person who was seeking help.

In short, the time was now ripe for a new perspective, including a form of treatment which would take into account some of these new insights, and which would make it possible to extend the treatment process to include groups of individuals whose problems seemed to be dovetailed together in complementary ways.

It needed the near laboratory conditions of the small group, in one room with an observer, to identify the processes at work and to provide the concepts and techniques that were needed. The family had to be turned from an often largely unseen network of interdependent roles and relationships into a small face to face group whose interaction could be directly observed and experienced by the therapist.

"The family is the problem"

One of the pioneers of family therapy, John Elderkin Bell,[2] described the point in his own professional development at which he passed from seeing the family as a group of separate if related individuals to seeing the family as a psychological entity with its own unique processes and problems and solutions.

"I had to wipe clean the blackboard of my mind and find a fresh piece of chalk to write large: 'The *family* is the problem.' I learned to reject the notion that the child who brought the family to treatment presented the problem with which I was to work. The child might be *a* problem, his behaviour having provided the occasion for starting treatment, but I learned that I must not regard him as the problem for therapy. *The problem is the family.* Here was the crux of the matter. Here was the transition in thought that I must make. This is the new idea, seemingly so small, but actually so major. 'The family is the problem'."

From this time onward, there have been rapid developments in the progress of family therapy and its applications. It may seem paradoxical, however, that this progress has been made at a time when the very existence of the family seems to be coming under increasing threat, and when families are breaking up, or breaking down, at an accelerating rate. It seems as if a mould has been broken, but to our mind, the purpose of family therapy is neither to repair the mould nor to find a new one. We would agree with Kubie[3] that "The psychoanalyst is not a marriage broker, nor a marriage saver, nor yet a marriage wrecker".

But although we do not consider that family therapy can be given the task of preserving the unity of families, it does need an acceptance on the part of family members of some notion of the family. There has to be some consciousness of a family structure, even if, at the same time, doubts are being expressed as to the nature of that structure. Both the awareness and the doubts are needed. We venture the thought that where there are no doubts there can be no possibility of change. In the past, when there were rigidly structured patriarchal (or matriarchal) families, there was no room for any doubt and so no opportunity was offered for therapeutic change. This perhaps may explain why family therapy has developed along with an increase in family turmoil and vulnerability.

Group therapy and family therapy compared

Knowledge about families has to come from many directions, and the new discipline of family therapy did not draw upon group dynamics and group psychotherapy alone, important as these were. It has also taken theoretical concepts and inspiration from many other sources, often seeking out theory after first establishing practice. These sources include systems and communications theory, encounter methods, family casework, sociology and anthropology, as well as all the knowledge of family life recorded and communicated in myth, literature and art.

We are for the moment going to put these other sources aside in order to pursue our main theme of the group process from which the central concepts of the family process are to a large extent derived. We are going to set family therapy alongside the group work which we have been discussing, the family process alongside the group process, and relate the two. These two may ultimately be similar processes, but there are also important distinctions to be drawn between them, for the family forms a special and unique group. The similarities and the differences are revealing, and throw light upon both treatment modes.

In discussing the group therapy group, we have emphasized the following points. The members of the group are strangers to each other: they are not expected to meet each other outside the therapeutic sessions: there is no direct contact between what happens to them within the group and their relationships elsewhere. Problems existing within these relationships are transferred into the group, in the expectation that any improvement which takes place within the group will find its way back into these outside relationships.

There are some physical similarities between the group therapy model and the family therapy model. In both these forms of treatment a small group of patients comes to sit in a circle with the therapist.

The family group may, however, contain young children whose communications are still largely non-verbal, and who may require special provisions if their contributions are to be recognized and accepted as part of the whole. They will be within the circle, but they may be on the floor with play or drawing materials, or they may be moving freely among the other members and adding to, or interrupting, the conversation.

The family group members are not strangers to each other, and their important personal relationships are not left outside the treatment room. Whereas the problems and solutions brought by group therapy patients have different sources, the family members have problems and solutions in common, coming from the same family network. Prominent in the sequence of events which has brought the family to this encounter is likely to be a complaint about the behaviour of one of the children.

The traditional child guidance model

Compare this family therapy model with the treatment model of traditional child guidance practice.

In this model, a treatment programme would be focused upon the child who was being brought along as patient, and any work with other members of the family would be secondary and undertaken in the interest of that child. If the mother, for example, were offered treatment because of her involvement in the problem that had been presented, it would not be "in her own right", since she was not seeking help for herself and neither was anyone seeking it on her behalf. There had to be one patient, a child, whom the clinic team was authorized to treat. This was following the traditional medical model which has served for centuries, and on which psychology as well as physical medicine has been based: the one patient with his illness, the one individual with his own psychological processes, the one treatment and the one cure.

But, as we have seen, there has been a change which has brought a departure from this time-honoured model. This model is now under challenge within psychiatry and even within much of general medicine. The notional family that we have been carrying in mind, coming for help with its "problem child", is now being given an opportunity to move away from traditional practice and fit into a new pattern of family therapy. This pattern is the one that the family therapists are carrying in their minds as they reach out for the techniques that can give it concrete form and bring the whole-family concept to life in the treatment room.

A family bringing a child for help is now likely to be offered the idea that the problem is not confined to the one child with the symptom, is not even seen as centred upon that child, but, rather, is the problem of them all equally and in conjunction. It is, in fact, now seen as a problem of the family system of which they all form a part.

The family as a whole

Whenever treatment is offered and accepted, it is expected to lead to some change. The change that is being sought in family therapy is no longer change limited to, or focused upon, one individual. It is change in the family system as a whole, and in the total pattern of family relationships.

When a family opts for (or is induced to accept) family treatment, and the family members agree to come together for therapy, they are relying upon the therapist to hold this total pattern in mind, to look beyond the individual and to direct intervention to the whole. The therapist will perceive each family member in relation to this perceived pattern which encompasses them all, and will not single out individuals and attribute responsibility or blame. The concern is with the family as a whole.

This focus is comparable to the focus of group therapists, and, as with the small face to face groups already considered, this encounter in the one room has to provide conditions which make it possible for the interaction among a number of people to be viewed as a whole in a concentrated and encapsulated form. It is here that the family problems and the factors which created them have to be identified. It is not a question of how A behaves, or of how A behaves towards B, or of how A and B behave when C is present. ABC makes up a whole, and any single piece of behaviour derives its meaning from this total context. For the therapist, it is a question of the total behaviour of a network which includes them all.

In the treatment room, the family is to be observed behaving in its habitual ways, with all its harmonies and dissonances, compromises and rigidities, understandings and misunderstandings, and all the patternings of its roles and relationships. The full range may not be openly demonstrated at every session, but all the potentiality is there and cannot be left at home. The family therapists have to make use of what is going on in front of them: they require no other information, for all that is needed is contained here if only they can see it and make use of it. And the therapists, too, form part of the total pattern, contributing along with the family to what is taking place.

Furthermore, the main emphasis is placed upon what is happening in front of them all, witnessed by them all, rather than upon events that are experienced by one member and then reported subsequently to the others or to the therapist. What is said by any one member in the session becomes a commitment which cannot be denied or conveniently forgotten. The members of the group are committed to their own insights, in the words in which they have revealed them, and cannot easily withdraw from the new position achieved.

The family group matrix

In family therapy, it is not merely the individual family members who are linked together to form part of a single entity: individual events can also be treated in the same way. Every event which takes place in the family treatment room can be related to every other event, and to the family process as a whole; and so every event can throw light upon the problems which have brought this family into treatment.

We can apply to the family the concept of the group matrix formulated by Foulkes.[4] Applying this formulation to the family, we postulate a family group matrix which is built up of all the past happenings in the family and the meanings that the family has ascribed to them, including the family myths and traditions, the memories and the secrets, inherited from past generations. This matrix is the family inheritance seen as a whole, and every event in the present is related to this matrix and contributes to it.

Every detail is important. The question of who sits in which seat; of who speaks first, and of what, and to whom; the challenges and the withdrawals; the responses and the silences; all these have their significance in this context and all form part of one total pattern. Perhaps mother enters the room first and directs the others where they are to sit: perhaps father and one child sit close together: perhaps another child edges his chair away from the circle. None of these happenings are seen as random events. Each has its place and its relationship to the family matrix, to the family problem, and to the pattern of relationships as a whole. It may fall to the therapist to recognize and (where appropriate) to reveal these relationships.

But this is not a therapy group of strangers in which all the members start on the same footing, and in which the therapist has as much and as little knowledge and experience of the group itself as has any other person present. Here, in the family treatment room, is the real-life family network itself. The confrontation is with the actual problem *in situ*, the raw, unprocessed situation within which the distress is to be found.

Unlike the group therapist, the family therapist does not start on an equal footing with the other people present. The therapist is the one outsider, who does not know what was said yesterday, or last year, in this family group.

The other members of the group have a long, complex and intricate experience of life together, a whole history of which the therapist will never know more than a fragment. The therapeutic group of the family (whatever structure may be contrived for it by the therapist who is carrying family concepts in mind) remains part of the continuum of a particular family's life. Whatever happens in this group is still only a part of that family life. It is an addition to it which comes in order to make change possible, and any change introduced here will go on developing when the therapist is no longer present.

The assumptions of the therapist

The group therapist and the family therapist respond to the needs of their respective treatment situations with different sets of assumptions.

One assumption that the family therapist has to make in order to carry on the work is the assumption that family life is all of a piece, and that the portion before him contains a decoction of it all. Family life has to be thought of as a bowl of soup, in which one spoonful is sufficient to convey the flavour and quality of the whole, rather than as a plate of mixed salad which may contain disparate and unrelated elements. Every little interaction, every gesture and every word spoken, is considered to contain something of the problem within it. Like group therapists, family therapists work with the processes before them, and, equally like group therapists, they inevitably contribute to these processes. Unlike group therapists treating stranger groups, however, they have to relate the processes to the on-going life of the group which continues when the therapists are not present.

"The power to guess the unseen from the seen"

A social worker once said that she did not need to go inside the house of one of her clients in order to know what it was like. It was enough for her to stand on the doorstep, to see the knocker on the front door, the tiles in the hall, and the curtains at the window. Making these observations, she would then know what she would find in the sitting room and in the kitchen. In saying this, she was making two assumptions. She was assuming that the rest of the house did exist, so that what she was able to see was not all. And she was also assuming that what she could not see, although different, was, at the same time, "all of a piece" with what she could see; that the relationship between the one and the other was such that clues as to the nature of the one could be found within the other. She was also, of course, claiming that she had the experience and the knowledge to make these assumptions.

A very similar idea is expressed by Henry James.[5]

"I remember an English novelist, a woman of genius, telling me that she was much commended for the impression she had managed to give in one of her tales of the nature and way of life of the French Protestant youth. She had been asked where she learned so much about this recondite being, she had been congratulated on her peculiar opportunities. These opportunities consisted in her having once, in Paris, as she ascended a staircase, passed an open door where, in the household of a pasteur, some of the young Protestants were seated at a table round a finished meal. The glimpse made a picture; it lasted only a moment, but that moment was experience. She had got her direct personal impression, and she turned out her type. She knew what youth was, and what was Protestantism; she also had the advantage of having seen what it was to be French, so that she converted these ideas into a concrete reality. Above all, however, she was blessed with the faculty which when you give an inch takes an ell, and which for the artist is a much greater source of strength than any accident of residence or of place in the social scale. *The power to guess the unseen from the seen, to trace the implication of things, to judge the whole piece by the pattern, the condition of feeling life in general so completely that you are well on your way to knowing any particular corner of it,—this cluster of gifts may almost be said to constitute experience . . .* " (our italics)

Whatever the range of observations available, we have no choice, when working with families, but to act upon the basis of the small part which we can perceive, and to assume that it is not random or arbitrary. Indeed, all of psychotherapy, whatever school it represents, is based upon the inference of the whole from the part.

Freud,[6] in his *Interpretation of Dreams*, dealt with the point that he had in fact no direct knowledge of the dreams which he was claiming to interpret; that all he had to work on were fragments, mutilated by the untrustworthiness of memory, and embellished by subsequent false elaborations. He based his work upon an assumption that a direct relationship existed between the unconscious processes, which had given rise to the unknown dream, and the distorted fragments presented for analysis, these "arbitrary improvizations, hurriedly patched together in the embarrassment of the moment", so that the very distortions and the selectivity of the recollections were not themselves arbitrary but part of the same mental processes that had brought the dream into being. The part and the whole are all of one piece, linked together through pervasive processes from which there is no escape, and the one contains the essence of the other.

Perhaps Freud, as he concentrated exclusively upon the inner world of his patient, was able to make a virtue of necessity, using the part to lead him to a whole.

Therapists in general are faced with a similar necessity as they struggle to make sense out of the fragments they observe. To find this sense, they have to add some fragments of their own. This brings the very real danger that they might come to reconstruct a complete drama out of their imaginations and out of their own personal family experiences. Their interpretations are based upon the few lines from the script that are being played before them, and they take it for granted that this bit of the action is the equivalent of the original play which they can never completely know.

The analogy of a play is irresistible. For the therapists, it is as if the stage curtain rises for a moment and all the action is before them on the stage. Only a fragment is seen, but the assumption has to be made that all the essentials are contained within it, including the theme of the play as a whole. Nothing can be treated as random or arbitrary, everything is taken to be significant and full of meaning. The task is to bring these fragmentary observations into some sort of meaningful order, and to arrange them into a pattern. This can only be done through the use of the therapists' past experiences, the professional framework, and the concepts and theories that happen to be available.

Bertrand Russell[7] used an analogy from the theatre in his *Sceptical Essays*. It serves as a warning against the dangers implicit in any such task.

"*Hamlet* is a well-known play, but few readers would have any recollection of the part of the First Sailor, which consists of the four words 'God bless you, Sir'. But suppose a society of men whose sole business in life was to act this part; suppose them isolated from contact with the Hamlets, Horatios, and even Guildensterns; would they not invent systems of literary criticism according to which the four words of the First Sailor were the kernel of the whole drama. Would they not punish with ignominy or exile any one of their number who should suggest that other parts were possibly of equal importance?"

The danger is particularly great, it seems to us, for the family therapist, and all those others who work with family systems and are given the task of intervening in the whole drama on the basis of an observed fragment. But there is no choice. In working with family systems, it has to be assumed that the fragment that is available is enough for the immediate task.

To vary the analogy, archaeologists with a few pieces of pottery can infer the existence of a whole culture; but before they can claim to do this there are a number of stringent requirements that have to be met. Archaeologists have to have a disciplined approach, familiarity with the skills of digging and handling artefacts, and a knowledge of the shapes of pots previously discovered. In addition, it is necessary to have a knowledge of cultures in general, and the ability to enter into another culture free from the distorting influence of one's own. Family therapy needs no less stringent requirements.

The need for a storehouse of knowledge

The fragments of family life observed in clinical situations can only be understood in the light of an understanding of the broad sweep of family life, of individual families and of families at large, both inside and outside the particular culture in which one is living.

For this sort of knowledge, we have to draw not only upon clinical observations but also upon the work of the historian, anthropologist, novelist and dramatist. We have to study family life as a continuing saga spanning generations. We have to escape the confines of our own experience, so that we do not risk finding that the only family which we can use as a template is one based upon (falsified) recollections of our own.

This wider knowledge has to come from many sources. It has to come through personal experience and through entering into the lives of others. It has to come through the work described by doctors, nurses, health visitors, social workers and other helping professionals. It can also come through reading newspapers and novels, seeing plays, and listening to gossip in bars, supermarkets and railway stations. All this and more is needed to give the would-be family therapists, and others in this field, a storehouse from which reference points can be derived, similarities and differences discovered, patterns recognized and validated or discarded, anomalies noted and remembered. The need for such a storehouse precedes the need for the disciplined structure which comes with formal training.

The two-way traffic in knowledge

All this is a two-way traffic. Family therapy has done more than add another option to work with families in distress and open up a new therapeutic approach. It has also added a new dimension to the study of human behaviour at large, and it has brought new insights into the field of literature and the arts. In this, the impact of the new whole-family psychology could be compared with the advent of psychoanalysis as a metatheory outside the consulting room, which led to a major reappraisal in, for example, the fields of history, biography, and literary criticism. It also fundamentally affected the work of other professions. For example, we have already noted how a large proportion of social workers began to describe themselves as psychoanalytically orientated. They were not psychoanalysts, they continued to consider themselves social workers and to practice their original discipline, but they mastered and applied many psychoanalytic concepts. When these concepts were truly incorporated and assimilated into existing practice, they enriched and extended it.

As in the case of the concepts of psychoanalysis and group psychotherapy, the concepts of the family process are not the exclusive property of the family therapists who first formulated them, a possession to be passed on within a closed profession. Family therapy, with the group therapy that preceded it, must be our starting point, but we do not rest here. The next stage is the outward movement of ideas and concepts first developed within the practice of family therapy, a movement which leads out into the work of other disciplines, and then beyond that into the understanding of human behaviour at large.

From the point of view of the helping professionals, the new insights which have been developed within family therapy are being returned to the fields of work from which so much of the original impetus first came. The task now is to facilitate such a return of concepts across professional boundaries, and, in addition, their transfer into fields that are new.

Notes and references

1. Skynner, A. C. R. *One Flesh: Separate Persons* Constable, London, 1976.
2. Bell, J. E. A theoretical position for family group therapy, *Family Process* ed. Ackerman, Basic Books, New York, 1970.
3. Kubie, L. S. quoted by Dicks, H. in *Marital Tensions* Routledge and Kegan Paul, London, 1967.
4. Foulkes, S. H. *Therapeutic Group Analysis* Allen and Unwin 1964.
   Foulkes, S. H. *Group-Analytic Psychotherapy* Gordon and Breach, 1975.
5. James, Henry *The Art of Fiction.* 1884.
6. Freud, S. *The Interpretation of Dreams* Vol. V stnd. ed. 1963.
7. Russell, B. *Sceptical Essays* Geo. Allen and Unwin, London 1960.

10

The Family in Action

Family problems seeking solutions

Groups exist to carry out certain functions, which may be explicit or implicit, within or without the conscious awareness of the group's members.

The specific functions carried out by a family group are likely to include the creation of a home base, the provision of economic support for the family members, the nurturing of children, and the satisfaction of social, emotional and sexual needs. In common with all other groups, the family has one first and overriding task on which all other tasks depend; namely, the task of staying in existence. The successful performance of this task requires the creation of sufficient cohesion within the group to contain the disruptive forces.

Let us consider this task in the terms of an analogy.

Imagine an established family with all its acquired possessions moving into a new house. These possessions are both an enhancement and a limitation. There is a fixed amount of living space, divided up into rooms in a particular way. Into this space the family members have to fit themselves, their furniture, and their pets; and here they have to make provision for the carrying on of their family life. For example, space has to be found where the little children can play and where the older children can entertain their friends, where mother can do her sewing and father his carpentry (or vice versa). They have to fit in their bedroom suite, their dining-room table, and their piano. They have to rearrange the garden so as to fit in a toolshed and a rabbit hutch. They may not be able to find room for everything, some of the furniture may have to go, and some of their original ideas may have to be relinquished. There will have to be compromise and adjustment. However, the final outcome is likely to be an arrangement in which some provision is made for the major family activities, and in which the individual members are left feeling sufficiently satisfied, even if they have all had to surrender something.

If you visit the family, you will be shown what they have done. You will see the wall knocked down here, the partition put up there, the space found on the landing for someone's desk that could not be fitted in elsewhere. What they are showing you is the solution which they have established for their problem of living together, physically, as a family. This problem is their own unique problem, and you cannot know its exact nature and extent. You may come away thinking that you would have arranged the house differently. But then the problem that you yourself and your own family would be attempting to solve would be a different problem requiring a different solution.

The visitor will not only see how the family has arranged its living space and its possessions. He will also see how the different family members interact and respond to each other, the types of behaviour which are permitted and the types of behaviour which are discouraged. He may well, if he looks carefully and perceptively enough, think that he can discern an overall pattern in which the behaviour of each member is linked to the behaviour of each of the others. He may go on to discover that he cannot understand this overall pattern by considering the behaviour of the individual participants alone. In the same way, one cannot understand the positioning of the desk upon the landing unless one knows about the competing claims for space in the family living-room of the piano and television set and the bookcase inherited from Uncle George.

We have taken a notional example to illustrate the way in which families work towards a solution. Everything that is presented to the observer, the spoken and unspoken communications, the behaviour no less than the physical setting, the family style and the way of life which has been established, forms part of the solution to a family problem at which one can only guess at first. In order to understand the solution, it may be necessary to work backwards and to try to uncover the problems which are being solved in this way.

At one level, each family is working on its own unique set of problems. But, at another more general level, it can be said that all the family problems are the same problem. They all have to arrange their living space so that they can continue to stay in it; and they all have to regulate their behaviour so as to be able to stay together as a family. Sufficient satisfactions have to be provided for each one of them in order to keep that person within the family circle, contributing to the satisfaction of the needs of the others and to the continuation of the family as a whole.

And the needs that have to be provided for are complex and diverse. They are the needs of people of both sexes and of different age groups. They have social, sexual, emotional, intellectual and physical dimensions, and they will be constantly changing both absolutely and relatively to each other. They may at times be antagonistic, at times complementary. No satisfactions are ever complete; but in a fortunate, relatively harmonious, family they will be complete enough; and everyone will be given something, and will have the experience of giving something back in return.

Family solutions concealing problems

In some families this problem solving process is unobtrusive, and proceeds without drawing attention to itself, leaving conflict and anxiety contained within manageable limits. The problems are there nevertheless, and it is through the continuous attempts to find solutions that family life, in every family, becomes fashioned into certain characteristic patterns.

According to this formulation, a family is in distress when its solution is no longer containing the problem, or is containing the problem at too great a cost. The solution that a family has managed to establish may be restricting or distorting its functioning to an unacceptable extent, or it may be bearing too hardly upon one particular family member or sub group. Alternatively, or in addition, it may be causing trouble between the family and the world outside.

The family that signals its distress to the helping professionals could be asking for one of a number of different things. It could be looking for support and confirmation of its chosen solution, or for extra strength for a solution that is not proving strong enough to contain the disruptive forces. It could be asking for help to make a solution unanimous within the family, or more acceptable to others outside the family. Even when the family comes with a complaint about the behaviour of family members, or about a defect in the family circumstances or in the style of life, what we are seeing is still an attempted solution to problems the nature of which has to be inferred.

Crisis theory

Sometimes a family may come seeking help to ease the transition from one solution to another. The need for this transition may have come upon the family suddenly or it may have come gradually, through an anticipated event or through an unexpected accident. It is often at such a point of transition, where a change in circumstances makes the habitual solution no longer appropriate or possible, that help is likely to be most acceptable and most effective.

This concept has been put forward cogently in the Crisis Theory primarily associated with Lindemann[1] and Caplan.[2]

According to Caplan's formulation, an individual is faced with a crisis when, as a result of changed circumstances, important life goals can no longer be achieved by established problem solving methods. The changed circumstances could be the result of a bereavement, or other loss or threat of loss, or of any other changes in the individual's life that disturb the existing solutions. During the ensuing period of distress and disorganization, the individual will be trying to adapt existing coping mechanisms to the changed situation and to find a new solution. Lack of success is likely to bring a further increase in tension, stimulating the mobilization of yet more internal and external resources.

This state of affairs presents both a danger and an opportunity. The danger is that the crisis may not be successfully surmounted, with the consequence that the individual will have to fall back upon earlier coping mechanisms that had seemed to have been outgrown. Use may be made of regression, or denial, or else a physical or mental illness may develop. The opportunity, on the other hand, is that a resolution of the crisis could bring with it enhanced and expanded coping mechanisms, and a chance to resolve at the same time any linked problems which may have been carried over from similar unresolved crises in the past. Crisis theorists point out that it is at these times, when established patterns of behaviour are being disrupted, that the individual is both particularly vulnerable and particularly responsive to help.

Crisis theory can be applied to the family unit in the same way that it is applied to the individual. A family crisis, breaking up existing patterns of family behaviour, provides an opportunity for the establishment of different and more effective ways of coping with the problems of family life.

Sometimes a bigger unit than a family may be involved and sometimes the crisis may seem to belong to the helping professionals as well as, or even more than, the families that they are trying to help. There may be solutions which are experienced as satisfactory by the families concerned, but which pose problems for the guardians of community standards.

Example: The Dartie family

For example, one could consider the Dartie family, once known to one of us. Mr. and Mrs. Dartie with their eleven-year-old son Benny and their nine-year-old daughter Carol were showing no overt signs of distress and asking for no help. No one paid any particular attention to the problems and solutions of the Darties until a school medical officer decided that Carol Dartie was grossly overweight. The medical officer asked to see Mrs. Dartie, a stout and cheerful woman, and gave her a diet sheet for Carol along with an embargo on sweets and snacks between meals.

At the next medical inspection, the doctor was dismayed and somewhat annoyed to find that Carol weighed more than ever. Mrs. Dartie was at first bland and smiling, apparently unaware of any problem, until pressed by the doctor when she became at first belligerent and then tearful. She insisted that she had tried to cut down on fattening foods. She agreed that Carol was rather big, but then so were all the rest of the family and it had never seemed to do them any harm. She thought it was right to try to feed children well, and cruel to limit their food.

The doctor asked the social worker attached to the school health team to visit the home. The social worker found a cheerful and affectionate family, all extremely overweight; a family tradition of good eating, and the frequent distribution of sweets and ice creams. It seemed that this was more than a long established habit; it was an integral and essential part of the life of this family, and a pattern of behaviour in which they were all involved.

It was inferred by the social worker that Mrs. Dartie could only experience her goodness as a mother through generous over-provision, and the satisfaction she derived from heaping plates high and never withholding food. Conversely, rationing, denying and disappointing, signified badness. The giving of food had become the language through which this mother communicated with her children, and they had learned to read these communications. They had come to know that all was well and love was certain as they ate their way through lavish family meals. The family seemed to have no other effective means for conveying this message.

As for Mr. Dartie, he needed to be able to look upon himself as a good provider for the family, and he had come to find confirmation of his value in the well-stocked fridge and the generous margin they all consumed over and above their basic needs. He was also satisfied with the love and attention his wife showed him through the big teas which greeted him on his return from work.

Their happiest times were when they were all sitting around a table together. As other families might share other activities, they shared eating. But it was more than eating. Earning money to buy food, shopping for food, putting food upon the table, sitting about in the kitchen while mother cooked, also provided the structure within which the family could hold together harmoniously. The consensus about food seemed to be complete, and any interference in their eating habits became an attack upon the harmony.

But this was not what the doctor had seen. The doctor had seen an unhealthy child and a feckless mother who was ready to subject her child as well as herself to all the physical and social handicaps of obesity.

What the doctor saw as a problem was, in fact, the solution to the fundamental problem of the Dartie family group, holding them together and successfully promoting family cohesion. It was an entrenched and inflexible solution, and it worked. There was none of the distress which is found when a solution is less than adequate, when it is unequal, or unfair, or restrictive. There was no sign of the turmoil that comes when one solution is being abandoned in favour of another.

The solution did, however, bring the Dartie family into conflict with the standards of the society around it. It is not enough for a family to be a harmonious self-contained unit. A family also needs to maintain smooth relationships, as a system, with the larger system of which it forms a part.

The nature of the problem underlying this solution was recognized by the school health team. Collectively, they were able to place the problem within a bigger context. They now saw the difficulty, even the danger, of any attempt to introduce change into these family patterns. They were able to look on the family as a developing and changing unit from which the children would eventually emerge. They hoped that the children would be able to develop interests outside the home which would lead them in other directions, towards other possible solutions. They hoped that the children would be able to find alternatives even if it seemed that their parents had none. Otherwise, the current family solution would, in all likelihood, be passed on as a family legacy, so that for Benny and Carol and their children the centre of family life would be forever a groaning table, and love a plate heaped high.

Thus the school health team came to a position which they could share with family therapy practitioners.

As we understand family therapy, it is not an attempt to move a family from one fixed pattern of behaviour to another one that the family therapist considers to be better, (though there are times when this type of work may need to be undertaken by other workers in other contexts). Family therapy, in whatever setting and by whatever means it is provided, is an attempt to open up alternatives so that a family may have a wider range of choices as it reconstructs the solution.

Here, of course, family therapy has much in common with family casework, and it must be remembered that the family caseworkers were the first in this field, and that they were taking the family to be their unit of concern when psychotherapy was established as the treatment of individual patients. Caseworkers have been successful borrowers, and they have also been successful lenders. Now they are often the means through which whole-family formulations, built to some extent upon the foundations they laid down, are borrowed in their turn from family therapy to be passed on to a wider audience.

We have not finished with the Dartie family yet. At another, and perhaps "deeper" level, one might have wondered about the nature of the underlying problem which required such a solution. Why, one might have asked, did they have to evolve this exclusive method of communication? Was there, somewhere, someone's massive deprivation for which they were having to make amends? Whose hurt, whose feelings of insecurity, were having to be assuaged? What hazard, or calamity, was it feared another pattern of behaviour might bring, and what sort of emptiness and depression might then be exposed?

Though these questions might come to mind, no one, in this case, was authorized to seek the answers. This family was not asking for any form of treatment, let alone family therapy. But the concepts of family therapy were nonetheless relevant. Whether treatment is an issue or not, the lessons learnt in the practice of family therapy can be transferred to all the professions which provide a service to the public, informing and refining their interventions in many different situations.

The fear of a calamity

The mention of the fear of a calamity, which another pattern of behaviour might bring about, recalls the concepts of Ezriel[3] which were mentioned earlier. His formulation is worth restating.

Ezriel considered that the groups which he observed were trying, through the operation of the group processes, to establish a particular pattern of behaviour or relationships. The main purpose of this pattern was to prevent the establishment of an alternative pattern from which the group wished to escape, because in the unconscious collective phantasy of the group this alternative pattern would bring a calamity upon them.

This calamity may be related to the loss of the leader, to the outbreak of rivalrous feelings, or to fears of persecution from within or without. A shared fear is established in which all the individual fears of group members find a common ground. The group as a whole struggles to maintain a pattern of activity which will permit the threatened disruptive forces to be contained, denied, given symbolic expression, or projected elsewhere. In this, families are no different from all other groups.

Finding a beginning point

A family, enduring over time, and playing a more central and more fundamental role in the lives of its members, is a more complex entity than a therapeutic stranger group. Family solutions take a more permanent form, become woven into the fabric of a family's life, and receive powerful support. They may be passed on from generation to generation. But not every solution is as monolithic as that of the Darties. For the most part the solutions develop gradually, and they are always in the process of being reinforced, modified, adjusted and augmented. At times a solution will be abandoned altogether in favour of some other pattern of behaviour. Most families have at any one time a variety of sub-problems, within the fundamental problem of staying together, each of them simultaneously seeking a solution. These problems can only be accommodated through constant compromise and rearrangement.

The family process is a continuous one, but within this continuous process it is possible to distinguish successive family units, each of which has a history of growth and development with a beginning and an end. It is convenient, in looking for a point at which to begin to start with the young couple as they first set up house together.

Although assumptions about this relationship can no longer be made with any confidence, for people set up house together in a variety of different ways, the reality is still that a pattern has to be established. And, whatever the pattern, an idealized or rejected image of a close union of two people will play a part from the beginning. The relationship is a new one, but both partners inevitably bring with them much from their previous life experiences and from their families of origin. Often, it has been observed, they bring with them similar problems, with fears of a similar calamity, and with a shared propensity to seek one sort of solution rather than another.

The newly attached couple have quickly to negotiate a customary way of behaving together so that, over time, every activity does not have to be set up afresh, and every decision debated. The result is a relatively autonomous system based upon the maintenance of relatively stable interaction patterns.

They soon establish, for example, that one makes the breakfast, that they both have toast and coffee, and one locks up at night and puts out the cat. And so on, throughout the day. They both have to modify their original expectations, conscious and unconscious, about each other. These expectations come largely from their prior experience in their parents' homes (or where ever else their formative early years were spent), including the needs carried over from the earliest stages of life of which they are not consciously aware. But the modifications should not have to go too far, and at least some of their original expectations and needs should be satisfied, if their solution is to be a viable one.

As time goes on, it becomes settled between them that there are some decisions which he makes, and some which she makes, and some which they make jointly. For example, he finds that there are areas in which he must not query her decisions. She finds that she can rely on his support in some of her activities and not in others, and that she needs to give this support a certain amount of acknowledgement and appreciation if it is to continue. And so on. They need to reach an unspoken agreement about how they will behave towards each other, and to feel sure that this agreement will, by and large, be honoured. They begin to say "we always do so-and-so" in an acknowledgement that their life together is patterned in a certain and mutually reinforcing way, according to an unspoken code of behaviour. Problems may then arise if just one of them seeks to introduce change into a system that has become relatively fixed.

Rules which regulate family life

The pattern of family life continues to be built up from an accumulation of small details and individual transactions which unite into a repetitive pattern. It is from these details on which agreement has been reached that general principles or rules are evolved by which other details can be regulated.

An outside observer sees the details, such as who sits in which chair, who gets up to make the coffee, which television programme is turned on, or off, and who speaks first, and to whom.

The observer notices, perhaps, that there is only one comfortable chair in the living-room and that father is sitting in it. Or he may notice that the living-room floor is covered with toys, that the women are drinking coffee in the kitchen, that no one is helping mother to clear the table. Like one compass reading, one observation is not enough to plot a position or draw tentative conclusions about the implicit rules in a family; at least two compass readings, converging upon the same point, are needed. Or, as Sherlock Holmes said, "When you follow two separate chains of thought, Watson, you will find some point of intersection which should approximate to the truth."

There may be rules within the awareness of the family which come to be openly stated. "We are a democratic family in which everyone has a right to be heard". "We all share the work, and everyone knows what jobs they have to do" "We don't believe in rules and want everyone to do as they like." There are also rules which are not stated: "Mother does all the nasty jobs", "No one has to take any notice of father"; "We never show how angry we are with each other". Sometimes these spoken and unspoken rules appear to be in conflict with each other. There are also other rules which operate outside the conscious awareness of the family altogether.

"Science advances by relentless examination of the commonplace," wrote Jules Henry.[4] "If a man reads a newspaper or watches television; if there is dust or no dust on the furniture; if a parent kisses or does not kiss his child when he comes home; if a family has eggs or cereal for breakfast, orange juice or no orange juice, and so on through all the trivia of everyday life—this is significant to me." This recalls Jane Austen[5] writing to her sister Cassandra and appealing for news, "you know how important the purchase of a sponge cake is to me." She too understood all the complex issues involved in the purchase of sponge cakes.

The metaphorical unity of the family

The big events may give the signals about the problems and solutions, but we enter into the family process through the small change of family life. The regulation of this small change, and thus of the rules, stated and unstated, conscious and unconscious, takes place through the interplay of the cohesive and disruptive family forces and so through the action of what we have called the family processes.

In order to reach this level, which transcends individual activity, we have to treat families, like the small groups discussed earlier, as if each family were a single psychological entity. This has been made easier for us by recourse to metaphor.

The individual body is seen to have its physical boundaries, and most people are prepared to take the individual as constituting a separate and distinct whole. But, in fact, the unity of the individual could, in certain contexts, be considered to be no less notional than the unity that we are now attributing to the family.

The unity of the individual is a concept which is needed in order to describe certain activities, but which can be abandoned in other instances when there is a need to consider the individual as a collection of different and separable parts. Sometimes it is important to be able to give separate descriptions of the endocrine system, the central nervous system, the autonomic nervous system, and so on, and to trace connections between these systems and the activities of respiration, metabolism of foodstuffs, and the chemical and electrical activities within the tissues generally. All these systems interact, but all the same it may sometimes seem a desirable aim to intervene exclusively in one or more than one of them. Sometimes the emotional life is treated as a separate existence, but this, too, can also be related to activities in these other systems.

Thus the individual can be considered as a unity; but, for other purposes, the individual can be considered as a collection of different systems related to each other in different ways. Thus an individual, depending upon the viewpoint of the observer, could be considered as a system, as a collection of subsystems, or as a subsystem that forms part of a larger system such as a family or group.

The concept of homeostasis

One of the characteristics of the individual, which can be described only by assuming a unity made up of interrelated systems, has been given the name of "homeostasis". In an individual physiological sense, the term "homeostasis" is used to describe the tendency for an organism to return to a state of physiological balance after a disturbance of metabolism.

There is nothing inevitable about this return to the previous state, but such a tendency has actually been observed and so a word is needed to refer to the observation. Through repeated use the term has become to some extent reified, and, in consequence, people sometimes talk as if there is some force called "homeostasis" actually in existence. From here it is not difficult to make the further assumption that it is through the properties of this homeostatic force existing in the individual that the return to a state of physiological balance takes place. But we are still talking about a tendency which can only be observed if and when it is present. It would be more correct to restrict ourselves to the statement that this tendency for the balance to be restored, when and where it is observed, can be referred to as "homeostasis". And, in fact, there is no guarantee that, after an upset, such a restoration will ever take place.

The concept of family homeostasis

The family group, then, can be considered as an entity which operates according to a system of "rules", some inside and some outside conscious awareness. These rules limit and circumscribe individual behaviour as they work to establish and maintain a viable family solution to the family problems.

Within this limiting system of rules, the amount of flexibility permitted may be small or it may be great; there may be much leeway or there may be very little. But, in every family, however securely it appears to be able to handle the disruptive forces, there must come a point where deviations from the code of behaviour which the family has established as its norm have to be corrected.

The family which is based upon a democratic conception of family life, in which no one dominates any one else, may not be able to allow one member to take charge. A family based upon the principle that "father knows best" cannot allow father's authority to be seriously challenged. A family in which there are shared fears of separation and loss will have difficulty permitting risk taking. If a rule has any force at all, then it must mean that any family member stepping out of line is pulled back before he can get too far.

Suppose we have a family which has established a tacit rule that certain topics which could cause friction are not to be discussed openly at family gatherings. This rule, of course, will itself be one of the things that cannot be discussed. Suppose that one family member draws dangerously near to the forbidden topics. Family cohesion is threatened and there is fear of the release of disruptive forces. At once there is tension and unease, a withdrawal from the person who seems to be about to flout the family rules, perhaps an attempt at a diversion, or a display of the symptoms of physical illness. For example, mother may develop one of her headaches, serving as a reproach, a warning or a distraction. It becomes very hard for the deviant member to proceed further. The moment of danger passes and the rule is tacitly re-established.

There may be other times when a challenge to the rules leads to some appreciable change in the family system. The family may find that the rules have somehow come to be modified, that the boundaries to what is permitted have been extended, and that more deviations from the former norm can now be tolerated, without any increased fear that the family will be put in danger. Conversely, there may also be times when the response to challenge is a tightening of the rules. At such times, any threat, external or internal, to the established family solution, is likely to lead to an attempt to do something to increase conformity and cohesion, and strengthen the solution.

It is here that we can make use of the term "family homeostasis". We apply it to describe the way in which deviations from the norm which a family has established for itself are corrected through some process in which all the family members are involved. But, as with the application of the term homeostasis to the individual, there is a danger the term family homeostasis may be used as if it were describing something with a reality of its own, apart from the perception of the observer who is using the term because he needs some language with which to enclose his observations.

The use of the term applied to the family group is as valid as the use of the term applied to the physiology of the individual, with the qualification in both instances that it is only valid if and when the individual or family group can be seen to restore a balance after a disturbance. It is improper to speak of homeostasis as a force before such an observation has been made. And family homeostasis also resembles physiological homeostasis in another particular; there are times when the balance is *not* restored.

For many families, some sort of working balance is usually maintained. Solutions are created which fit with sufficient comfort into the fabric of family and social life, changing and developing to meet changing circumstances, so that for many families it is only occasionally, at some particular point of stress, that the nature of the underlying problems becomes apparent.

There are transition points in the lives of all families, which strain the existing solutions and demand adjustments. These are among the "crises" described by Caplan and already referred to. Transition points provide opportunities for growth and development and the establishment of better solutions, but they can also lead to the return to a former solution that seemed to have been outgrown, or to the adoption of other more restrictive coping mechanisms. Such a transition point could be, for example, the death of the grandparents, the departure of the adult children, or a change of job, all having an impact upon the family problems and family solutions.

The family and its environment

A family is not a closed system, and so it is in a constant interaction with the larger system of which it forms a part. The nuclear family is embedded within the extended family, within neighbourhood, community, and the wider society at large. Dynamic interchange is always taking place, and information is being passed back and forth through the permeable boundaries of all these interconnected systems. No solution at any level is ever established in isolation from the environment, and no solution can be maintained without the co-operation, acquiescence or collusion, of other people and other groups.

A cohesive family, like the Darties, whose solution achieves its purpose and is not challenged within the family, may be able to maintain that solution for a time even in the teeth of opposition from outside. But there are many other families who have to seek external help in order to strengthen a solution, to reduce a threat to a solution, or to minimize the cost of maintaining it. Many solutions require, and receive, the active participation of social, medical or educational services.

There are families which appear so disorganized, so inconsistent and inefficient in carrying out the family task, and so incomplete as a psychological entity, that only repeated activity on the part of helping professionals can keep them together. These are among the families who become well known to social service departments, to probation officers and to health visitors. There are other families that obtain the help they need from elsewhere, and a relative or even a family friend may play a similar, though probably more concealed, role.

There are also families that are held together by solutions which appear to be satisfactory to themselves, but which are considered too deviant or too anti-social to be acceptable to others. These are the families that are delinquent, or that offend in some other way against the standards which the community they live in counts as normal. Sometimes they are pioneers, pursuing a different lifestyle which will become generally acceptable in the next generation. Sometimes they are clinging to standards which their contemporaries are abandoning.

The Darties can be considered in this context, since their family solution, satisfactory to themselves, came to be challenged by the school medical service. In this case, the Darties seemed to "win". Such a challenge leads to change somewhere in the system, but it is not always the identified "deviants" who do the changing. The result in this instance may have been a change in the conceptions of the school medical team itself rather than a change in the system that the school medical team was trying to modify.

Notes and references

1. Lindemann, E. Symptomatology and management of acute grief, *Amer. J. Psychiat.* **101**, 141.
2. Caplan, G. *An Approach to Community Mental Health* Tavistock Publications, 1961.
3. Ezriel, H. A psychoanalytic approach to group treatment *B.J.M.P.*, Vol. XXIII, Parts 1 and 2, 1950.
4. Henry, J. *The Pathway to Madness* Cape, London, 1972.
5. Austen, Jane, *Letters* O.U.P., 1952.

11

Splitting and Scapegoating

Questions to be asked

Professional helpers, faced with families or individual family members in distress, might, at some point, ask themselves the following questions:

What implicit rules has this family established in its attempts to regulate family roles and relationships?

What solution is this family group establishing to the problem of controlling the disruptive forces and staying together?

What is the calamity that this family group fears and is trying to ward off?

What part is the presenting problem playing in the life of the family, and how is it related to the family's efforts to stay together and ward off the calamity?

Let us take, for example, the case of a family with the problem of an asthmatic child. Perhaps it is the very illness of the child (a burden and sadness to the parents) that is staving off the calamity of a family break up. When the child comes to be sent away to hospital or special school, in the interests of his treatment and with the parents' approval, they may find that they cannot preserve their marriage any longer in the new situation. Sometimes, in such a case, another shared burden and preoccupation, equally distressing, will appear to replace the one that has been temporarily removed.

Introducing the Spencer family

One such child and one such family comes to mind to illustrate this.

Mr. and Mrs. Spencer came with eleven-year-old Andrew to the psychiatric department of a children's hospital. Andrew's asthma had brought them to the hospital in the first place, and subsequently they were referred to the psychiatric clinic because of their complaints about his defiant, rebellious behaviour and his aggressive attacks upon his younger sister.

Mr. and Mrs. Spencer had both been brought up in a commonwealth country, where Mr. Spencer worked as a commercial artist. They had come to this country 9 years earlier, shortly after the birth of their daughter.

The journey to England by boat, meant to be a holiday, was a bad experience for them. Mrs. Spencer was taking a long time to recover from a particularly difficult pregnancy, and had no energy for anything other than the care of the baby. Mr. Spencer was preoccupied with his work, and worried about his prospects. Neither parent could give much time to the care of two-year-old Andrew, and he was left in the ship's nursery for most of the day. Mrs. Spencer was told afterwards that he cried continually, and his asthmatic attacks started at this time.

During the next few years, when Mr. Spencer was struggling to establish himself as an artist in this country, and money was short, Andrew had repeated admissions to hospital with asthma. His aggressive behaviour became harder for his parents to tolerate. Their daughter, in contrast, was described as a good tempered and biddable child, and she was frequently the victim of Andrew's malicious attacks.

We shall discuss this case in terms of family solutions.

The search for a scapegoat

If we were to try to classify family solutions, there is one pattern of family behaviour frequently brought to the attention of professional helpers which he might call "the solution of last resort", since it comes along so often when other solutions have been tried and have failed. If this one fails in its turn, there seems to be no alternative way in which the unacceptable aspects of family life can be contained. "No alternative" is a powerful demand on the professional helper who may be enlisted by a family to make an unacceptable solution acceptable.

In individual psychology, we recognize strategies whereby an individual deals with unacceptable parts of the self which cannot be integrated into the whole. Unwanted or unacceptable feelings may be repressed, denied, or else projected on to some other person, group or institution, so that they can be attacked and repudiated. A personality may split in an attempt to hive off the unwanted part, causing psychosomatic symptoms or an apparent loss of control over the split off part.

Families, viewed as a whole, may behave in ways which can be understood within a similar formulation. They, too, have their unwanted and unacceptable aspects. Events may have occurred that the family needs to be able to forget, or to repudiate. Events may be still occurring that threaten the family and which cannot safely be permitted to continue, but which cannot be openly confronted either. Repression, denial, and projections, can be a part of the psychic life of a family as well as of an individual.

Some external object may have to be found to receive the family projection. Someone or something outside the family, a hospital, a local housing department, a school, or even a neighbour's dog, may be used to represent a bad object, to be attacked for its misdeeds and to carry the blame for all the family misfortunes. Thus a family may be able to put its energies into a long-standing battle over the children's schooling, the housing provision, or the medical care that it has received or failed to receive. It could set itself against its neighbours, or even the whole community, keeping itself going through perceiving all the badness outside itself and all the goodness within. Many a family has kept itself intact for years by means of a quarrel about the garden fence, or the condition of the communal stair.

But, for many families, it is not easy to obtain a lasting relief from tension through an external "scapegoat". Unless there happens to be a sitting target, other people and institutions often appear too powerful, and success too uncertain. There is the fear of inviting reprisals and the return of the hostility that has been projected on to others.

For that matter, it is almost equally unsatisfactory for this purpose if the chosen adversary is too weak and capitulates too easily, for this once more reinforces the family's fear of its own destructiveness.

It is for these reasons that, for many families, it is easier to find a scapegoat within rather than without, despite the pain that this causes. And so it seems to have been for the Spencer family.

The use of the term "scapegoating" refers to the Old Testament theme of the scapegoat which became the symbolic receptacle for the sins of the whole community, and which was driven out into the wilderness, carrying away within itself all the unacceptable aspects of community life. By analogy, a family group deals with its unacceptable parts by projecting them into one of its members, or a minority subgroup, which can then be repudiated as sick or deviant.

Splitting

The use of the term scapegoat implies that one member of a family is the victim who is chosen by the remainder for discrimination or exclusion. Although this impression is often given, it is only part of the picture. We prefer to use the term "splitting" so that we can more easily acknowledge the fact that all the family members, including the deviant one or so-called victim, are playing a part in the same process and for the same end. The member who comes to play the part of scapegoat is often no less actively involved than the others, and may elect to take on the part of the alienated one, or at least may accept election to that role.

Such splitting is found in individuals in families, in groups, and in communities, societies and nations. It can occur in all situations in which the unity of the whole is threatened by disruptive forces which refuse to be controlled or find more acceptable means of expression. In the individual, some part of the personality may be split off; and, in the case of a family, some part of the metaphorical "family personality" may be split off from the whole and come to be represented by one member or by a subgroup.

The treatment of the scapegoat

When Mr. and Mrs. Spencer came to the child psychiatry department with Andrew, they left their daughter, who was giving them no trouble, at home. The clinic staff saw a tense and sulky child; a quiet, slow speaking father who seemed detached from the problem; and an angry and embittered mother who did most of the talking.

Such a family would probably be offered family therapy at the outset in many clinics today. But, at the time the Spencers came for help, techniques for seeing whole families together were not as well established or widely practised as they have since become. It was, however, recognized that the whole family was involved in the problem, with the parents' psychodynamics and marital relationship intimately connected with the child's difficulties.

It was arranged that Andrew should have individual psychotherapy, and that the parents should bring him to the clinic together and see a social worker at the same time. The treatment for the parents would be in support of the treatment being given to the child, and the child remained the sole identified patient. It was a children's hospital, not a family therapy centre.

The parents appeared to assent to this, but it so happened that they never came together to the clinic again. Sometimes one parent came, sometimes the other, and sometimes Andrew would be brought by an au pair girl. It was said that they could not spare the time to come together, although they both wanted to "keep in touch" with his treatment by coming separately from time to time to hear what the social worker had to report to them. When this was challenged, they said that they did not want to talk about themselves or to "have things stirred up again".

Their family life was so much better now, they said, and they did not want to have this improvement jeopardized. Although Andrew's bad behaviour continued, they were now able to manage him. Mr. Spencer was beginning to establish himself in his profession and had received some important commissions, and Mrs. Spencer was happier and was thinking of studying for a degree. Neither of them showed any sign of distress now, and they were both equally detached and evasive.

In psychotherapy, Andrew was making little progress. He was always quiet and compliant, and his mood often seemed depressed. His asthma attacks continued and, despite his high intelligence, he was not doing well at school.

The professional workers had now been drawn into the family solution, and were playing a part in supporting it.

It happens that professional workers are very often drawn into solutions of this type, for such solutions are hard to maintain without some outside collusion. The presence of doctor or probation officer, social service department or child guidance team, is very often necessary to keep the solution going.

The family members may not like the situation they are in, but while they appeal for help to reduce the pain, they resist any fundamental change for fear that it will bring a greater problem upon them. They come for a confirmation and acknowledgement of the sickness and deviation of one member, and a mitigation of its more painful consequences. The alternative to their chosen solution would be the confrontation that they have been trying with all their strength to avoid, the "calamity" described by Ezriel. So it was with the Spencers.

The choice of scapegoat

Very frequently, it is one of the children who is cast in the role of scapegoat, or carrier of the family disturbance. Very frequently, it is a disturbance manifesting itself in the behaviour of a child that leads to family therapy. It is usually easier to recognize scapegoating when the scapegoat is a child.

This is not inevitable. It is possible to recall instances in which one of the parents remained balanced on the periphery of the family with problems or disorders which the others repudiated. Either parent may accept the role of scapegoat in a way that is more subtle and less apparent than when the scapegoat is a child. The mother who is seen as incompetent in worldly affairs, but carries the burden of household tasks as an unappreciated drudge, may be felt to be the limiting factor on the family's progress. The father who is an unlucky loser in the rat race may be held responsible for the low level of material provision and the physical ill health of an overburdened mother. There may be an understanding, never made explicit, that one senior member's inadequacies can be held responsible for the lack of success of all the other family members.

But, nevertheless, there are reasons why parents, for the most part, escape being elected to this role. The continued existence of families largely depends upon the effective presence of the parents, and their services are too important to the others to be jeopardized. Moreover, parents are better able than the children to resist the pressures to take on the scapegoat role, and are more skilled in imposing this role upon others.

Children are in the more vulnerable position. There is their dependency upon the parents and their relative plasticity: there is the fact that they do not have the physical resources to get away from the situation: there is the fact that the incapacity of a child does not endanger the material survival of the family. Finally, most children have stages in their natural development in which they find it rather easy, and also rather gratifying, to be the family rebel and the family disrupter.

The parents are the originators and the architects of the family, and theirs are the original problems and the original solutions. The children arrive to join in a process which their parents have started.

There are many life tasks which parents expect their children to perform on their behalf. They may require children to succeed where they themselves once failed, to fulfil their own unachieved ambitions, or to reflect credit upon the family through intelligence, good looks, or athletic prowess. They may wish to have from their children compliance, docility, affection or admiration, or they may require sparring partners or delinquent alter egos.

But the children, as they grow, may come to challenge rather than support the family solution which has hitherto helped to maintain the intact happy family. And if, at this point, one of the children were to fall ill, the illness might serve to reduce the tension which has been building up, diverting attention from the hidden trouble, and enabling the whole family to come together again in shared concern for the ill one. In such an instance, the illness could contribute to family cohesion at a critical point and become something hard to relinquish. A pattern could become established, and subsequent change or recovery might be resisted.

The scapegoat is sent away

In the case of the Spencer family, attempts to include the parents in the treatment process did not succeed. After several months, the clinic staff decided that Andrew could not be given enough help in isolation from the rest of the family, and that they were unlikely now to be able to introduce change into the family situation as a whole. Perhaps a chance to do this had been missed. The problem now seemed to have become crystalized into a particularly resistant form. Andrew seemed to have been cast in the role of the ill one, who had to be held responsible for all the difficulties in order to allow the other family members to see themselves and each other as "normal".

Looking for an alternative, the clinic staff decided that it would be better to remove Andrew physically in the hope that he would do better in a less adverse environment. So, with the parents' ready agreement, a place was found for him in a boarding school.

The biblical scapegoat was driven out into the wilderness, but, when it comes to a family, the sending away of the split off part rarely provides the hoped for relief. The presence of the split off part is needed in order to provide some manageable expression for the disruptive forces in which they all have a share. Thus it is found that, very often, when the child whose behaviour is unacceptable is placed away from home, these forces have to find another avenue of expression within the family, and another scapegoat has to be selected.

Ambivalence has already been mentioned. Co-existing feelings of love and hate, often outside conscious awareness, are a component of relationships between family members, and these feelings also have a part to play in the family process as a whole. If there is hostility and antagonism towards the split off family member, there is also love and genuine concern. This member, no less than the others, is locked within the family system even while active steps are being taken to exclude him. It is important to remember that it is not, in fact, the victim or scapegoat that the family wishes to exclude so much as these aspects of their family life that he has now come to represent.

At his boarding school, Andrew settled quite well; his asthma cleared up altogether and his school work improved markedly. However, there were still times when he appeared depressed and he was observed to be quiet and solitary. When he went home for the holidays, his asthma always returned.

Within a year of Andrew going away to school, both his parents had become ill. Mr. Spencer had a breakdown with depressive symptoms, and had to have a period of treatment in hospital. Mrs. Spencer began to go to her doctor complaining of headaches and insomnia.

It seemed that when Andrew went away to school, he could not take all the family badness away with him. Some of it remained behind, and had to be parcelled out amongst those left at home. The essential requirement for the maintenance of this family solution was that the badness should remain within the family but be confined and controlled, and for this the actual presence of the scapegoated one was essential. But the pain that this solution created was too great for the family to tolerate on its own, and so the aid of professional helpers had to be enlisted. In this case, the professional helpers found themselves supporting the solution, and then made the decision to make it unworkable. At no point were they able to make the redefinition of the problem, in terms acceptable to the parents, that would have enabled them to work at the level of the family as a whole.

5

The Family Process in Practice

12

The Therapist in the Family Group

Comparing group therapy and family therapy

When we compare family therapists and group therapists (without making any attempt to review them comprehensively), we find that they have a central commitment in common. This is their commitment to introduce change at the level of the group as a whole. Both of them work with and through the processes that operate in all interpersonal networks.

But, as settings for therapy, there are important differences between groups made up of strangers and groups made up of close relatives: and so there are important differences in the therapeutic opportunities that these groups provide and in the type of demands that are made on the therapists.

A treatment group of strangers is a group made up of people who come with unrelated problems and unrelated solutions. Even if the group members are selected on the basis of similar problems, as, for example, in a group composed of alcoholics, the problems and solutions are still individual ones, and the group will include a range of different attitudes and responses. This diversity is important. Even in such a group, there are likely to be times when it will become a collusive alliance of people united in their efforts to maintain a shared solution and resist change; but the fact that the group includes members with different histories and different and conflicting viewpoints will take some of the force from the collusive alliances and prevent them from hardening into more permanent groupings.

In a group of strangers, the leader can expect that the natural processes taking place in the group will, in the longer run, help to challenge existing solutions and discourage the establishment of entrenched positions. It is through the operation of these processes that much of the therapeutic result is achieved. While monitoring what is going on, the leader is usually able to keep interventions to the minimum required to release the natural potential of the group itself.

In a family group, however, the position is in many ways reversed. This is no group of strangers. On the contrary, it is a collection of people who are bound together permanently by the most intimate of ties; by a complex web of obligations and expectations and by a common history of inheritance. These family members have solutions as well as problems in common, established by collaboration, perhaps inherited from a previous generation. Also in common they will have potent family traditions, and family myths and secrets, in which they have all come to have a share.

Moreover, the members of a therapeutic group come on an equal footing. Not so the family members, who are part of a hierarchical structure of young and old, weak and strong, inexperienced and experienced, inarticulate and articulate. They enter the treatment room within their family roles, as spouses, parents, children and siblings. Since these are the roles that they recognize as relevant to the treatment process, they may come with the intention or the expectation of leaving other aspects of themselves outside. What they are bringing into the treatment situation is not something transferred from family networks that have been left behind at home; it is the living family network itself *in propria persona*.

It follows from this that, in the family group, we do not have an assortment of different problems and different solutions brought in from various outside contexts. Instead we have family members who are sharing the same family problem and joining in the establishment of a common solution in which they all have some serious investment. It is a solution which is now under pressure, having become too painful or too inadequate for changing needs, but the family is tied to it because of the difficulty of finding an alternative. Some family members may be protesting against it, or may appear to be excluded from it, but they cannot escape for their very exclusion forms a part of this family solution.

The activity of the family therapist

One of the paradoxes of family therapy is that while, on the one hand, the family is appealing for help and seeking change, on the other hand the family is struggling to maintain its familiar solution and is fighting to stave off the "calamity" which a different pattern of behaviour might bring. Present pain may have brought the family into treatment, but that very pain is likely to be part of the means by which the family is avoiding another situation which would be even more painful. In systems language, the family is occupied in trying to maintain a steady state by means of its relationship rules and pattern of mutually reinforcing transactions.

It follows from this that any challenge to the family's established pattern of behaving, any proffering of alternatives, and any exposure to new possibilities, is not likely to come through the processes that are already operating within this particular group itself. Some new element is required that will challenge the established solutions. The person in a position to introduce this new element, and bring the possibility of therapeutic change into the family group, is the family therapist.

Family therapy is practised in a number of different forms. There are now several well recognized schools of family therapy, each with its own adherents.[1]

Family therapists bring to their work their understanding of family structures, systems, and processes (within the particular framework in which they have done their training) and their conceptions of change and of the ways in which change can be introduced. They bring their experience; and they also bring their own personalities which they have to put to disciplined use. Personal styles and preferences have their importance.

Some schools of family therapy have been founded by powerful, confident and charismatic personalities who believe in intervening actively in the treatment sessions in order to challenge and sometimes to disrupt the existing patterns of behaviour, attempting to force the family to behave differently. In contrast, there are others who keep their own value systems and their own personalities in the background, allowing themselves to experience, and react to, the family pathology, so that they can then share their understanding of what is happening.

These two different ways of working tend to be based upon the family systems approach on the one hand and on the psychodynamic approach on the other, but these bases are far from being exclusive.

In the systems approach, the primary focus is upon the problem in the present and on the current pattern of interaction by which the symptoms are being maintained; and the aim is to introduce, or even force, change into the here and now situation in the treatment room.

Therapists with a psychodynamic approach place the problems within an historical context in addition to the immediate social context. They feel that there is room in family therapy for concepts of the transference of attitudes and relationships formed in the early childhood of individuals. At a more specifically family level, such concepts relate to the internalized models of past family members, and to the family history, myths and legends inherited from the past generations. These therapists are ready to work more slowly, uncovering and working through past influences which are affecting current relationships, developing insight, and identifying and removing the obstacles which are preventing the family from finding an alternative solution to its current problems for itself.

Beels and Ferber,[2] who have attempted to classify the activities of the leading family therapists, have divided them into the "conductor analysts", those who actively force change, and the "reactor analysts" who try to free the families in order to allow them to improve on their own solutions. They add a third group, the "systems purists", made up of those family therapists who look for the pattern of established rules which govern the behaviour of the family as a system, and try to expose, challenge, and alter, these rules as they are demonstrated in the treatment situation, including in this the relationship with the therapist. They are, so to speak, trying to disrupt the game in progress by moving the goal posts.

In the literature there may appear to be clearer distinctions between these different ways of working than is found in practice, where the differences are

often more of emphasis than of exclusive orientation. There are many practitioners of family therapy who do not identify themselves exclusively with
any one school, but feel free to draw from a range of different formulations
and techniques.

Family therapists of different orientations, comparing their work with
other forms of therapy, frequently emphasize the need to take a more active
role. The very strength of the family group, which makes this necessary, also
makes it possible for the therapists to move more freely and intervene more
directly, drawing upon their own personalities and experience within their
professional discipline. The family as a unit is less vulnerable to the effect of a
therapist's intervention; and transference, though considered important by
many family therapists, is not the main therapeutic tool that it is in individual psychoanalysis. In the family group, transference is present in a more
diluted and dispersed form, and an additional or alternative focus can be
found in the interaction taking place in the present situation.

Roles

By the very nature of their function, all family therapists have one thing in
common. Unlike group therapists, in their treatment groups they start off in
a very unequal position *vis à vis* their patients. In this situation, they are the
outsiders, the newcomers, with a very powerful alliance set in opposition to
them.

Whatever their orientation and their personal style may be, family
therapists inevitably become more quickly (and more completely) drawn
into the conflicts of their family groups than therapists in other situations
would be, and they are less able to maintain some detachment from the problems confronting them. Should family therapists try to remain outside the
conflict, they risk appearing to the family as intrusive aliens, inviting it to
close ranks as it would against any other threat coming upon it from outside.
Nor can the family therapist appear to be exploiting existing divisions within
the family, and searching out the chinks in the family armour, without the
danger of aligning a family sub-group in opposition, and thus increasing the
splitting and polarization. This has to be taken into account, and there are
family therapists who are willing deliberately to incur this risk and then to
deal with the splitting.

In order to take on the role of catalyst, or facilitator of change, family
therapists cannot altogether escape the double role of participant and
observer. Whatever their framework and orientation, they have to enter into
the family process and become part of it, while, at the same time, they have
to remain outside it. They have to expose themselves to the family means of
communication, and experience the operation of the family processes; but
they must remain apart from what is going on in order to challenge it. If a
therapist is to become, at least temporarily, a member of the family group, it

must be as the one member who is not caught up in the family fear of a calamity, and who is able to reduce such fears while challenging the family defences.

Many of the practices of family therapy have been developed on the basis of this ambiguous position of the family therapist. There are number of different modes of working, and strategies, which provide family therapists with space and a measure of detachment from the problem. The conflict may be dramatized, participant members being given different roles to play (their own or those of other members of the family as they perceive them). There is *sculpting*, in which each member of the family is invited to create a living tableau representing the family relationships as he or she experiences them. Families may be given games to play, or specific tasks to carry out, inside or outside the treatment session. Family trees may be compiled. These techniques have several advantages. In addition to providing some structure for the therapist, they can be used to provide access to more material, to allow the expression of a wider range of feelings, and to encourage the active involvement of all the family members in the treatment process. We should also mention here co-therapy, in which colleagues work together to support each other and monitor the involvement; and the one-way screens which permit colleagues to have a part in each other's work as observers, supervisors, or even as participants making contributions from time to time, although remaining outside the visual range of the patient family.

The therapist who moves into the current family struggle and is taken into the fold, has to take or accept some position within it and become aligned in one way or another with the family activities.

There are a number of different possibilities here, and different positions available. The therapist cannot be impersonal, and is allocated some position or succession of positions in a gallery of traditional or archetypal family representations.

It could be, for example, that the therapist will be experienced by the family as if a member of the grandparents' generation, representing and highlighting the inheritance from the past and from the parents' families of origin. Alternatively, contact might be made by the therapist entering the family as if another parent, challenging existing assumptions about parenting and authority, and even modelling a different parental role (which the family may need to reject). Another possibility for the therapist would be to enter the family processes as if in the position of one of the children, accepting exposure to the experience of the family pathology as it impinges upon a child, acting as a mirror or a sounding board, and articulating the experiences of the younger and weaker members who are not able to do this for themselves. Sometimes a therapist may move through all these positions and more.

This is the transference situation, and it plays its part in the therapy. The different roles may be consciously assumed by the therapist, but they are also a product of the minds of the family members. Which aspect predominates will be influenced by the extent to which the therapist is actively setting out to introduce new experiences, or concentrates upon responding to what the family is bringing.

There is an ambiguity about generational roles. As a matter of physical maturation, the distinction in the behaviour of these different roles is perfectly clear. But, psychologically and emotionally, an adult carries living traces of former levels at all times, and there are occasions when earlier levels may reassert themselves and dominate behaviour.

The transfer of generational attributes can take place in two directions. As the infantile parts of the parents are never completely outgrown, and remain included within the family relationships, so the desired and undesired qualities of the grandparents, and of the parents themselves, may be absorbed by the children and given a new expression.

The overlapping of roles takes place at different levels and in different ways. In the natural course of the development of families, different members are permitted from time to time to relive earlier stages or to anticipate later ones. When a member is not well, there is an entitlement to be nursed like the precious infant; or, to take another example, a junior school child may be given a brief taste of later independence when going on a school trip. This can be permitted because of an understanding that a restoration of the previous state will follow.

Thus, in appearing to take up one particular position in a family, the therapist can be making contact with them all, at all the different generational levels, and with the family process as a whole.

Boundaries

The boundaries between different individuals and different generations make up an important part of the structure of family life. One of the functions of a family is to help in the formation of boundaries between individuals, starting by enabling the infant to differentiate the self from the other, and going on to provide sufficient security for the growing child to ease the transition from one developmental stage to another.

A family has its natural history of growth and development, and is always placed at some particular point in a life cycle which ranges through the establishment of the newly wedded couple (or, in these days, newly committed partners), the symbiotic relationship of mother and infant, the child's achievement of a sense of personal identity, and the breaking away of the adolescent. At every stage of family life there is some balance of togetherness and separateness, which is shifting all the time. Those who have been held securely at the appropriate stage, when their dependency needs were uppermost, are able to let go later on with confidence and trust. But, at any stage, an inappropriate separateness leaves the family unable to perform its tasks, and the individuals unnurtured. By the same token, an inappropriate togetherness freezes the family at an immature level with the infantile problems unsolved and the inevitable pathology preserved, divided out, and passed around amongst them.

It is usually thought necessary to the well-being of a family that boundaries between the roles of the different members should be recognized. Roles and boundaries provide limits and controls; and they also confer entitlements and obligations, so that the individual members better understand what they are expected to do themselves and what they can expect from the others.

Difficulties arise when these boundaries are poorly defined, but they can also arise when boundaries are rigidly maintained. In some families, the expression of individual opinions is discouraged and there is a family line which has to be adhered to: in other families, each member is assigned to set attitude from which departure is not permitted. There are other families in which roles become reversed. For example, father is "just a little child", excused or denied a father's role, leaving a gap which has to be filled by someone else; or a young girl is expected to take on adult responsibilities and be "a little mother" to her younger siblings, losing her right and freedom to engage in the individual activities appropriate to her age group.

Some family therapists would directly challenge the inappropriate roles. Others, who do not see their therapeutic task as one of commanding change, might give recognition to the need to behave in a particular way at a particular time, while also giving permission to change the behaviour. All members of the family can have an urgent need to be taken seriously in their (temporary) roles before they can relinquish them. Therapists may be able to demonstrate, through the questions they ask and the responses they give, that change is more possible and less dangerous than the family believes, and establish conditions in which some safer experimentation is possible. Some change takes place in the sample of behaviour which is brought into existence in the therapeutic session, and is there to be explored, and for every member of the family to witness, take part in, and remember. What takes place in the family session is progress which cannot subsequently be withdrawn.

Communications

Problems with communications and problems with boundaries go together, so that attention paid to the one usually includes attention to the other. In fact, all aspects of family life are interrelated, and intervention at any level can introduce changes which percolate throughout the family system.

Since the application of general systems theory to families, particular attention has come to be paid to the interpersonal communications taking place within a family; and there are many family therapists who make this level their main focus. These therapists may define their primary task as that of clearing up the muddles and mystifications, clarifying the conflicting and incompatible messages, and removing the blocks and obstacles placed in the way of clear communication which are a feature of the life of disturbed families. Sometimes a few of the family members seem to be trying to resist the passage of certain communications; sometimes all the members of a family are colluding to this end. There may be things that are never referred to, and other things that have become secrets to be shared by some family members and withheld from the rest. Communications have become blocked and can no longer be made openly, but they may erupt in the form of physical or mental symptoms—illness or disturbed behaviour—perhaps located in one particular family member. When some communication is then made, it is likely to be given in an incomplete, distorted or ambiguous form.

It was Bateson et al.[3] who first labelled a communication containing two contradictory messages a "double bind".

Many examples can be found. A child may be praised in one sentence and all the approval snatched away in the next. A child may be urged to go to school, while at the same time the urging contains a subtle message about the dangers of the playground. Boys are expected to stand up for themselves but must not be rough. "I'd like some help with this—but its too late now to be any real use". "I do want you to go out and enjoy yourself—I don't mind being left on my own again." Words may say one thing and gestures another; for example, an embrace may be stiff and unyielding.

The escape from this situation lies in pointing out the ambiguity and asking the speaker for elucidation. But in some families there is too much fear of hurting and being hurt, and of something unacceptable emerging, for anyone to be able to challenge double sided messages. Children in particular are frequently too vulnerable and too dependent upon their parents to be free to question the communications.

If there is no way of pleasing, and any response at all is held to be wrong, if you are "damned if you do and damned if you don't", the tendency is to make no response. At the extreme, where there is no escape from the situation, the victim who is doubly bound may withdraw into a personal inner life with phantasies which have their own satisfactions. This formulation has been used to explain the origin of some cases of schizophrenia; but the process is familiar enough in all families, at varying degrees of intensity.

Communications in the family are of interest to all family therapists. Some family therapists who pay particular attention to this level work by exposing themselves to the consequences of the faulty communications in order to be able to demonstrate what the family members are doing to each other, receiving the ambiguous messages and drawing attention to the confusion which makes it impossible to know how to respond. They may identify and highlight all the hidden messages—the two edged communications and the latent hostility—doing what the family members have become unable to do for themselves. They may ask firmly for clarification whenever confused communications, verbal or non-verbal, are made. In this, as in other situations, the therapist who feels confused always needs to say so clearly.

Satir[4] quotes the following interchange to illustrate her own methods:

Daughter to mother: May I go to school?

Mother to daughter: When I was a little girl, I never had an education.

Therapist to mother: Now your daughter asked you if she could go to school and I'm wondering if she got an answer from you. Should she go to school or shouldn't she?

Those therapists who play a more direct and active role may take control of the family communications system themselves in order to reshape it. They may, for example, refuse to allow one member of the family to speak on behalf of another, silencing the parents perhaps so that the childrens' views have to be heard, or controlling the noisy behaviour of the children that is being used to silence the adults. They may make it impossible for the family to communicate in their habitual way, breaking up the existing pattern and making the family go back to the beginning and start all over again. Their interest is likely to be focused upon the present rather than the past, on the current manifestation of the problem rather than on its origin and function within the family developmental process.

Problems from the past

Those therapists (including many of the ones who Beels and Ferber have classified as "reactor analysts") who look at the family process reductively within an historical framework, are interested in the way in which problems develop and are passed on and perpetuated within families. They look beyond the immediate observations for the hidden origins of the problems and are ready to consider long sequences of time. Some of the developments in systemic family therapy have come as a reaction to what has been seen as the slowness of this type of work, and its reliance upon inference and interpretations. It is also criticized for tending to preserve a linear model of causality, in which events are assumed to have prior causes, in place of the circular model of continuous interaction.

Therapists who work psychodynamically may look, for example, for the particular area of family functioning in which the fears seem to be located, and may feel that the most relevant point of intervention is where unmet needs are carried over from the parent's families of origin, so that the unsolved problems of former generations are being passed on to involve the children of today. This is an approach which may well use object relations theory and the formulations of Melanie Klein[5] at a family level. Sometimes family therapists go back over the history of past generations of the family in a structured way; drawing up a family tree, or geneogram, in order to uncover and demonstrate the means through which the family pattern is continued and problems from the past are being carried over into the present. Lieberman's[6] work on the theoretical development of transgenerational family therapy is an example.

Byng-Hall[7] has described work with family myths and legends, those episodes of family history which are told and retold to successive generations. He finds that these stories are often moral tales which convey the rules and obligations, and the shared beliefs, convictions and assumptions, of family life; and which are subtly adjusted at each telling in order to retain their relevancy within current family preoccupations. They play a part in controlling or discouraging change within the family system, and so can act as powerful defences, all the more powerful because they are so difficult to challenge. To the therapist, family myths and legends can be a valuable source of information, and they are also a powerful tool for the introduction of change, since challenging and re-editing the family myths and legends can lead to a reformulation of the family rules.

The long past and the immediate present

A distinction can be made between two broad groups of family therapists in terms of their use of time. On the one hand there are those we have just been mentioning who work with long sequences of time, with segments of family history, and who look for the control processes, or "governing concepts"—the family rules, and the family myths and legends which support them—which keep patterns even of dysfunctional behaviour in existence, to be transmitted from generation to generation. And on the other hand there are those other family therapists who concentrate upon the current situation, the "here and now", and deal with the small segments of family behaviour that are presented to them, finding family pathology within the short sequences enacted in the brief duration of a therapy session, and making their interventions at this level without looking any further than at what they are witnessing in the present.

Two different models of change are involved. In discussing the ways in which these two models are related to each other, Cooklin uses the analogy of the holograph: the photographic plate, containing a three dimensional image which changes according to the position from which it is viewed. If the plate is shattered into fragments, each fragment continues to contain an image of the whole object but the image is now a much smaller one and represents one single viewpoint.

Cooklin[8] describes the two different contexts in which change can be introduced as being related to each other in a way that is analogous to the relationship between the whole holograph and its fragments. The different approaches have had to be distinguished for purposes of clarity, but the distinctions can be misleading if the relationship between them is not also acknowledged.

The same family problems and family solutions can be viewed in both these different time contexts, and they can be identified and treated as they are passed on within long sequences of family history, or as they are enacted within short sequences of family interaction. Family therapists may focus their work upon one of these two levels, but many carry both levels in mind, and there are some therapists who are able to work at both levels and move flexibly from the one to the other.

Changing the means by which family transactions are regulated over time is undertaken on the assumption that changes at this level will lead to changes in the short sequence interactions between family members in the future; and such change can only be introduced within the current family context. The past is gone and cannot be altered now; but new meaning can be given to it in the present.

Equally, active interventions within short sequences of time are made in the belief that each small sequence contains the pattern of the whole, and that the parts are linked together, in time as in space, in such a way that change introduced in one component will affect every other component and bring change throughout the whole.

The family of therapists

Whatever may be the chosen focus and mode of intervention employed, the central feature of all family therapy seems to be the need for the family therapist to assume the role of principal change agent.

Out of this need for a conscious and controlled personal involvement has come the widespread use of co-therapy, with two, or sometimes more than two, therapists participating together and monitoring each other's involvement. For many therapists, this provides a safeguard against the dangers of being sucked personally, and not always appropriately, into the family pathology: it could also provide some protection against the danger that one therapist's interventions might come to dominate the family interaction. It also reduces the disproportion between the united strength of the patient family in resisting change, and the weakness of the single therapist.

In this conjoint work, the family group is confronted with another group in the form of two or more members of a therapeutic team, i.e. a "therapeutic family" ready to demonstrate another shape of family interaction, and to model alternative solutions to interpersonal problems. The therapeutic team needs to be aware of the existence of interpersonal conflicts and show that it is not afraid of them. No apology need be made for differences of opinion among the team members. They are not claiming freedom from the type of conflicts which are contained in the patient family, and are ready to display differences and difficulties spontaneously and demonstrate that there are alternative ways in which such differences might be handled.

Thus the diversity in the therapeutic group restores to family therapy some of the advantages of group therapy which the seemingly united nature of families had taken away.

Whatever their training, family therapists have to construct for themselves their own ways of working, drawing upon many sources inside and outside themselves. In few other areas in the helping professions can it be harder to define the role of the key worker with any precision.

Looking back to the three systems of group work

If we look back to the three systems of group work formulated earlier, we have to conclude that something from each of these three systems is contained within the practice of family therapy.

Family therapists often need to employ the comprehensive range of skills of the group therapists, including the ability to handle unconscious processes at both interpersonal and transpersonal levels.

They also require the freedom of manoeuvre, and the ability to focus and limit their work within a comprehensive framework which is more characteristic of the work of a group counsellor.

In addition, family therapists may need the skills to handle sensitive themes at an abstract level, and this brings us to group discussion. We have, in group discussion, an educational process which has a personal application to all the participants, even if this is not always made explicit, and even though the communications may focus upon abstract and general topics. The power of the group work here depends upon the way it reaches these areas of unconscious as well as conscious personal concern of its members. This is not the place for the group leader or therapist to ride an ideological hobby horse, but general questions may be asked and some generalities may be thrown into the discussion to be picked up and developed by different members of the group.

Many problems of parenting are approached at this level, as are the problems of growing up and handling interpersonal relationships in family, school and peer group.

In addition, amongst our family groups are those who have moved from one culture to another, creating something greater than a generation gap between parents and children. It is difficult to explore the interpersonal problems which these families bring without some reference to the generalities of cultural adaptation. This is not in itself part of the therapeutic process but we feel that it cannot be excluded from it, even if its deployment is unobtrusive and incidental for most of the time.

Three systems co-existing in every group

The separation of group work into the three systems of therapy, counselling, and discussion, was made to provide boundaries and to clarify the different roles of different types of group leader. It was felt that it was important to do this in order to make it possible to set limits to "therapy" and release the group process for disciplined use by a variety of professions who are not primarily group workers. Likewise we believe that many professional workers who are in no sense family therapists can enrich their professional work with families through a knowledge of the family group processes.

The consideration of family therapy has now added a strength to our belief (and made this belief explicit) that the distinction between these three systems is not absolute, and that work may co-exist at all three levels.

The distinction between these three systems still has to be made in order that the nature of the transactions between group leaders and group members in different situations can be clarified. The leader will always be exercising a specific and limited function, and needs to understand what this function is, and to abide by its limitations. The authority that is given to the group leader is an authority to make direct and acknowledged use of one of the three systems as a professional tool in one particular context.

In discussing the use of the family process, inside and outside family therapy, we still have to take these considerations into account. But we also have to recognize that there are some common factors in all groups; and it is these common factors that we carry into other forms of therapeutic work including family therapy.

The framework that was useful for the study and application of the group process has been applied to family therapy and has served its purpose. In order to take the discussion of family therapy further another and additional framework or formulation, which we are borrowing from psychodynamic theory, has now to be added.

Notes and references

1. Skynner, A. C. R. *One Flesh; Separate Persons* Constable, London, 1976.
   Walrond-Skynner S. *Family therapy—The Treatment of Natural Systems* Routledge and Kegan Paul, London, 1982.
2. Beels, C. C. and Ferber A. Family therapy; a view *Family Process* **8**, 280, 1969.
3. Bateson, G. *et al.* Towards a theory of schizophrenia *Behavioural Science* **1**, 251, 1956.
   Bateson G., A systems approach *Int. J. Psychiat.* **9**. 242–244, 1971.
4. Satir, V. *Conjoint Family Therapy* Science and Behavior Books Inc. Palo Alto, 1964.
5. Segal, H. *Introduction to the work of Melanie Klein* Basic Books, New York, 1974.
6. Lieberman, S. *Transgenerational Family Therapy* Croom Helm, London, 1979.
7. Byng-Hall, J. Family myths used as a defence in conjoint family therapy *B.J.Med. Psych.* **46**, 239, 1973. Family legends: their significance for the family therapist *Family Therapy* vol 1. ed. Bentovim A., Gorell Barnes G., Cooklin A., The Academic Press, London 1982.
8. Cooklin, A. Change in here-and-now systems vs. systems over time *Family Therapy* vol. 1. ed. Bentovim A., Gorell Barnes G., Cooklin A., The Academic Press, London, 1982.

6

Wider Applications of the Family Process

13

A Psychostructural Model

The use of metaphor

Mental processes, whether we attribute to them to an individual or to a group, can only be described by means of analogies or metaphors. The very term "mind" is itself an abstraction rather than a term used to denote an entity. It is a term which enables us to speak of the mental processes of the individual as forming a system of related parts, so that the separate experiences of thinking, feeling, loving, hating, remembering, forgetting etc., can be brought together into one whole. For convenience, we group all these processes together, and then we acknowledge their relationship by bestowing upon them a common identity which we call "mind", although all that we can know are the activities themselves. We need such a device, or figure of speech, in order to simplify a complex field so that it can be brought under scrutiny within the range of our mental capabilities.

In a comparable way, Freud, at different times, arranged his ideas about mental activities into a number of models so that he could discuss mental functioning more easily, each model serving as a separate metaphor.

We need metaphors of mental activities in order to deal with these complex abstractions, but we need to use them with caution and constantly remind ourselves that they are only metaphors. Otherwise there is the danger that abstract processes will become reified in our thinking and will be given a spurious existence of their own.

"The right word is always a power, and communicates its definiteness to us in our actions."[1] So wrote George Eliot in "Middlemarch". She might well have added the reminder that the wrong word can have power too, with its misleading capacity to communicate a definiteness that does not exist.

Borrowing Freud's structural model

This discussion of the use of metaphor introduces the fact that we are going to borrow one of the most celebrated of all metaphors, one of those structural models of mental activity already mentioned which Freud found necessary for the formulation of his concepts. We refer to the tripartite spatial division of mind into ego, superego and id.

We are, furthermore, going to transfer this metaphor from the level of the individual to the level of the family as a whole. We are going to discuss family activities in relation to a notion of a family ego, family superego and family id.

If its use is to be justified, a metaphor has to have some reference to a reality which is difficult to describe in direct terms. The metaphor, however, may gradually come to acquire a life of its own, and additional meanings may come to be added to enrich the original ideas. There is a danger that we may be distancing ourselves yet one more stage from the reality to which the original metaphor refers.

If, however, we heed this caution, we believe that we can use this borrowed metaphor to describe some essential ideas which would otherwise elude us. The metaphor is the vehicle which carries the ideas.

"It is astonishing what a different result one gets by changing the metaphor,"[2] said George Eliot in another of her novels. As we shall show later, treatment may be at its most effective when it seems to involve nothing more than discovering an alternative metaphor.

The use of this model of Freud's enables us to recognize and approach processes within the family, and within individuals within a family context. We have found, in particular, that it gives us a framework in which different forms of intervention carried out by members of different professions can be related to each other. This last point is important in so far as different professions have a tendency to look upon their own particular contributions in isolation, and to ignore what others have to offer.

Freud's structural model recalled

Let us first recall Freud's structural model as he applied it to the individual. Although very well known, it needs to be briefly restated here in order to avoid misunderstanding.

Freud divided the human mind into three parts in order to be able to talk about different aspects of mental activities which can only be approached with the help of some such physical construct. "We assume", he wrote, "that mental life is the function of an apparatus to which we ascribe the characteristics of being extended in space, and of being made up of several portions".[3] In time, he himself came to write about these parts as if they had indeed not only a separate existence but even a physical location. Subsequent writers have followed him in this.

The term "ego" was first used by Freud in order to separate out the organized part of the self, the conscious self in action, which is able to carry on its daily life and its relationships with the rest of the world in a fairly coherent and purposeful way. But there is more to the self than is found at this level alone.

At a different level there is the "superego", that part of mental activity which is formed by the individual taking into himself the standards of society, of his parents, and of others who have influenced him from his earliest years. The superego provides a rule of conduct, criticizing, prohibiting and restricting the drives, phantasies, feelings and actions, which are inconsistent with such standards.

But before the ego and superego there is the id. This term is used to denote the level which is not directly available to introspection, and the presence of which has to be inferred. The id represents the earliest form of mental activity, predating the ego and the superego, and is the main source of mental life from which, in time, the ego separates. It is non-verbal, and unconscious, and contains the primitive drives which supply energy to all ego activities.

Added to these original sources of mind is the material which was formerly conscious but which, for some reason or other, is no longer acceptable to the individual and which therefore has to become repressed.

These two sources of unconscious mental processes which form the id tend to emerge into consciousness from time to time. They may be perceived as something incongruous with an individual's perception of the self; or, alternatively, they may be welcomed as indications of personal creativity.

If these manifestations of the id are denied contact with the ego, and remain repressed, they can become the source of disturbance and illness. The alternative to complete repression is to allow these unacceptable manifestations to find some disguised expression in substitute activities which the ego can find acceptable.

The family ego: organized family activity

If, first, we are to look for evidence of some counterpart to the individual ego, we look for the shared family activities through which the family as a whole carries on the business of its day-to-day life, and organizes and maintains relationships between itself and the world around it.

In every family there is a rational organized aspect of family life, in which all members are involved, to which all members contribute in different proportions, and by which the activities of all members are regulated on relevant occasions. This aspect of family life is conducted according to norms, rules and clichés; and these are expressed in all the daily transactions in which the members of the family are involved, either together, or separately or on the family's behalf, and which affirm the family's continuing identity. There is a recognizable pattern of behaviour, and there are forces at work which tend to preserve this pattern, which we have already described by means of the metaphor of family homeostasis. This is the level of family functioning to which we can apply the metaphor of family ego.

Examples of the transactions which are made possible through the operation of the family ego are the finding of a house, housekeeping, cooking family meals, spending money on the family as a whole as against individual purchases, and the arrangements for joint family activities such as meal times and bed times. There are also all the leisure pursuits and hobbies which are shared rather than individual, in contrast to those activities which are personal and private (as far as anything in a family can be personal and private).

The family ego is also expressed in individual activities which are approved and taken by all members to be an expression of the family ego, enhancing the value of the family in their own and other people's eyes.

Family defences

In the day-to-day life of a family, there will be shared activities and separate activities, there will be approved and disapproved ones, and these activities will all be brought into some sort of balance reflecting the position of cohesive and disruptive forces in the family as a whole.

A family is made up of individuals who wish to continue to live together as a family and to pursue the family goals efficiently and harmoniously. At the same time, the family is made up of the very same individuals wishing to pursue their own separate goals unencumbered by family restraints and hindrances. In the same way that individual defence mechanisms are needed to preserve the individual ego from destructive forces within, family processes have their defence mechanisms which serve to contain individual strivings without impairing the unity of the whole. Both in the individual and in the family, there are always some parts at risk which require defending.

In individual psychodynamics, there has been a tendency to look upon defensive processes as something to be deplored. It is important to acknowledge, however, that there is often something that is worth defending. In the complex processes of the individual mind, the ego defences serve a useful purpose and need only be considered pathological when they absorb too much mental energy and leave the individual personality depleted. We visualize the defences of our family ego as playing a comparable role. There is no need to expose all the inner workings of family life if they do not seriously threaten the family structure.

Controlling the disruptive forces

For there to be a satisfactory balance between cohesive and disruptive forces, there needs to be a sufficient number of shared or approved activities to give the family ego some strength and to diminish the effect of disapproved individual activities.

Each family will have its own way of coping with threats to its integrity. Many of the minor, or even moderately serious, disturbances which threaten families are made tolerable by the use of family clichés which diminish the importance of disruptive activities and help to hold the family together.

"It's just one of your father's little ways." "It happened on one of Mum's poorly days." "All the men in our family have hot tempers/weak chests/no sense of direction/an eye for a pretty face."

Some of these phrases may sound patronizing when we quote them, but they are in regular use. They do for the family what so called ego defences do for the individual.

Another way in which the impact of disruptive forces can be reduced, and the balance maintained, is through the use of stereotypes which give some members of the family permission to be divergent and still be thought of as normal within that family pattern. It may be taken for granted, for instance, that someone studying for an exam, or with a very strong particular bent or interest, or a member of the family chosen for some particular outside activity, can be excused the evasion of shared responsibilities without the importance of these responsibilities being reduced. Even a few oddities of personality can be used as an explanation for some unsatisfactory behaviour which might otherwise be experienced as dangerously disruptive.

"He takes after Uncle George," may be used to explain away such incidents as minor delinquencies, relating them to the family's continued existence, and, at the same time, making the behaviour more tolerable because the person who is alleged to have set the precedent had some likeable qualities which kept him within the family, and for which he continued to be valued.

"But the girls in the Smith family have always settled down in the end," removes some of the threat from awkward behaviour by placing it within a family tradition which is recognized and accepted, so that the individual does not have to be considered deviant. This is the process of normalization which is part of flexible family growth and development, enabling the range of the acceptable to be changed or increased to fit the changing reality of a particular family.

There are some "magic" words which sometimes help in an awkward moment. Every family will have some particular ones of their own, but they will include "please", "thank you," "I'm sorry," and "it was an accident". When misused, the same words only make matters worse. "I'm sorry" is all right until it becomes "I'm sorry. I've said I'm sorry, what more can I say?" Used in this way, it only increases the threat of disruption.

Maintaining the balance, or homeostasis, in the family means the application of constant repairs, sometimes requiring an amount of family effort (and often including unequal amounts of individual effort) which may seem disproportionate to the advantage gained. We do not believe that homeostasis can always be left to look after itself without some conscious attention.

There are reparative activities which drain off so much energy from other more positive family undertakings that they leave the family unit weaker rather than stronger, and so less well equipped to deal with subsequent threats. Opportunities may have to be relinquished, and controversial undertakings abandoned, in order to keep a vulnerable family unit together. Individual members may have to remain within the limitations of their socially defined family roles in order not to fracture a rigid family structure.

The family ego ideal: family aspirations

The family ego represents a level of family functioning which has many different aspects. We need to include here the concept of a family ego ideal, which in this context represents a level of family activity in which the selected goals express conscious or unconscious family standards. The family ego ideal is the name we are applying to the model which the family strives to attain, and the picture which it carries in its (metaphorical) consciousness of what it would like to be, as it sets about organizing its day-to-day business.

The way in which a home is arranged and furnished may often indicate the prototype which is being utilized. The model may be a museum, a senior common room, a stately home, a nursery school or a private zoo. One family may seem to see its home as a haven from the world, while another family may see its home as a launching pad.

The family superego: family standards

At a different level from the family ego, more complex and less conscious than the ego ideal, is the area of family functioning which we are calling the family superego.

This the metaphorical representation of the standards by which families value themselves in comparison with other families, and which they struggle to maintain and to pass on to the next generation.

Family superego preserved

As with the individual superego, the family superego is influenced by the preceding generation and by the standards and values of contemporary society. Because the family superego emphasizes the separate existence of the family, and because it develops at a point where standards are shared and passed down from generation to generation, it can come to be represented by actual possessions and conscious ways of behaving. The traditional aspect of the family superego may be given physical representation in some possession which is handed down from generation to generation: a sewing box which belonged to Great Granny, the family bible which records family history, portraits, service medals, certificates and photographs.

Continuity may also be provided by the transfer of first names from generation to generation, by family cooking recipes which are only passed on within the family, or by home remedies, or little sayings which come in handy in times of trouble.

The family superego may also be embodied in a particular individual who has become entrusted with this role, somehow holding the family together and managing to settle quarrels while maintaining the family standards and sense of value. Later, the memory of such a person may continue to perform the same function, so that it is enough to say "What would Grandma have thought of that?" Or another member of the family may inherit Grandma's mantle, assuming functions and adopting attitudes against which he had formerly tended to rebel.

The operation of the family superego may also be discerned in many activities which incorporate standards which have come to be valued as characteristic of the family in some unique sense. There are traditions of hospitality, the open house, the weekly salon, the kettle always on the stove. Or there may be traditions of unquestioning family support which excludes any sharing with strangers. There are the traditions of giving to charity, of church membership, of political activity, or of financial prudence.

"Of course, we've always been Liberals," it may be said, or "Of course, we've never owed a penny" There is no argument when people say "Of course, we've . . . " (until, of course, the time comes when somebody does start to argue!) The younger generation may pull away from the family traditions, but there is often an assumption that they will, in time, return.

The family superego can be a powerful cohesive force. It can also act as a family straitjacket which eventually has to be cast off. It may end up by being eroded through the action of forces within the family, and through the operation of cultural change operating from without.

There are strong families which develop and maintain superegos which are in opposition to prevailing standards in society. And there are also families in which effective superegos fail to develop altogether.

We believe that even those people to whom the word superego comes fresh are likely to find that they have been making certain assumptions in relation to the families they encounter as if such a concept were already in their minds.

The family id: unconscious family processes

Lastly, we come to the third level of mental functioning, the id. This is the level, non-verbal and outside consciousness, which presents the most difficulties. It is the hardest level to understand and describe in individual terms, and difficulties are compounded when we try to find its counterpart at a family level. Nevertheless, it is a concept which we have found ourselves able to put to good use.

It is most convenient to begin, as we have done, by describing the ego and the superego, which are potentially within our conscious awareness, and then to say that all that is not contained within these two concepts approximates to the id. From another viewpoint, we can say that the id is the beginning of mental life from which all the rest is ultimately derived.

Primary and secondary unconscious components

At the individual level, the id represents the main reservoir of the mental life with which the infant is born, and from which the ego gradually develops as more and more of the infant's experience is differentiated and brought into conscious awareness. Although distinct from the ego, the id does not remain completely separate, but continues to have an influence on any and every thing through which the ego is expressed.

The id is, in the first instance, the primary, unorganized and irrational part of the self. It is that aspect of mental activity which has not become subject to control and organization through becoming included in the rational, purposive part of the individual personality, neither has it come under the influence of standards imposed by the superego. More positively, it is the source of the basic energy which activates all other mental processes and allows human beings to interpret their perceptions of the external environment, and it provides the creativity behind all human activities which alter that environment.

It is difficult for us to grasp the idea of mental activity in the absence of words in which self awareness can be expressed. But, in fact, the id being non-verbal, its essential attribute is the absence of words that can be used to describe the nature of its existence.

Ego comes into existence through the recognition of external perceptions; and it requires an outside world, sense organs and a nervous apparatus, if it is to receive, recognize and store these perceptions. The id is the power which makes this possible.

In addition to this, the scope and content of the id is enlarged by the continual addition to it of material for which the ego can no longer give a place. This discarded material was at one point included in the ego in the form of wishes, impulses, drives and memories; but, in time, some of these latter came into conflict with the developing superego, and so became a threat to the harmony of the ego. They were then split off and driven out of consciousness, returning by repression to the id. The ego may be obliged to continue to make strenuous efforts to prevent their re-emergence into consciousness, and these efforts may lead to recognizable illness as well as to all the psychopathology of everyday life. It is on this process, and this conflict, that the psychoanalytic explanations of mental illness are based.

According to this formulation, a distinction can be made between two aspects of unconscious mental activity.

There is the primary id, which is the energy source behind all other mental processes, and which remains outside consciousness and therefore unverbalized, although the effect of its activities may be unconsciously recognized and represented in indirect and symbolic form.

Then there is the secondary, unconscious component of mind, the repressed component, made up of mental activities which have formerly had some representation in consciousness, but which now have been forbidden full expression. These activities fail to be verbalized, or reverbalized, because words would be too dangerous and would threaten the ego in its current stage of development.

In every discussion of unconscious processes, in the theoretical systems of clinical writers from Freud up to the present day, it is the secondary id, made up of those elements which have passed out of consciousness as the result of conflicts resulting in repression, which has received the most attention. This is because the concept of the id was first formulated in the study of pathology. A result of this has been the practice of looking on the unconscious as something abnormal or undesirable, which is a threat to the normality ascribed to the ordered aspects of the ego. Thus the relationship between the ego and the id has largely been described as one of conflict. We, of course, shall also be dealing with the conflict, but, in addition to this, we shall also be giving recognition to the creative and positive forces which are equally outside the current range of our conscious awareness.

Looking for the family id

It is clear that the term id cannot be applied to the family in the same way that it is applied to the individual. The historical process in which the ego grows out of the id through differentiation is not present in the family. We have to consider whether the concept of a family id has any meaning or purpose; and any justification for the use of such a term has to be made here on empirical grounds.

When work with whole families was first undertaken, it was in the absence of established concepts, and much of it had to be carried out by improvization. In order to formulate what was being done, and to pass beyond the stage of improvization, there had to be concepts and a vocabulary that would make it possible to deal with the family as a whole at all relevant levels. Much has been done to formulate family concepts, but the work is far from complete.

At one level of family treatment, intervention has to be directed at processes which are not consciously formulated, but which cannot be fully understood in terms of the unconscious activity of individuals alone. Some term is needed which will allow us to recognize and to enter into the unconscious or unverbalized activities of the family unit as a whole. It is for this purpose that we propose to use the term family id.

The term must be used with caution, and with an awareness of its limitations. The differences between the family id and the individual id need to be carefully borne in mind. We conceive of the family id as developing after the nuclear family has come into existence, within the dynamics of interpersonal relationships and the needs of family life. But it has precursors in the unconscious processes in the ancestral families going back beyond the immediate parents to earlier generations. These unconscious family processes include but transcend the unconscious processes which operate at the level of individuals.

Creative aspects

With the family, as with the individual, there is a temptation to find manifestations of the id mainly in terms of the divisive aspects of integration, that is, in those aspects which become unacceptable and which cannot be expressed without a risk to family unity. It is probably here that the clearest and most dramatic expression of the activity of the id can be found. We shall be using our formulation of this aspect of the id to clarify the interaction leading to the disruption and disintegration of families, including the splitting and scapegoating which has already been mentioned, and which indicates that family unity is being preserved by sacrificing a part in order to preserve the whole.

But this is not all, for the id preceded the disruption and the splitting. There are other family attitudes and activities which remain outside family consciousness. In the family, as in the individual, there are unconscious reservoirs of creativity which give life to the activities which family members share.

Every family builds its own distinctive way of life, a whole which is made up by the fusing of many different actions and decisions. In some families decisions are made as the result of open discussion. In other families decisions seem to be reached through agreement at a non-verbal level, so that things "appear to happen" without being made explicit and are accepted with little or no prior discussion. These things are often matters of significance which shape a family style.

We would suggest that such a family style is formed to a large extent through the operation of unconscious processes at a family level; through the activity of the family id which is unifying and creative as well as disruptive and destructive, and which is the non-verbal counterpart of the family ego. The family id has something in common with the unconscious, non-verbal processes which have been identified in all group situations, but the family context gives it more dimensions and makes it altogether more complex and more intricate.

This is no more than a figurative way of describing an aspect of the interaction between members of a family, and emphasizing that there are unconscious forces within a family which are helping to draw it together into a cohesive whole at the same time as the disruptive forces within the family are trying to pull it apart.

To take one instance, the desire of a couple for a child may or may not be openly discussed between them. Whether they discuss it or not, they will each bring to their marriage attitudes towards birth and parenthood at an individual, unconscious level; and these attitudes will incorporate unconscious elements from their families of origin, carried over from earlier stages in their lives. This desire may find some joint expression in the activities which they undertake together without any conscious discussion or choice. For example, it may be expressed in the plays which they see together, in the books which they share, by the arrangement of the furniture, or by the introduction into the home of plants and animals which renew their lives.

The oedipal situation

The concept of the family id may help us to understand the sexual drives which permeate the family as a whole and which go far beyond the physical sexuality of the adult family members. What has come to be called the oedipal situation is the re-creation in the next generation of the sexuality of the parents. It does not have to be thought of as pathological, but rather as the overture to mature sexuality, although it includes unexpressed and unacceptable aspects.

Descriptions of the oedipal situation in the past have tended to concentrate upon its representation in the individual growing child, and therefore upon individual unconscious processes. But the oedipal situation is now beginning to be placed in a wider interpersonal context. In this context, both father and mother have an active part to play, as do the other children; and each member of the family comes to react, not only to the sexuality of the parents, but also to all the diffused sexual reactions between parents, between parents and children, and between child and child. Older children become the additional and intermediate models of mature sexuality to the younger ones, even while they themselves have as yet been given no endorsement of their sexual role. All are drawn in. The concept of a family id, of unconscious processes at work involving the family as a whole, operating at a primitive non-verbal level and making a link with the unconscious processes of the previous generations of the family, provides a useful framework for the understanding of this situation.

Repressed aspects of the family id

If we pass on to the secondary (repressed) aspect of the id, and try to discover how this concept can be usefully applied to the family, we come to those aspects of family life which are no longer allowed any expression in the family consciousness. Some family activities, family wishes or family aspirations, may be tacitly or consciously dropped when they conflict with the image of itself which the family wishes to preserve, and when they are felt to endanger the standing of the family with outside society. Other family wishes and aspirations which conflict with the family superego may never be allowed to enter consciousness in the first place. Though the attitudes of individual members will vary, within the family as a whole there will be standards which all value as part of the family cohesion.

Everything that takes place within a family, at conscious or at unconscious levels, does not only belong to an individual family member, but is also the property of the family as a whole and becomes part of the family group matrix. Every single event resonates through the family as it elicits reactions and influences interactions.

Family secrets

Particularly powerful resonators are the "family secrets", whether these secrets be individual, shared between family members, or the property of the family as a whole. There are acknowledged secrets; and there are also the secrets which are pushed outside conscious awareness through family collusion so that they have to achieve indirect expression through myths and fantasies, or through family patterns of behaviour and family solutions, which may be passed on from parents to children. Working their way down from generation to generation, family secrets can bring with them pathological processes that become too painful to be ignored. Only if they are finally challenged and exposed, and if the family feelings can be given expression, will the family be freed from their terrible power.

Universal family themes

Family secrets are ultimately derived from the universal mysteries of birth, procreation and death, the powerful family themes explored in the dramas of Sophocles, of Shakespeare, and of other great playwrights from that day to this.

In Sophocles' myth of Oedipus the familiar themes of incest and patricide were preceeded by impregnation through rape, attempted infanticide and child abuse, as well as a concealed adoption, adolescent rebellion, and the desertion of the adoptive home. These are themes of current importance; and they are related to the mistreatment of children with tragic consequences which seems beyond the comprehension of any of us, even when we have a professional commitment. There are some explanations to be found in terms of past experiences, of deprivation, and of failure to mature; and although these explanations are often brought into good use, there still seem to be elemental forces involved whose nature escapes precise definition at a conscious or individual level.

These themes recur throughout classical literature, and are found in the case reports of contemporary professional workers. They are also found within the secrets, myths and legends of present day family life. For the most part they are not acted out, and remain at the level of myth and fantasy; but even the fantasy can be denied expression and become a part of the family unconscious.

These elemental themes underlie the conflicts which arise within the family, and in the psychopathology of ordinary family life. Conflicts among and between individual family members are going on all the time in all families, threatening the family unity; and the capacity to find a continuous, flexible, family solution to the conflicts is an attribute of the successful family unit.

Traditional psychiatry aimed to find distinguishing characteristics of mental disorder which would differentiate the insane from the sane. Then psychodynamic psychology emerged to question this distinction, looking for universal processes which all humanity shared, and no longer finding a difference in kind between the mentally disturbed and the presumed normal. This attempt was felt as a threat by many who preferred to have the distinctions preserved.

At a family level, we now have a similar process. The assumptions of psychodynamic thinking are now being applied to the family, and therefore to all families. They are not likely to be universally welcomed either, for there are many who would prefer to maintain the distinction between their own families and those other ones that they see depicted on the stage or read about in newspapers.

With family therapy has come the recognition that severe family disturbance is a consequence of processes which are themselves universal, but which more fortunate families are able, in part to transcend.

Notes and references

1. Eliot, G. *Middlemarch.*
2. Eliot, G. *Mill on the Floss.*
3. Freud, S. *An Outline of Psychoanalysis* Vol. 23 Std. Ed., 1964.
   See also:
   The Analytic Experience Lectures from the Tavistock. Free Association Books, London, 1986.
   Greenson, R. *The Technique and Practice of Psychoanalysis* Hogarth Press, 1967.
   Ellenberger *The discovery of the Unconsious* Allen Lane, 1970.

14

The Psychostructural Model Applied

The model in practice

The tri-partite psychodynamic model, borrowed from Freud and adapted for our purposes, now has to be tested in actual practice, and applied to work with families and to work with individuals who come as carriers of their families' distress. If this model has any validity, it lies in its function as an additional tool which can enable workers to respond to more of the data, and to re-arrange their observations in different ways.

We ourselves have found that this model can provide us with a useful framework, whether the work undertaken includes the whole family seen together in family sessions, or a part of the family, or is confined to a single individual. It has enabled us to put problems within a range of different contexts, and to choose different modes of intervention, selecting those that appear to be more available or more appropriate, and linking them with other possibilities.

What we have found this model to offer, in general terms, is an idea which allows workers to see their activities as being directed to some particular part of the family process, and which helps them to relate the work that they are doing at one level to the other levels of family functioning as well as to any other interventions that may be taking place.

Whole-family work, with whole-family problems, may also require its focus. Problems may have their origin in one particular level of family functioning. One level of family functioning may be more accessible, or more relevant, than another. The training and the terms of reference of the workers involved may provide a qualification and an authorization to work at one level and not at another.

Despite this, however, we have to remember that when we separate out the different levels of family functioning, we are doing this for our own purposes. We may choose to consider them separately, but must bear in mind the fact that they are closely interconnected, that all need to be recognized, and that every intervention that is made at one level has an effect upon the whole.

We are going to discuss the use of this model through work with three families.

The Wells family. 1

The Wells were a designated "problem" family, and their problems were multiple. Mr. Wells had frequent periods out of work, during which he seemed to spend most of his time in bed, and had served at least one prison sentence for receiving stolen goods. The family lived for most of the time well below normal subsistence levels. On the occasions when they had access to extra money, from charitable funds or possibly as a result of Mr. Wells' illegal activities, they spent lavishly on luxury food and toys while the rent remained in arrears.

Although not yet thirty, Mrs. Wells had had nine pregnancies, and there were seven surviving children. At the suggestion of doctor and health visitor, she had attended the family planning clinic and had been supplied with contraceptives, but it was thought that she had little intention of using them. At times she appeared genuinely to wish to avoid having further children and to be able to concentrate her resources on improving the material lot of her existing family. At other times, she would hint slyly that she just might be pregnant again, and barely conceal her wish to have another baby, using this possibility in a teasing way, as if to demonstrate the impotence of the professional workers who were trying to help her (in contrast to her own potency).

Within this "problem family" culture, Mrs. Wells seemed unusual. She enjoyed being "a character", and would look back at herself with humour and mock herself, while she teased the people who allowed themselves to be exploited by her. At the same time, she was self deprecating and self punishing, sometimes genuinely losing the money which she had, with great effort, managed to accumulate in order to pay off rent arrears or other pressing debts.

In spite of all this, the seven children seemed (all but one) well cared for, and they had a warm contact with one another and with their mother. The one exception was a four-year-old girl who was, in Mrs. Wells' view, different from the others, and who seemed to be singled out for slaps and verbal criticism.

A health visitor knew the family well, and, rather to her surprise, found something to admire in Mrs. Wells despite the insatiable demands she made. One frequent demand was for dried milk for the baby, who, she said, would have to go unfed if the milk were not provided. Often the health visitor responded to these demands, although Mrs. Wells' undertakings to pay at the end of the week were rarely honoured.

Discussion

It could be said that, for a time, the health visitor attempted to work with the family ego, as a representative of the community which gives support to families in general, and as an individual member of a caring profession giving help to a particular family. Her practical help staved off crises and provided the family with an additional resource and an experience of mothering and being mothered for parent and children alike. She did this with an appreciation of the mother's likeable qualities, and an acknowledgement of the goodness of her mothering, and she carried in mind the concept of an enduring family to which she was giving some temporary support. She was the more able to do this because, amidst her exasperation, she found herself recognizing some genuinely good qualities in this family.

This is an example of the help that many a health visitor is able to bring to many "problem" families, entering the family when the children are infants, and remaining a supporting presence, knowing that she is necessary to see the family through the next few years, but expecting that they will be able to manage as soon as the children are all at school. This is very skilled work, which involves relating to ego strengths as well as ego weaknesses. It also involves carrying in mind a model of the family as a system passing through different stages in its development and retaining a longer term capacity to survive. This work is often done intuitively, without being put into words; at other times, it is done as a conscious and deliberate part of a worker's repertoire.

There are many instances of family distress presented for help in which it is appropriate to consider first whether a family would be helped through work at this level, work designed to strengthen the level of conscious family awareness necessary for confident functioning which we have called the family ego.

This is the most accessible level: work at this level is likely to cause the least disturbance and is also often the most effective. It can accompany and give force to all the practical assistance designed to improve the family's ability to function as a family. Included here are many of the interventions of doctors and social workers which aim to improve the level of physical, mental, economic and social functioning. There are also the community workers, the clergy, teachers and family lawyers, and sometimes others such as home helps and undertakers, who provide services for families in difficulties. These workers too can carry in their minds, during the course of their contact with a family, the concept of the family as a whole, and find some family strengths even in times of great family weakness.

This does not always have to be a professional contribution. A similar service may be performed by a "family friend". This is a friend of the family as a whole, with a lasting relationship and allegiance which is not so much to any individual family member as to the family itself. Such a friend may have memories spanning more than one generation, and in his or her person represent a continuity and a cohesion along with memories of family roots and traditions.

Families may seek a family friend, and some family friends seek families. It could be a member of an older generation, who remembers important family members who are now dead. It could be a neighbour, a distant relative who can remain detached from the immediate problems of the present, or it could be the man in the corner shop. At one time there were many families for whom an old family servant, perhaps the nanny who had cared for more than one generation of children, carried a clearer concept of the family as a whole than did any of the family members. Although the prototype of the family friend is a non-professional one, members of some occupations fit readily into this role. In settled communities a head teacher, park keeper or pharmacist, for example, may be an ego support for a number of local families.

Professional workers are usually in a less permanent relationship than these "family friends", and they often enter the situation when the family ego is already weakened or under attack. Their task may be to offer assistance by serving as an "alter ego" for a limited period, during the time that the family ego is temporarily weakened, or when the family is passing through some crisis or transitional stage in its development. There are times in the histories of all families when such support is particularly needed, when the family is at risk because of illness, loss, or economic misfortune, and the family ego needs to be augmented, and existing family strengths validated and confirmed.

It is an advantage for professional helpers to recognize and acknowledge this role even when their contact with the family is for a limited time and for a limited purpose, and even when it would appear to have little to do with the family therapy that takes place in family therapy centres. If the different modes of intervention can be set alongside each other within the one comprehensive framework, the different workers involved may be able to identify their own area of work with more confidence, and relate it to the work that may be being carried out by workers of other disciplines.

There are times when work that remains at the level of the family ego is sufficient to enable a family to maintain or improve its chosen solutions. There are times when changes introduced at the level of the family ego can lead to changes at other levels which then percolate throughout a family system. There are also times when this level is not sufficient, and when conscious attempts have to be made to introduce change at other levels as well.

So it was with the Wells family.

The Wells family. 2

The time came when the health visitor decided that a different level of work was needed by the Wells family. Her anxiety about the welfare of the four-year-old child was growing into a fear that the child might come to harm within the family, and was making it hard for her to continue. She turned to the school medical officer, who also knew the family well; and then to the community mental health service, who arranged a visit to the home.

Throughout the contact that the psychiatric team had with this family, Mr. Wells remained unreachable. Wherever he might be (and no one was ever sure) Mrs. Wells could only be approached upon her own terms, and these terms included the acceptance of herself as the sole parent. On these terms, she agreed to accept treatment, and was ready to acknowledge her own anxieties about her four-year-old daughter and express her conflicting attitudes. At times she said that the child was abnormal, and asked to have her cured or removed; and at other times she blamed herself histrionically for being such a wicked woman to so mistreat a poor little child.

It seemed that one thing which Mr. and Mrs. Wells shared was a reluctance to conform to accepted standards, and this seemed to include a reluctance to conform to each other's expectations as well. They appeared to be able to tolerate this in each other: at any rate, Mrs. Wells made no complaints about her marriage.

Mrs. Wells was taken to be the key figure in any intervention that might be attempted, and the treatment that was arranged came to be directed at her personally. But she was not seen alone. The treatment took the form of weekly visits to the house by a team that was composed, unconventionally, of the psychiatrist, the psychiatric social worker, the health visitor, and also the school medical officer who knew the family well. These last two were the workers who were going to continue working with the family after the psychiatric contribution was over, and it was felt that no work should be undertaken without their participation.

It was an unusual approach, but it was felt that this family required unusual measures. It was made with the assumption that the family was to be kept together and that the pre-existing professional involvement would be maintained. This apparently expensive use of professional time would in the end be much cheaper than the cost of taking a child into local authority care.

During the interviews the children were always present, and they played an active part, clambering on to the knees of their mother and of the visitors.

Although addressed to one person, the psychotherapy was related throughout to the family interaction. It could be said to be directed to the individual id of the mother, but in this id the children played a part, and in particular the one child who had been made the receptacle for some of her mother's "badness."

Some of the topics in the interview were treated in a way which utilized psychoanalytic concepts of ambivalent transference, that is, the transfer of conflicting feelings from one person or situation to another, including the relationships within the family and with all the professional people involved. Discussion alone was not enough. It needed the presence of the young children in the interview for it to be possible to demonstrate the primitive part of the relationship between the mother and the rejected child, to whom, in fact, she was very close. She was able to come to understand that this child represented the rejected part of herself.

She appeared to obtain a greater sense of her own value, or, rather, a diminished sense of her own worthlessness, through her positive relationship with the male psychiatrist. She even managed for the first time to lose some small part of her enormous weight: though, even here, she retained her histrionic self mockery, scrawling the word DIET with a child's crayon in foot high letters on her sitting-room wall.

The health visitor had carried, and would continue to carry, the brunt of the work. As often happens, the psychiatrist was only called in at the point where family breakdown was feared. The health visitor, because of the part she was playing in supporting the family, was able to authorize the intervention of the psychiatrist and make it more acceptable to Mrs. Wells as part of the ongoing process on which she knew she depended. In this setting, and with this support, the psychiatric team was able to penetrate to unconscious levels that affected them all, with the children involved and listening.

Here it becomes clear why it had seemed particularly necessary to include the health visitor (and also the school medical officer) in the treatment. Their presence alone gave sufficient coherence and strength to the family ego to make this sort of treatment viable. A treatment group had first to be created with sufficient coherence to provide a basis for a family ego, and sufficient strength to support change now and in the future.

Discussion

Here we might usefully call to mind the concept of the "minimum sufficient network" formulated by Skynner.[1] He uses the term "network" to describe "a set of psychological structures which need to be connected to one another if the total system is to be autonomous—that is, capable of intelligent response and adaptation . . . The addition of the words 'Minimum sufficient' indicates that we must include as much of the network as is essential to achieve our aim, but that we do not wish to make our task more complex than is absolutely necessary and so wish to exclude from consideration any elements whose influence is sufficiently small to permit them to be safely ignored".

There is another reason for the need to include the health visitor in every stage of the treatment. If we were to take as our starting point the consideration of the problem to be solved, and were to ask "Whose is the problem" and "Who is complaining?", the answer must be "The health visitor". It was indeed her problem and her request for help which started off the whole treatment process. She was asking how she could continue to work with this family. The psychiatric team came in to make this continuing work possible. It came to support existing workers and not supplant them, and therefore it declined to take on the case as a separate referral and to institute treatment as a separate process.

There was also a danger. The father was being left out and the health visitor was being brought in. She was there to fill a gap in the family network, to strengthen the family ego and to enable the family to function as a sufficiently coherent autonomous system. The psychiatrist, too, was entering a gap in the family structure. It was important to remember that any intervention brings a risk, and can make things worse rather than better, and family egos weaker rather than stronger.

If one looks again at the way in which the health visitor was holding this family together, one might decide that there was a sense in which the health visitor was acting as the parent of them all. In some ways, the mother was the eldest of the children and to the professional workers she often played the part of the clever child, pert, provocative and seductive.

She needed to be ever surrounded by young children herself, and if she was able to meet their demands, as she often was to a remarkable degree, it was because some of her own very similar demands were being met in their turn. It was through her children and through her motherhood that this provision for her own needs became possible, and it did not seem that her husband played much part in this. So what would become of her if she stopped having children?

The primacy of her own needs was acknowledged in the form that the treatment took, and she responded to this. She was not only seen in the derived role of mother, in which she was aware that she could be criticized, but there was also recognition of her own unusual qualities, and her readiness to enter into discussion with the psychiatrist on equal terms.

In such a family, it is not only the family ego that is insufficiently developed. Any community worker who attempts to work at the level of the family ego is likely to become directly drawn into work at the level of the family superego as well. A family superego is needed to provide a value system that will help to give a family coherence and shared goals, and to form a bridge between that family and the community of which it forms a part.

There are agencies and workers who are particularly placed at the interface between the family and the community, and who may have to make a bridge between the two sets of standards. Here we place the law enforcement officers, and others who have the representation of law and order as part of their task. These will include not only probation officers, education welfare officers, but also teachers, doctors and social workers who are employed by public services or represent particular professions. Most helping professionals, in fact, will do some of their work some of the time at this level, (though this does not preclude the fact that these workers may also be critical of the community standards that they are being expected, to some extent, to represent).

To coin another phrase, "an alter superego" can play an important part in reinforcing standards that are failing and so in restoring a family's self esteem. It may, of course, equally play a part in helping those who are having to abandon the standards imposed by an obsolete or punitive family super-ego and who have been unable to evolve a workable alternative on their own.

Much valuable work is done at this superego level. Bad work, on the other hand, may be done when an appeal is made to an inappropriate or unassimilated superego, perhaps one passed down from the previous generation with standards that have not been implemented. For example, we recall the comment of the head master to the delinquent child who came from what was considered to be a "good" family.

"Don't you realize how you are upsetting your father and mother—and after all that they have done for you!"

Such a situation requires the consideration of dynamics at other levels. Perhaps the underlying and main purpose of the behaviour was, in fact, to upset the parents.

We can also recall here the story of the father saying, as he beat his son, "This is hurting me more than it is hurting you," and the son replying, "Keep it up then, Dad. I can stand a bit more."

The most successful work at one level is done with an awareness of the existence of the other interrelated levels. Good work can, and often does, take place without such awareness, but it tends to be haphazard and fortuitous rather than professional and planned. There are also dangers for the unwary. Supporting the family superego may be damaging if there is no recognition that the superego could be in conflict with the family id, and that the family id may be finding expression through the activities of one family member although it belongs to them all.

It is a not infrequent occurrence that the child of a well-known figure and public representative of high standards of morality turns out to be delinquent, as if it has become necessary to disclaim a publicly presented ego ideal which is denying the imperfections that exist in all families. The ego ideal has to come under attack because it has within it the unconscious component of the intolerant, primitive, family superego. Both aspects are exaggerations, the blatant imperfections as well as the blatant perfections of behaviour and standards.

The family ego, family superego and family id, are all aspects of the family as a whole. They may, however, come to be personalized and allocated separately around the family to different members or sub groups. One parent may perhaps publicly represent the superego while the children openly take upon themselves the task of representing the spontaneity and disruptiveness of the family id. They are all sharing in the same conflict, and require each others co-operation to work through it, but the conflict has had to be split up into different parts.

It is not unusual in a family of two children for the elder child to become the responsible one who supports family standards while the younger child is given indulgence for a certain amount of non-conformity which may end up exceeding the limits that the family finds tolerable.

The parable of the Prodigal Son describes a situation in which this indulgence is maintained to become a family virtue, even at the cost of the supplanting of the good son. There are other cases in which tolerance is completely absent and the family member who excludes him or herself from the family notions of virtue is thrown out from the family but kept in mind as an awful example.

There we have come back to the concept of splitting or scapegoating which was discussed earlier. This can now be related to the concept of the family id containing material which has been repressed because it is inconsistent with family standards and so forms a threat to the family ego. Because the repression is incomplete and unsuccessful, the conscious representation has to be split off so that it can be repudiated and dismissed. (This process needs to be compared with the splitting described in the formulations of Melanie Klein as a characteristic of the very early stages of normal development, and which comes to be considered pathological if it persists into adult life.)

If the aim of the professional intervention is to repair a family that has split in this way, then the work may have to be aimed primarily at the family id rather than at the family ego or the family superego. Formally structured work that concentrates on this level of family functioning is likely to require the special training and authorization of the family therapist, and a treatment process in which unverbalized family processes are brought into conscious awareness. But the phenomenon of splitting and scapegoating is found in all families, though to very different extents, and in the case loads of all helping professionals. Responses outside the practice of family therapy have to be found.

This is illustrated in our next case.

The Chubb family

The second case is that of the Chubb family, and we are again going to use the intervention of a community psychiatrist, and describe a joint visit to the home paid by the psychiatrist and a social worker. Both of them were accustomed to using dynamic family concepts, and, although at this interview only one family member was present, work was done and formulations were made which introduced progressive change throughout the family as a whole.

The family consisted of a recently widowed mother and three children aged 14, 10 and 8. One of the children attended a special school; and the staff of this school, aware that there were long-standing difficulties, and that there had been a recent bereavement, became worried by Mrs. Chubb's apathy and referred the family to the social worker.

The father of the family had died a few months before, after a long, progressive illness. The children consisted of John, 14, who was on probation as the result of a transitory involvement with a delinquent gang; Daphne, 10, the focus of concern, who attended a special school for educationally subnormal children and was epileptic; and Geoffrey, 8, at a junior school, and said to be passive and dependent on his mother.

The social worker visited the home, searching for the depression that appeared to be there yet refused to reveal itself. Then she asked the community psychiatrist to join her on her next visit.

In preparation for this visit, Mrs. Chubb was asked to suggest a time at which the children could also be present, but when the psychiatrist and social worker called they found her alone. This was accepted, for to pursue the reason for the children's absence would have been to start the interview with a criticism. If they were to enter the family system and explore it, it now had to be done through work with a single family member.

The home was a well-kept council flat, and Mrs. Chubb a tall, fair woman in her forties who seemed stiff and controlled. The psychiatrist, as soon as they had sat down, began to question her actively. Being there at the request of a third party, and not at her request, he had to start by declaring his interest; he could not wait for information to come, as he might have done in another context. He mentioned all the points that the school and the social worker had raised, including the death of her husband and the problems that he had heard about in connection with each of the children. He put all his cards on the table, and waited to see which one she would pick up.

She talked about the children. She began with Geoffrey who would cling to her and be reluctant to go out and play with other children. He wasn't a boyish boy at all, not a bit like John. John was "a real boy", but he had made some bad friends and it had ended up with his being put on probation. She thought he was over that now, but she still worried about his restlessness and dislike of school. All the same, she thought she would be able to manage the boys now, if only it were not for Daphne. Daphne's fits had become less frequent, but her behaviour seemed to be worse. She was always doing "silly, daft things", and had started wetting her bed again lately. These last six months had been very hard.

All this had been gone over before, and there seemed to be no way of intervening, at this stage in the problems of the children, without the introduction of some new factor; perhaps something related to the father's death.

It was six months since the father had died, and the psychiatrist took up the oblique reference to this and asked about him. They were told that he had been nursed at home for the nine months before his death.

The psychiatrist, looking for what was not there, noticed that there was no picture of the dead man in the room, although other family photographs were displayed. He asked Mrs. Chubb if he could see one. The only picture in her possession was in a drawer in her bedroom, and she went to fetch it. It proved to be a snapshot of Mr. Chubb standing with a neighbour; there was apparently no picture of him as a member of the family group. There seemed to be something lacking here.

The psychiatrist then asked about his work, and learned that he had been a furnaceman.

"Hot work?"

"Yes."

"Thirsty work?"

"Yes."

"Did he drink?"

"Yes."

"A lot?"

"Yes."

"Too much, perhaps?"

"Yes."

There are two points to be made about this interchange.

Having recognized an anomaly in the absence of a family photograph of Mr. Chubb, the psychiatrist knew that the subsequent interchange would contain some clues, if only he could recognize them. What, he was wondering, was the missing factor which had placed the father outside this family?

It was within his knowledge as a doctor that men who work in extreme heat perspire freely, lose salts, and, if they drink plain water, suffer from cramp. Beer comes to be preferred to water, (although it must be said that some firms do supply drinking water containing replacement salts). Those who drink large quantities of beer are likely to suffer from alcoholism.

The perception was instantaneous, but it would have aroused too much tension if the question had been asked outright. It is often necessary to ask questions in steps which make them appear part of a gradual process of discovery to which the informant is also contributing, and which can help to demonstrate how situations like the excessive drinking came about. Here the progression allowed the widow to realize that her husband's drinking behaviour had a natural explanation in his circumstances and was not being condemned. It also allowed her to admit that it was a problem to her just the same.

After this interchange, other information came freely. She had married late, giving up a good job as a trusted cashier, and in opposition to the wishes of her family. Mr. Chubb's relations were not the class of people they were used to. She thought her family was wrong, but, in fact, she herself had never liked her husband's friends, and after a very short happy period they had grown apart. He had his friends, and she had hers, and he thought her friends were stuck up just like her family. There was never enough money. He kept a lot of his wages for himself. He smoked, and he went to pubs, and he often came home the worse for drink. She had felt ashamed, and hadn't encouraged her family to visit, although she never said anything to them.

Then he had fallen ill. In fact probably the best part of their marriage for her had been this last year when he was ill and needed looking after. He had been grateful for her care of him, and she hadn't been left alone of an evening wondering where he was. But it had been too late. She had grown bitter and couldn't forget.

It was hard for her to experience his death as a loss. She was better off financially as a result of it. She had used some of the financial benefits she derived from his death to refurbish the house according to her own tastes, and it now seemed that there was nothing left of the husband that could fill any perceived need on her part or preserve his memory.

It had to be concluded that marriage for this woman had mainly been a disappointment. It had brought loneliness and deprivation. She may have hoped that after her husband died a load would be shed. But she discovered that what had been wrong was not what was there but what was missing. And after her husband's death it was still missing. This sense of loss made it difficult for her to give any acknowledgement to the fact that at times there had been some satisfaction and happiness in her marriage.

The social worker took up the question of the children, and their response to their father's death. Mrs. Chubb said that they had taken it quite calmly. However the difficulties with all three of them were now worse rather than better, although she had expected an improvement without the strain of a sick man in the house, and with more of her time and attention to give to them. She went on to say that he had not been a bad father, and when he was well he had often played with the children. But it did seem to the two professional helpers that, since she was unable to mourn, the children had been denied their opportunity to mourn too. And perhaps they were missing qualities in their father of which she was unaware, or which she would not allow herself to recognize.

It also seemed to them that Mrs. Chubb had other losses which she was unable to acknowledge, including the loss of her family when she married against their wishes, the loss of her hopes, and the loss of the brief happiness of her early married life. The incomplete mourning could be a defence against the experience of further loss. It could also be an attempt to maintain the separation she had made between her standards and those of her husband. And yet, in spite of the high personal standards of her family of origin, she had not gained the satisfactions that those high standards might have brought.

Discussion

The problems that had been disclosed could be looked at at different levels of functioning. They could be related to the operation of the family ego, and linked to an inability of the family unit to develop into a cohesive whole which could support further growth. Yet, for all the difficulties, there did seem to have always been a functioning and caring family unit. But what was there, it seemed, was being threatened from within. Within the family system as a whole there was a lack of energy and a lack of coherence.

A family superego is needed to enable a family to pursue a consistent goal, and this had never developed. Mrs. Chubb had become the sole upholder of a superego which was in some ways inappropriate to their needs, but which she endeavoured to carry in such a way that it could include the whole. There were no standards which they could share and be comfortable with. Nothing came from Mr. and Mrs. Chubb as a pair that could be transmitted to their children with pride.

Turning to the family id, it seems possible that at this level the parents did maintain some contact. There was perhaps an implicit agreement between them that he could represent in their partnership all the socially disapproved aspects of life which her family had never allowed her to enjoy. He could taste the forbidden fruits for both of them. She had come to be ashamed of his coarseness, and attempted to hide it from her own family, but there must have been a time when she had been attracted by it. Then the accident of Daphne's epilepsy and low intelligence came along to embody for her the pathology of the family system, including the hidden uncontrolled urges, the fits, and the sexuality, in fact all her negative feelings about her husband and his despised or disapproved social background.

The other two children had their roles, too, in this sharing out of different aspects of the family problem. John came to acquire a delinquent record, and thus embody another aspect of her fears. Geoffrey, on the other hand, represented that part of the family relationships which she had come to find most gratifying; the dependency and the closeness to the home.

From the point of view of Mrs. Chubb, it seems as if three different aspects of her problem were separated out, to be externalized and embodied in her children who thus became participants in her inner dilemma. But, conversely, from the point of view of the family, a family problem in which they were all involved had come to be encapsulated in the mother. And from the point of view of the professional intervention this meant that the family problem could be approached through work with the mother alone.

A therapeutic aim was established. If a therapist could find and acknowledge both the goodness and the badness in the marital relationship, the satisfactions along with the dissatisfactions, help could then be given to Mrs. Chubb to acknowledge them too. She might then be able to permit the children to show traits which she identified with their father, and she might recognize that there was now a gap in the family which she could not fill by attempting to be both mother and father herself. If she could recognize that something was now missing, she might be able to allow herself to mourn, and so allow the children to mourn too.

It did, in fact, take only one or two additional interviews, building upon all that had taken place in the joint interview, for the social worker and Mrs. Chubb together to bring a substantial change for the better in this family.

The work was focused at first upon Mrs. Chubb's unexpressed sorrow, her ambivalent feelings about her marriage and widowhood, and the regrets which she had not been able to acknowledge to herself or to anyone else. She had indicated the lack of value that her husband had in her estimation. This devaluation had spread in subtle ways into her valuation of her own self and of her children. After these issues were ventilated, she and her children became able to mourn the past together. The expression of some of her feelings about her husband, and about her own relatives, and more open discussion with the children, made it possible for John to take on more of the eldest son's role. He then gave up much of his delinquent acting out, and became increasingly able to be the responsible helper to his widowed mother. After this Geoffrey became more independent of his mother, and made some friends, and a little later Daphne stopped wetting her bed. Family processes at all three levels seemed to have been affected.

Any therapeutic process that took place with this family did not come from exposing and sharing dissatisfaction and loss alone. The identification of all the positive aspects of their family life, and the help that Mrs. Chubb was given to discover and rediscover them for herself, were essential parts of the process. The workers had to be able to find their way to these positive experiences, and relate them to everything that was going on now and that had gone on in the past. All the interactions between the workers and Mrs. Chubb had to include this awareness, and a visible respect for her and for all the members of the family, alive and dead, as well as for the family as a whole.

The Fernandez family

A terminal care team, like some other workers in other settings, has to intervene in family situations but does not usually have the authorization or the opportunity to practise family therapy as such, (or marital or individual therapy either for that matter). In addition, terminal care teams, by definition, have relatively little time in which to do their work. They are required to respond immediately to the critical situations that confront them, making use of what is available to them in terms of practical opportunities and concepts, and leaving on one side anything in the history or the circumstances that is not clearly relevant to the crisis that has brought them in.

In the following case, we are going to focus upon the work of the social worker, bearing in mind that what was being offered was integrated care in which the social workers, doctors and nurses collaborated closely.

The patient was a man of 44 with advanced gastric carcinoma who was referred to a home care team attached to a hospice. He came from East Africa, was of Indian racial origin, and had lived in England for 20 years working as an electrician. He was married to a Scottish woman from a large, close knit, Glasgwegian family, and had two children aged 12 and 11.

First visit

The social worker paid four visits to the family during the last two weeks that the patient was being cared for at home.

On the first occasion she accompanied a nurse, and, while the nurse was attending to Mr. Fernandez, she was taken into the sitting room by Mrs. Fernandez to join her sister and another female relative. All three women were in an exhausted state, but there was also an air of excitement. They described how Mr. Fernandez had spent the night roaming about the house in a disorientated condition, at times appearing hallucinated, talking to absent relatives, brandishing a screwdriver, and speaking in a wild and threatening way. No one had slept, and they had all been frightened that Mr. Fernandez would do an injury to himself or to someone else. They described this behaviour as if it fitted into a pattern of family expectations. It seemed as if Mr. Fernandez was already seen in the family as a wild and alien person whom it was impossible to understand.

It seemed likely that Mr. Fernandez' behaviour was linked to the medication that he was receiving for the pain. After this had been discussed with the family, the social worker talked with them a little longer, and heard that they had had a number of recent misfortunes. The wife's father had died the year before. Her sister had recently had to have a leg amputated, following a fall. They felt that bad things had happened to them, and that perhaps more bad things were to come. There were references to badness and to blackness— "This is a black time for our family." The two relatives were offering Mrs. Fernandez their attention and their concern, making it clear that they had come down from Glasgow to support and protect her in her trouble. They knew about Mr. Fernandez' illness, but found it hard to think of him as ill and weak, let alone dying, because he was still capable of outbursts of vigorous activity.

This interview raised several specific problems. First, there was the problem of the composition of the family and of the unit of work. The focus of the team had to be upon the patient, but the social worker had the task of considering the illness within the family context. Mrs. Fernandez indicated the family group that she wished to be involved, and the people who were playing an important part in terms of the current family dynamics. This was the wife's extended family, and it was this group which was defining the patient as "deviant" in ways which included but went beyond his illness.

There was the problem of the present situation and its relationship to situations in the past. It seemed that current reactions were being largely determined by past events. These past events included the marriage of Mr. and Mrs. Fernandez with its problems, and the attitude of Mrs. Fernandez' family, as well as the other family misfortunes.

In this interview, the social worker allowed Mrs. Fernandez to define the family unit. Within this unit, the social worker represented the home care team, bringing an assurance that help was available, explanations of strange behaviour, and help with practical problems.

She encouraged discussion of current and past family events, letting the connections emerge, but indicating that the connections were not inevitable.

Feelings from the past were undoubtedly involved, but the current problems were different and could be considered separately. At this interview, there was no opportunity for the social worker to spend time talking to Mr. Fernandez.

Second visit

Two days later, the social worker visited again, this time accompanying a doctor. Two more members of the wife's family had now arrived, another sister and a teen-aged niece. Another discussion with the wife and her relatives centred upon fears of irrational behaviour and of dying. They all seemed frightened, and said that none of them was able to sleep at night, although the patient had become quiet again after an adjustment to his medication and there had been no more confused or irrational behaviour. They thought that he too was now frightened of something happening at night. The wife joined in to say that her own family was very different from her husband's family, regretting that he had never known family closeness. He was not talking to any of them now, and she did not know what he was feeling. Once again, the social worker tried to help them to express their fears, and to separate present reality from fears and expectations carried over from the past.

The social worker then joined the doctor in talking to the patient. Mr. Fernandez began by asking if it would be possible for him to go back to East Africa "to my own people", although he indicated that he knew he would not be strong enough to travel. He described his weakness, and his fear that the pain would get out of control. He was also afraid that his wife would not be able to go on looking after him for as long as he needed her. He showed a fear of being abandoned, and referred to two occasions when he and his wife had separated and she had gone back to her family in Glasgow with the children. He talked about a GP who had "struck him off his list" without explanation. His fears of being abandoned evidently included both his wife and the home care team.

Mr. Fernandez also spoke of his illness as a "badness" inside him. He asked about the options that would be available to him if he could not remain at home, and, when the options were described, he showed an interest in the possibility of coming into the hospice. Having been restless and agitated, he became calmer.

Third visit

Five days later, when the social worker visited again, all the relatives had left taking the two children away with them. Mrs. Fernandez said that this had been at her wish.

It now became possible to change the focus to Mr. and Mrs. Fernandez and their life together, although it still was not possible to talk to them together in one room. Mrs. Fernandez urged the social worker to talk to her husband on his own, and firmly declined invitations to join them.

Mr. Fernandez talked about the children's fears.

"Wouldn't you be frightened if you had to watch your Dad die?"

This was discussed at two levels. There was Mr. Fernandez' concern about the children, and his role as a caring parent. Then there were also his own fears, and his feeling that he was having to watch himself die.

He asked the social worker to talk to his wife about the children. He said that sometime soon he would like the three of them to have a talk together, "but not today". He was too tired now. He asked about the possibility of admission to the hospice. "Is it still on?" Would his family be allowed to visit? Fears of abandonment seemed to be present again. The social worker said that a hospice bed would be offered very soon. She said that she would pass on to his wife everything that he had said. He appeared pleased and said "She is looking after me well."

Seen on her own, the wife said that the children had shown their fear that their father would die at home when they were there. It was accepted that this represented her fear too, as well as her concern for the children. The social worker discussed with her the fears shown by the different members of the family, including those fears which she shared with the patient, and their joint concern about the children. She said, "He's a good Dad".

The following day the social worker visited to say that a hospice bed would be available for him on the morrow if he wanted it. The patient appeared pleased to hear this, but did not want to talk any more.

The wife again wanted to talk on her own. She spoke of regrets that her marriage had been "bad", that she was joined to a morose, irritable man whom she had never understood. It had been a long illness, and now she wished it could be all over. She had sent the children away to her family because she could not handle the children's feelings as well as her own. Now they had gone away she was inclined to regret it because they formed the main point of contact between herself and her husband. She was having to give him constant care now, and he still hardly spoke to her. But sometimes she sat with him and he seemed to like her presence.

Three days after this, Mr. F. died in the hospice. His wife was with him.

Discussion

Looking back on this case, four different areas of work can be distinguished.

First, there was the involvement of the wife's extended family. At the first interview, the wife presented herself as a member of this family, although her husband was excluded from it. His illness had returned her to her culture and him to his, alienating him in both senses of the word. Current events were being given their significance within this context, so it could not be ignored. It was not until some work had been done in this area that the wife could separate herself from her relatives and place her husband's illness in the alternative context of their marriage.

The intervention of the home care team as a whole came at the level of the family ego, bringing additional support to the nuclear family. At the same time the social worker, while sharing in work at the family ego level, also had to take into account the fears and phantasies which were less conscious and which emanated from the level of the family id. It was because of these fears that the stereotype of the blackness had been extended to include the illness and increase the isolation of the patient.

Secondly, there was the area of the patient on his own. In this individual contact, work was focused upon his feelings as a loner, shut out by his wife's family; upon his fears of being abandoned; and upon his fears of his "badness". These fears had become encapsulated in his feelings about his illness and his knowledge that he was dying. The expression of these fears, and the safety provided by the home care team, reduced some of the anxiety.

A third area of work was the relationship between the patient and his wife. Although it was not possible to talk to them together, the social worker was able to some extent to communicate with each of them, and to share the feelings of each with the other. Through the presence of the home care team, the patient became a man who was receiving treatment and care, and this made it easier for his wife to accept him back.

Finally, work with the wife on her own enabled her to enlarge upon what had been hinted at during the family interviews. She found it possible to express these feelings, and yet continue to care for her husband and be a good wife to him at the end.

Brief interventions

We have been describing cases that were treated through team work and through interventions that could be, to some extent, thought about, planned and structured.

Professional workers who have to respond to the problems caused by family conflicts may find themselves contributing to a complex, multi-professional treatment plan: alternatively, they may find themselves on their own and being required to make an immediate response. Sometimes even a very brief intervention can be valuable.

For example, a general practitioner was treating a young married woman with terminal cancer. On one visit, the patient's mother, who was the principal carer, said to the doctor in the patient's presence, "I wish you could speak to my daughter's husband. He came home drunk last night and was sick on the kitchen rug".

The doctor exclaimed spontaneously, "Oh, the poor man", and saw the dying wife's eyes light up with gratitude.

The patient knew that the doctor was acknowledging her husband's grief at her plight, and the fact that "his grief was very great". The superego had been invoked by the mother, but the doctor refused to respond at that level. Instead he made his brief comment containing a (paradoxical) interpretation which recognized the underlying family conflict and offered an alternative perception. It extended his concern to include the husband, and it brought the husband's behaviour within tolerance, and back into the context of the family as a whole. It needed someone from outside the family, and with authority, to do this.

Although such a response can be unlearnt and intuitive, it is also part of a method of working which can be acquired: and it can only be taught on the basis of concepts which make it possible to approach the family interaction and family process as a whole.

Note

1. Skynner, A. C. R. The Minimum Sufficient Network *Social Work Today* 2/9.3. 29 July, 1971.

7
Epilogue

15

One Last Case

Miss Winefred C.

Our final case comes from a social worker employed by a local authority.

Miss Winefred C., recently discharged from a mental hospital, was in her mid forties although she looked older; a short stocky woman with frizzy greying hair, wearing wrinkled wool stockings and a dirty cardigan which incongruously gave her the air of an unkempt schoolgirl. When first seen by the social worker, she was sitting on the edge of her chair in the waiting room, ready to jump up when summoned, her expression expectant and anxious, as if all prepared to deposit her burden of misery and complaint into someone's lap.

In this and subsequent interviews her life history unfolded. She was an unmarried woman, a diabetic since childhood, who had never had a job and who lived alone in the little terraced cottage which had been her home for the whole of her life. Her father had been a tailor, a hardworking, respectable man, of quiet, retiring domestic habits; and, when visited at home, she would proudly bring out for display his great tailor's shears, which she continued to keep with great care. They had been a close, united family who "adored each other". Her parents were "the most wonderful parents in the world" and they gave her, (their only child) everything she could desire. If she ever wanted anything, she had only to cry for it and she would get it. It seems that she had cried often. They were particularly kind and indulgent to her after she developed diabetes (a family illness) at the age of eleven.

She recalled how her parents always made a point of being at home to welcome her when she returned from school. Then incongruously, she set against this another vivid memory. She remembered how she used to come up the little garden path to the front door, which opened directly into their living-room, wondering as she came whether they would be there or not; and starting to snivel as she peered through the letter box in case they had gone out and left the door key hanging on a string.

She left school at fifteen, her poor progress compounded by many absences. After this she stayed at home to be with her mother, and no employment was ever considered for her; she was too delicate, she needed looking after, and there was enough money coming in for her keep. Besides, her mother needed her company. She gave her mother some help in the house, which was always kept to a high standard with the brass gleaming and the kitchen grate black leaded. There was her father's tea to prepare every day. There were shopping expeditions; a summer holiday at Southend every year; and infrequent visits to relatives and neighbours. The visits were few because they did not have many friends. "We didn't need friends, we had each other."

And so her girlhood and young womanhood passed away, with apparently little change in her manner of living, until she reached the age of forty. Then, in the same year, both her mother and father died. Her father died of "stomach trouble", long taken for granted: her mother, who was also a diabetic, "just wasted away" and died a few months after her husband. Miss Winefred C. always wept when she came to speak of her parents' deaths. At times she would say, in a burst of anger, "How could they leave me . . . I never thought I'd be left . . . I never thought they would both go away and leave me like this."

She went on living in the little house, drawing regular small amounts from her parents' savings. It did occur to her occasionally that the sum was diminishing, and that when it had all been spent there would be nothing left; and at times she felt both angry and afraid. The house, which her father had kept in good repair himself, began to deteriorate. The roof started to leak; a gutter became blocked; plaster fell from her bedroom ceiling. She shut the door on the bedroom (it had been her parents') and moved herself back into the smaller bedroom which had been hers before.

A relative visited a few times; but then there was an awkwardness, something to do with money, and the relative stopped coming. There were neighbours who were quite well disposed at first, and she would borrow milk and a spoonful of tea from them when she didn't want to go to the shops, and call over the garden fence when she needed someone to talk to. But then they stopped being friendly; perhaps because her demands were too great and they became alarmed at the extent of her need. Whatever it was, they started to ignore her approaches, and no longer opened the door when she knocked.

As time passed, her frustration and loneliness grew. She began to cry, and then to bang on the walls and howl. The neighbours reappeared, suggesting that she should see a doctor, but she did not trust them any more. Eventually the doctor came, and then a social worker. They seemed concerned and kind, and she agreed to go into hospital for a while, "for her nerves". She liked the hospital. But now she was back home again with a bottle of tablets, a distant future appointment at the outpatients' clinic, and a referral to a social worker.

The social worker who was assigned to Miss Winefred C. ("you can call me Winnie, if you like" was the first thing said) found herself quickly caught up in a situation in which only her regular visits, and sustained personal interest, could prevent a recurrence of the disturbed behaviour. Attempts to bring about a change in Winnie's circumstances met with very qualified success, and only uncovered her paramount need to be coaxed and cajoled, to accept suggestions and then to be able to change her mind so that the process of explanation and discussion could begin all over again.

In all the group situations in which the social worker saw Winnie, in social club, welfare centre, holiday home and hospital ward, she was happy to the extent that she could find for herself a position as a specially favoured dependant. She strove to create for herself an interpersonal network in which her more pressing emotional needs could be met, manipulating the other members to provide the responses she wanted. Her aim was to be treated as if she were the one good child, the focus of parental approval: when this aim conflicted with the needs of the other members, or of the group as a whole, she changed from being the good child to being the defiant and destructive one. Always she was very alert to the effect that her behaviour was having upon others.

At the holiday home, to which the local authority sent her for a week, she was the youngest woman in the group and the only unmarried one, and afterwards she asked when she would be able to go there again. In the general hospital ward to which she was admitted for a few weeks for the observation and stabilization of her diabetes, she was the only ambulant patient, able to hand out cups of tea at the request of a motherly and responsive ward sister. In both these short term situations she seemed very content. In other group situations, where this role was not available to her, or where she met with competition, she became provocative and demanding. At a day centre, where some of the clients were more visibly disabled than she was, her behaviour was like that of a wilful child bent upon attracting attention and annoying the adults.

Her second admission to the mental hospital, again preceded by an episode of disturbed, histrionic behaviour, occurred while the social worker was away on holiday. This time Winnie was moved from the admission ward, where she had been before, to a back ward of chronic patients. Here she received the social worker tearfully and reproachfully, begging to be "rescued". But when her discharge had been arranged, she appeared to change her mind, and sought to be coaxed and persuaded to leave the hospital.

After some experience of Winnie's demand, of her vacillations, and of her changes of mood from ingratiating and compliant to wilful and obstinate, the social worker began to see Winnie as a child who was addressing her communications not to one parent figure but to two. The inconsistencies and shifts in position, the capriciousness in her relationship with the social worker, became easier to understand when her behaviour was seen as directed towards two people whose relationship with each other had come to be dominated by her. In other words, there were two people in her life who fell out about her, and she was the centre of their arguments. She was like a child who says something to cause dissension between her parents, and then sits back gleefully to watch their reaction. This was the situation she was still trying to create; but now she was in a relationship with one person, not with two. The social worker, attempting to establish a consistent and reliable relationship in which the two of them could work together on some of the problems, found that all her resources were needed to preserve the casework relationship against Winnie's manipulations. Later on, she came to perceive these manipulations as attempts to split her into two and "triangulate" their relationship.

When she came to make a final comment on the case, the social worker wrote as follows:

"The work I have been attempting to do with this patient reminds me more than anything else of child guidance. By this I mean that the problem is essentially that of a child in relation to her parents. The patient is a small girl born to a united and self sufficient couple who did not have enough space in their relationship to include a child. She is extremely dependent upon her parents, but has little confidence in their will or capacity to give her what she wants. She only feels safe when she is in a dominant position and able to control and manipulate them, and divide them from one another in order to make room for herself. She dare not leave them, lest she should find no place for herself when she returns. Neither side can break free from this circular situation, in which the parents' resentment at their bondage increases the daughter's mistrust, and hence her need to continue to manipulate them through her dependency. In such a case, there is little point in trying to treat the child on her own. The parents and the child need to be brought together, and the family unit treated as a whole. But in this case the parents have been dead for some years. The interpersonal problem persists, but the child guidance formulation is being made forty years too late."

Discussion

If we can go back in our minds to the period when Winnie was a young child, and attempt to reconstruct what was happening at that time, we can envisage a family situation that could have led, at a later date, to referral for child guidance or family therapy. The reasons for referral might have included school refusal, or sleep disturbance, or psychosomatic symptoms accompanying chronic ill health, depending upon the way in which the family shaped the problem and the way in which the helping agencies responded to the shaping.

Today we can identify a family group problem; but there was a time when some form of individual therapy would have been the treatment to be offered in such a case, with the child, and possibly the mother as well, being seen separately by individual therapists. Such treatment would have had little likelihood of success. Individual treatment requires a degree of separateness that did not exist in this family. Although all family members contribute to, and participate in, family processes, and help to create the family psychodynamic structure of family ego, superego and id, family members also have their own individual internal structure in which these three levels are represented. If the boundaries are not defined, if the individual egos and the family ego cannot be separated, then individual treatment is not likely to be effective.

In the case of the C. family, it would seem that the family ego had come to take the place of the individual egos, but was weakened by this lack of differentiation. Within a vicious circle, the weak family ego was unable to provide a firm framework within which a child could feel safe and go through the process of internalizing, projecting and re-internalizing, in the interests of growth and development. In the absence of this type of progress, there is likely to be difficulty in developing enough separateness to permit the child ever to leave the family circle behind her.

Alongside the weakened family ego of the C. family, we find a family superego that had to bear an extra weight. They had to rely for their sense of identity on the old-fashioned virtues which prevented them from sharing and enjoying the changing life styles of their neighbours. This increased the tendency of the family members to turn inwards and to cut themselves off from their community. The undoubted qualities which gave them a feeling of worth only increased their tendency to separate themselves from a deteriorating outer world, and left Winnie, the surviver, with insufficient resources to sustain her. Psychologically, one cannot live on superego alone: it is the ego processes which cope with the variations of present day life.

There was also the family id, giving rise to shapeless fears located by agreement in the outside world; turning the home into a much needed retreat from the dangers that might be encountered elsewhere.

Had it been possible to see this family together, the therapist might well have chosen to focus upon the family communications, upon the ambivalent messages and double binds which seem to have been a feature of the relationship between Winnie and her parents. This faulty communciation pattern was a necessary consequence of the absence of appropriate boundaries to their separate personalities. Clarity of speech would have revealed the hostile component and the anger contained in the ambivalent relationships. The ambivalence was expressed; but it had to be understood by inference. So the lack of the development of a coherent and recognizable family structure left fear and insecurity at the forefront of their lives.

The legacy of her early family life remained with Winnie into adulthood and middle age and was still very much alive when the social worker knew her.

We believe that the personality of every individual is to a large extent formed within family group situations in the first years of life, and continues to be permeated by early group experiences. It seems that the psychological processes, which we have in the past attributed to the individual personality, and which were once considered to belong *exclusively to the individual*, are derived ultimately from the group.

Although Winnie was never observed within the family group, she was seen in other group situations. She was seen entering existing groups, bringing with her, and transferring into these new situations, needs and expectations derived from her experiences in group situations in the past. These new groups tried to make room for her, adjusting their proceedings to accommodate her, and partially meeting and partially failing to meet her needs. When she did not obtain immediate satisfaction, she either left or responded vigorously with deviant behaviour, falling once more into the role of a demanding, and manipulating child which was the only option, it seemed, that was open to her, now as in the past.

Had group therapy been available, and had it been considered appropriate, it might have provided an opportunity for Winnie to have some different group experiences, in which her habitual responses would have been challenged and alternative responses offered to her, and in which she might have had a second chance to pass through the experiences that her family of origin had failed to provide. She might have tested the reality of her expectations and her fears, and learnt to relate to others in a different way, superimposing new experiences upon the experiences of the past.

Some group opportunities in fact were provided for her, or came her way incidentally. Although not designated therapy, they might have been some help by providing surrogate family situations. Some very limited changes did in fact take place, none of which proved to be lasting. It seems that they were insufficient and came too late.

We are aware that this last case could not be described as a success. But there is, as one of us wrote in another context, a creative aspect of professional work with human problems, and those who have chosen to extend and to go beyond traditional boundaries (and these include voluntary workers as well as those in established professions) have no reason to apologize for the occasions when their best efforts are not rewarded with success. Indeed, there are sometimes incidental advantages to be gained by the professional worker amidst the painful feeling of not having been successful enough. In professional practice, as in therapy, a measure of discontent is needed before the existing ways of doing things can be questioned. Cases like that of Winnie prick the bubble of our self-satisfactions, and set us off on the search for different formulations. After the formulations have been changed, the manner of working changes, because new thoughts lead to new kinds of actions. If a theoretical formulation is to be of any value, it must make a difference to what we do: and, conversely, if we absorb a new method of working it should make a difference in our thinking. The new understanding that each case gives us means that a repetition of past work is not good enough for the next case. This new understanding may come too late to help the current case, but we owe it to ourselves, and to the patients and clients for whom we wish we had been able to do more, to have something to add to the work next time.

Bibliography

Ackerman, N. W. *The Psychodynamics of Family Life* Basic Books, New York, 1958.
Austen, Jane *Letters* O.U.P., 1952.
Balint, M. *The Doctor, the Patient, and his Illness* Pitman, 1957.
Bateson, G. A systems approach, *International Journal of Psychiatry* **9**, 242–244, 1971.
Beeles, C. C. and Ferber, A. Family therapy: a view. *Family Process* **8**, 280, 1969.
Bell, J. E. A theoretical position for family group therapy. *Family Process* ed. Ackerman, Basic Books, New York, 1970.
Bentovim, A., Gorell Barnes G. and Cooklin, A., ed. *Family Therapy* Vols 1 & 2 Academic Press, London, 1982.
Bentovim, A. Theories of family interaction and techniques of intervention. *Journal of Family Therapy* **1**, 21–45, 1980.
Berne, Eric *Games People Play* Grove Press Inc., 1967.
Bion, W. R. Group dynamics; a re-view, *International Journal of Psychoanalysis* **33**, 1952.
Bowlby, J. *Child Care and the Growth of Love* Penguin Books, 1965.
Bowlby, J. *Attachment and Loss* Hogarth Press, London, 1969.
Byng-Hall, J. Family myths used as a defence in conjoint family therapy. *British Journal of Medical Psychology* **46**, 239, 1973.
Byng-Hall, J. Family legends: their significance for the family therapist. *Family Therapy* Vol. 1 ed. Bentovim, A., Gorell Barnes G. and Cooklin A., The Academic Press, London, 1982.
Caplan, G. *An Approach to community Mental Health* Tavistock Publications, London, 1961.
Cooklin, A. Change in here and now systems vs. systems over time. *Family Therapy* Vol. 1. ed. Bentovim, A., Gorell Barnes, G. and Cooklin A., The Academic Press, London, 1982.
De Haré P., *Large group perspectives*, Group Analysis Vol. **XVIII**, No. 2, 1985.
Dicks, H. *Marital Tensions* Routledge and Kegan Paul, London 1967.
Eliot, George *Middlemarch*.
Eliot, George *The Mill on the Floss*.
Ellenberger, H. E. *The Discovery of the Unconscious* Allen Lane, London 1970.
Ezriel, H. A psychoanalytic approach to group treatment, *British Journal of Medical Psychology* Vol. **XXIII**, Parts 1 and 2, 1950.
Ferrard, Margaret L. and Hunnybun, Noel, K. *The Caseworker's Use of Relationships* Tavistock Publications, 1962.
Foulkes, S. H. *Group-Analytic Psychotherapy* Gordon and Breach, London, 1975.
Foulkes, S. H. *Therapeutic Group Analysis* Allen & Unwin, 1964.
Foulkes, S. H. and Anthony, E. J. *Group Psychotherapy. The Psycho-analytic Approach* Penguin Books, 1957.
Freud, S. Standard Edition, Hogarth Press.
Glover, E. *Psycho-analysis* 2nd Ed. Staples Press, 1949.
Goffman, E. *Asylums* Doubleday, New York, 1961.
Greenson, R. H. *The Technique and Practice of Psycho-analysis* Vol. 1 Hogarth Press, 1967.
Halmos, P. *The Faith of the Counsellors* Constable, 1965.
Haley, J. Communication and therapy: blocking metaphors, *Am. J. of Psychotherapy* Vol. **XXV**, No. 2, 1971.
Henry, J. *The Pathway to Madness* Cape, London, 1972.
James, Henry *The Art of Fiction*, 1884.
Johns, T. T group traumas *Journal of Institute of Personnel Management* Vol. 1, No. 7. 1968.

Kahn, J. H. and Wright, S. *Human Growth and the Development of Personality* Pergamon Press, 3rd ed., 1981.

Kahn, J. H. and Carroll, H. C. M. Nursten, J. *Unwillingly to School* 3rd Edition 1981 Pergamon Press.

Kahn, J. H. and Earle, E. *The Cry for Help* Pergamon Press, 1982.

Kahn, J. H. The Newham Community Mental Health Service, in *New Aspects of the Mental Health Services* ed. Freeman, H. and Farndale, J., Pergamon Press, 1967.

Klein, M. *The Adult World and Other Essays* Heinemann, 1963.

Koffka, K. *Principles of Gestalt Psychology* Harcourt Brace, New York, 1935.

Kohler, W. *Gestalt Psychology* G. Bell, 1930.

Kreeger, L. *The Large Group*, Constable, 1975.

Leiberman, S. *Transgenerational Family Therapy* Croom Helm, London, 1979.

Lindemann, E. Symptomatology and management of acute frief. *Amer. J. Psychiat.* 101, 141.

Maier, H. *Group Work as Part of Residential Treatment* National Association of Social Workers, New York, 1965.

Minuchin, S. *Families and Family Therapy* Tavistock, London, 1974.

Moreno, J. *Who Shall Survive?* Beacon, New York, 1953.

Parkes, C. M. *Bereavement: Studies of Grief on Adult Life* Tavistock, London, 1972.

Parsloe, P. Some thoughts on social group work. *British Journal of Psychiatric Social Work* Vol. X, No. 1, 1969.

Pincus, L. and Dare, C. *Secrets in the Family* Faber and Faber, London, 1978.

Pines, M., ed. *The Evolution of Group Analysis* Routledge and Kegan Paul, London, 1983.

Rice, A. K. *Learning for Leadership* Tavistock Publications, 1965.

Russell, B. *Sceptical Essays* Geo. Allen and Unwin, London, 1960.

Satir, V. *Conjoint Family Therapy* Science and Behaviour Books Inc. Palo Alto, 1964.

Schoenfeld, P. *et al.* Long term outcome of network therapy. *Hospital Community Psychiatry* **37**, 373–376, 1986.

Segal, H. *Introduction to the Theories of Melanie Klein* (New Edition), Hogarth Press, 1973.

Skynner, A. C. R. *One Flesh: Separate Persons.* Constable, London, 1976.

Slavson, S. R. *Analytic Group Psychotherapy with Children, Adolescents and Adults* New York, Columbia University Press, 1950.

Speck, R. V. and Rueveni U. Network therapy *Family Processed* Ackerman, Basic Books, New York, 1970.

Stock Whitaker, D. and Liebermann M. A. *Psychotherapy Through the Group Process* Tavistock Publications, 1965.

Thompson, S. The group process in Chekhov's plays, in *The Evolution of Group Analysis* ed. Pines, M., Routledge and Kegan Paul, London, 1984.

Thompson, S. Working with families in a community service, *British Journal of Psychiatric Social Work* Vol. VIII, No. 4, 1966.

Walrond-Skinner, S. *Family Therapy: the Treatment of Natural Systems.* Routledge and Kegan Paul, London, 1976.

Winnicott, D. *Therapeutic Consultation in Child Psychiatry* Hogarth Press & Institute of Psychoanalysis, 1971.

Index